T0370456

HALLELUJAH

RENATA RIVKA

WESTBOW
PRESS®
A DIVISION OF THOMAS NELSON
& ZONDERVAN

All Scripture quotations, unless otherwise indicated, are taken from the Holy Bible, New International Version®, NIV®. Copyright ©1973, 1978, 1984, 2011 by Biblica, Inc.™ Used by permission of Zondervan. All rights reserved worldwide. www.zondervan.com The "NIV" and "New International Version" are trademarks registered in the United States Patent and Trademark Office by Biblica, Inc.™

Scripture quotations are from the Catholic Edition of the Revised Standard Version of the Bible, copyright © 1965, 1966 National Council of the Churches of Christ in the United States of America. Used by permission. All rights reserved worldwide.

Scripture taken from the American Standard Version of the Bible.

WestBow Press books may be ordered through booksellers or by contacting:

WestBow Press
A Division of Thomas Nelson & Zondervan
1663 Liberty Drive
Bloomington, IN 47403
www.westbowpress.com
1 (866) 928-1240

ISBN: 978-1-9736-0959-9 (sc)
ISBN: 978-1-9736-0960-5 (hc)
ISBN: 978-1-9736-0958-2 (e)

Library of Congress Control Number: 2017918292

Print information available on the last page.

WestBow Press rev. date: 02/12/2018

PROLOGUE

Everybody has a story. Some people's stories may include one or more of the following events: surviving physical abuse, verbal abuse, sexual abuse, drug abuse, or alcohol abuse, the loss of one or both parents, prejudice, accidents, etc. Then there are some who may not have had anything like these things happen to them and may not feel like they have much of a story. Well, as I know from family experience how much some people hate it when others pry into their business, and because I struggle with making myself draw people out, I do not always get to hear your story. For this I am sorry, because while I do not want to pry if you do not want to share, I love stories and would love to hear yours.

Right before I started to write my story, I had read a book called *More Than a Ring* by Don Beebe with Bob Schaller. I found it to be quite inspirational and in a format I thought would be easy for me to also write in as I wrote my own story as it looked like Don wrote an overview of his life's testimony and Bob then filled in more details. Up to then I thought and had tried multiple times to write my story in full rather than an overview repeatedly filled in more. In Don's book I really appreciated how he shared how the many different events the Lord had allowed Don to go through so that Don could share his story and people could learn about the Lord. That is what I have come to learn as well with my story.

So, I have chosen to write this story because of this saying of Don's, plus because of how at about the same time as I read this book, I heard a broadcast of Family Life on 91.9FM, which also advocated sharing one's story with others. Also, I once had a roommate, Ruby C, tell me how I should write a book telling my story. I did try a couple of times prior to this but never got very far. It was not until I read Don's book that I finally got further than just a few pages covering maybe a month to a year of my life. In fact, the very first paragraph of this prologue was one attempt at starting to write my story.

English writing has never been my strongest subject, but I hope that you will find my story inspiring nonetheless. By the world's standards, I have yet to find real success. But I know that the real measure of success is the Lord's, and I hope that I have been successful by his standards. This said, I will now share my story.

Due to the privacy my family always desires, the names of EVERYONE mentioned in this book other than when I am quoting those whom have indirectly influenced my life like sports, Biblical, other religious figures, etc. have been changed as have EVERYPLACE'S names. As my friend Rissa H said, the glory is for the Lord and not for any of the individual characters or places. May the Lord be magnified!

Renata Rivka

(I ended up choosing this name as I went on <u>meaning-of-names.com</u> as I tried to determine what name I wanted to use when my previously selected name got rejected from being a possibility. I ended up choosing Renata as it means born anew in its France origins and Rivka as it means servant of God in its Israel origins which is fitting as this book is written by a person who is a born anew servant of God.)

What Started It All

I considered going back in my mind's eye to when I was age ten which I usually refer to as being when a major life change happened and I then tend to credit many other life changes to that time frame too. On second thought though I am going back to when I was seventeen years which is when I started to think for myself rather than just following my grandmothers thinking.

In my mind's eye, I am sitting on the front porch of our two-story brick house in Lilac City by the front door which is on the west side of the house. The house which was built in the early 1900s has a door on every side of the house but the rear door on the east is the one most frequently used. As I'm on the front porch that would mean the neighbors in a similar looking brick house right across the road set back across a vast expanse of lawn aren't home as the only time I or my sisters are allowed on the front porch is when nobody next door is home.

Looking past the peony patch in the middle of our front lawn and the catalpa bush with another patch of peonies I am looking west at my neighbor's place. As mentioned earlier it has a two-story brick house, a couple garages and an old unused barn. Right behind their property my family's property resumes as a farm field. My uncle, Larry, owns over 200 acres of crop lands. Then across the field about a half mile away is some woodlands which my uncle owns, but it was probably when I turned 18 Uncle Larry sold the woods for enough money to get himself finally completely out of debt or maybe he already has, I cannot remember.

As that is as far west as I can see I sweep my gaze north. To the north of the neighbor's place is an old cheese factory. While it operated during my earlier childhood years it no longer is operating as a cheese factory. Instead the current owners appear to use it as a place to build up their racecars as throughout the week one hears the roaring of engines coming from the factory and we see racecars being pulled up and leaving from the area.

Looking further north past our twelve pine trees and solo birch tree I see a couple more operating dairy farms less than a quarter mile down the road pretty much right across the road from each other. Then about a mile north of our farm at the top of the hill are a couple more farms. One is a hobby farm and the other only has a few horses.

As that is as far north as I can see I then sweep my gaze south over close to one hundred acres of hay land as my grandmother feels that hay is the most profitable. My gaze skims over my uncle cutting hay in his big white Case tractor with an enclosed cab and then continues until about a mile south of our property my gaze comes to rest on two more farms. One is an operating farm while the other just has dilapidated buildings other than the new house that was recently moved onto the place after they destroyed the old house that used to stand there. As I draw my gaze back towards where I'm sitting, about a hundred yards from where I am sitting, I see a small wooded area which my sisters and I are allowed to play earning it the name Children's Woods. It consists of a very old maple, containing a branch as big around as my head to which a tire swing is tied to and many plum and honeysuckle trees. Just north of it is the big flower garden containing many rose bushes, peonies, lilies of the valley, honey suckle bush and raspberry plants plus a golden delicious apple tree which my mom bought and planted there.

From where I sit on the front porch I can't actually see any further but from memory I know that just east of the big flower garden is a gray shingled house built in the late 1800s which we call George's House. Nobody lives there since my uncle bought the place in 1976. It is here that my grandmother lets my sisters and me play. East of the house is several very old apple trees and some old wooden calf hutches. East of them is where our farm buildings start. On the south end, there is an upright concrete silo, behind it and going north is the blue tin cattle shed where the young stock are housed. Where the big red barn stretches east to west and the shed attaches to the barn stands another upright concrete silo which contents caught fire in my late teen years, in front of the silo stands the white milkhouse. To the north of the barn, built into a hill, is another upright concrete silo which my uncle had built to store corn. A bit further north and west of the barn is a corn crib and other older calf hutches with tin roofs and wooden frames. Next to them on the west is the big blue tin machine shed which stretches south to north. In the front of the machine shed is the garage where the family vehicles stand. They consist of a red Chevy Silverado and a blue gray Dodge Caravan which my grandmother picked out as being one she would feel comfortable riding in and have ease getting in and out of plus having enough room for all in the family.

Coming back toward the house which is separated from all the other buildings on the property by a U-shaped driveway and following the sidewalk to the house one sees the summerhouse just to the east of the house which Grandma Nancy had the family work together to build where we first started to get to watch TV again and which ultimately was meant to be where we held our recycling until we were ready to take it to the dump. At the house, one takes a couple steps up to the back door. Entering the back door, you need to be careful as in mere feet there is the stairways leading to the three rooms in the basement. Turning south away from the steps though you are in the entry room at this point containing a couple tables piled high with papers and projects, a bookshelf, a refrigerator, a gas stove, and an older chest freezer. Off the entry room to the south one sees the bathroom we use to change in and out of farm clothes. Then off the entry room to the west one enters the kitchen with a table set up in the middle. The kitchen contains cupboards all around the kitchen other than where an electric stove sits, three doorways and along the east wall. Going through the south doorway one enters the room which used to be the library room which got converted into the school room. It still contains a bookshelf of books and several other pieces of furniture all of them piled with projects. Off the library to the west is a full bathroom. This room also has projects piled all over. On the other side of the bathroom's other door is Grandma Nancy's room which she has piled high with school materials and games and other items. Then going through the door on the north side is the living room which has a pool table, bookshelves, a table, a couple rocking chairs, a divan with matching chair and a few other pieces of furniture all covered with projects other than the divan and matching chair as the divan is where my youngest sister now sleeps, Ma sleeps on the matching chair and I sleep on a full-length lawn chair. Along the north wall is a closet under the staircase leading upstairs to three bedrooms and another full bathroom at the far end of the hallway. If you go upstairs the first door on the east will be the bedroom where all but my uncle slept for many years and where my grandmother and older sisters still sleep. To the south still on the east side of the hallway is my uncle's bedroom. The only room on the west side of the hall is also my grandmother's room. It is here that she is usually found praying and watching the neighbors. Back down the stairs there is the remaining room on the main floor which is now the dining room which used to be the family room with the pool table. All the rooms which I had just toured in my mind's eye also contain projects in all but the main walkways and on the furniture which is still being used on a daily basis.

As I am sitting on the front porch at seventeen, I have come to the realization that my mom and grandmother had not waited until they were thirty to marry, like they were requesting of my sisters and me, but had both been married in their early twenties and had been done giving birth to their children by the age of thirty. As I contemplate this I realize that at my age they obviously then had likely had enough interaction with people of the other gender and maybe even been friends already with the guy they were going to marry. The thought makes me mad and hurt that my family would have isolated my sisters and me in this way. Also, as I take in the buildings on my farm I think in despair of the disrepair they have fallen into because of lack of money, lack of ambition and overall as distrust of others has truly taken its toll on the desire to maintain them in good condition. All these are fueling my desire today and has set me contemplating what I need to do so that I can change things so that I can become a part of society which they have so successfully cut me off from and made me scared of.

INTRODUCTION TO MY FAMILY

I was born a big chunky girl one-ounce shy of ten pounds to a 26-year-old Catholic woman in Wisteria City. I joined two remaining sisters that cold, wintery January day six years to the day after sadly Roe vs Wade made a woman's rights more important than protecting an innocent baby's life. I joined a skinny blond haired, blue eyed six-year-old sister, Dora whom I missed sharing a birthday with by just a few days.

Right around the time Ma was due to give birth to Dora she shares how she had been chasing some cows who had gotten loose. As she chased the cows she hit a patch of ice and fell. Upon falling her water broke but when she went into the hospital the doctors were unable to get her to go into labor. As Ma had a wedding she wanted to go to that afternoon she convinced the doctor to let her go home. A week later Ma went into labor and as it was going to be a dry birth, the doctors highly drugged her so she could escape most of the difficulty and pain associated with a dry birth and a first child. Ma says she remembers how several times during the labor process she would come out of the drugged state enough to realize how there were resident doctors also attending to the delivery. Ma remember how one or two of the residents she recognized having gone to school with them.

Then Ma likes to say how two years, two months and two days later Sandy another blond haired, blue eyed girl was born. Compared to Dora, Ma had a relatively easy time and really has never shared anything about her delivery other than after Sandy was born Ma called her brother Larry who at that time had moved from Wisteria City to

5

Lilac City to wish him a happy birthday and to inform him how he was an uncle again.

Then about a year later Ma and her family had an incredibly rough year as her dad, Robert and youngest brother, Nekoda battled cancer and passed away. Nekoda had had a lump on his upper leg for a while before someone else learned of it and took him in to the doctor to get it looked at. Robert I think was battling exhaustion when he was diagnosed. That same year Ma gave birth to another daughter, Nelly, who was quite sickly with everything she ate coming out one end or the other so she was never able to leave the hospital but was taken to the hospital in Crocus City where Robert and Nekoda also went for their treatments. By the end of that year all three had ended up passing away.

A few months after Nekoda had been diagnosed he had graduated from high school and that fall he and his mother, my Grandma Nancy, had started college. As the treatments continued and Grandma Nancy started to talk about discontinuing college to be able to spend more time with her sick family. Nekoda would say to Robert, "If Mom quits going to college we can quit fighting too, right Dad?" Grandpa Robert would then agree. So even after Robert and Nekoda passed Grandma Nancy continued to go to college even as family and friends questioned her decision.

Three years later was when I was born. Then just shy of seventeen months later, Ma went into labor shortly after midnight following Father's Day and shortly after she arrived at the hospital and before the doctor arrived she gave birth to her last daughter Abby. As she had tried to prepare me for having a little sister, Ma had taken to carrying a doll around instead of me. Up to the day Abby was born I had never walked on my own but when Ma came home carrying Abby, she shares how I had run to her calling "Dolly."

As Abby and I were so close in age, we usually did everything together with encouragement from the family. Grandma Nancy I remember was always telling us how sisters should make the best of friends like the sisters in the book *Little Women*.

While growing up I remember being the smallest in the family, and among my classmates during kindergarten through fourth grade which were the years I wasn't homeschooled, with my fine boned features. Abby was big boned so from the time I remember she was always about an inch or so taller than me. I was a petite girl with thin, straight shoulder length brown hair (until my teenage years when Grandma Nancy finally allowed my sisters and me to start growing our hair out), a light spattering of freckles, big blue eyes and a timid smile, usually not showing the teeth as Grandma Nancy did not like toothy smiles. I cannot remember why but she was always having us practice smiling our best smile without showing our teeth. Also, I was and still am a bit self-conscious of slightly overlapping teeth and a slight overbite that I have. Overall, I remember being a bright kid towards the top of the class especially when it came to reading as I remember being grouped with a few fellow students to read our readers while the teacher would work with another group which was struggling more. I also was timid among my peers. I remember how I would hopefully watch the most popular girls or older boys as they played during recesses hoping they would include me which I never was. While I was timid when I was included in play I wasn't much for role playing with classmates or more specifically with a classmate of Abby when Abby would let me join her and the classmate. That was because I hated being bossed around and would frustrate quickly with anyone other than adults if they tried to tell me what to do which is what I felt that Abby's friend would do as she would try to direct me in the role she wanted me to play. I am not sure if my discomfort with role playing was because Grandma Nancy discouraged us from making animal noises unless we held that animal, or car noises unless we had a car, etc. or if I just wasn't comfortable pretending. As I play with my niece I realize I still have the same discomfort with play acting and would rather read, play games, etc. than make believe with dolls. While growing up there were plenty of other friends of Abby's those four years of public school which I would join with in play but after a period just would get fed up with the pretend play. When at home I remember playing a lot with Abby with our toy cars, animals, dolls, etc. and not being fed up all the time so at this time I am not sure why it was such a big deal with Abby's friends.

My fondest memories growing up would include reading. I remember from some of my earliest memories sitting on Ma's lap or curled next to her as she read Abby and me nursery rhymes which progressed to Amelia Bedelia and similar books, then to Black Stallion, The Boxcar Children, Happy Hollisters and Trixie Belden and then eventually to Hardy Boys. Growing up on a farm, I remember fondly Ma smelling of hard farm work, a mix of sweat and dairy cows. I also remember often watching her lips as she read and how on the corners Ma's lips would stick together and slowly peel apart as she read. Additionally, I enjoyed spending time in a garden trying to make it so that the flower or vegetable which was planted could be seen and while I rarely made it weed free at least there were a lot less weeds or the weeds would be kept from blocking our view of the flowers or vegetable. Otherwise when I wasn't doing those things, school work, or farm work I was usually involved doing something with Abby. I have a ton of memories playing with Abby. They include cutting pictures out of magazines to create play house, paper dolls, paper animals, etc. Others include playing with a talking typewriter, Lite Brite, Etch a Sketch, our toy dolls (usually school as Grandma Nancy had been a school teacher and had lots of school materials we could have our dolls play) or our toy animals. Abby and I wished our cattle were horses and so we did our best to train them like a horse. When it came to halter breaking we actually were very good and it was beneficial to the calf and later the farm as they got lots of attention and were very tame. Also, I remember loving to do lots of crafts with Abby which included knitting, making homemade looms, making our own paper dolls and animals, etc.

Dora being six years my senior was always about a foot taller than me until my later teen years when I caught up with her at 5'4". She looked a lot like me as her blond hair darkened to brown and had a slightly bigger build, more pronounced freckles and as she had splashed chemicals in her one eye when she was younger that eye tended to be a lazy eye so she was required to wear glasses with the other eye patched. Usually she would not do so though. Being the oldest Dora tended to come across as being superior and the family bent over backwards to keep her happy. She and I often clashed because of how I felt she never cared to know my opinion on any matter. She often had her nose stuck in a book or newspapers as she sought to glean information so she could join adult conversations whenever the family would eat a meal together. Usually meals together were only for a family member's birthday or a holiday like Easter, Thanksgiving, Christmas and occasionally Fourth of July. Otherwise Uncle Larry was usually busy working off the farm or trying to complete all the farm chores which none of the rest could do (fixing the barn cleaner, silo unloader or most of the field work-Ma would try to help some with the field work but most of it fell to Uncle Larry).

Sandy being four years my senior also was always about a foot taller than me until my late teen years when I also caught up with her at 5'4". Her blond hair as a young girl had also darkened to a brown color around the time she started school. She looked a lot like me other than she was ganglier and had a pronounced overbite. She usually had a ready smile with teeth as her overbite was quite pronounced which she usually wore unless you had provoked her and had yet to make up with her. She also had a disability which put her mentally several years behind. Starting in her late teen years you would find Sandy where she could be listening to the radio which is why she often never rejected the chance to do chores as she could listen to a radio station or two in the barn. Then after I left the farm in 2001, Sandy started carrying a portable radio around with her most everywhere she went.

Abby in many ways was like the rest of us. Where she was different though was in how pale her complexion was which never tanned but burned, her brown hair was naturally wavy, course and very thick and she was big boned. She ended up surpassing all in my family in height ending at 5'7". She also had a ready smile and she was very bright. From the earliest age, she knew what was expected and knew how to get my family's approval in many areas which they might have been reluctant to do otherwise. An example is how when she was in kindergarten Abby shared a quote she made up and claimed a friend told her it. From that quote, my family still affectionately remembers her friend and had been willing to let Abby and her be friends. Abby had also been able to figure out how to knit, crochet and almost anything else she set up her mind to do just by watching others. She also became the family poet and wrote close to a hundred poems which she had always wanted to get put to music and to hear someday on the radio. I helped her get at least one song put to music in 2001 when I asked a friend if he could look through a pamphlet Abby had given me for Christmas which contained all the poems she had written to that point and put one to music. He had though as he played by ear the music had never been written down anywhere but was just a recording of him singing a song and playing his guitar. Ma surprised her once by typing all the poems up and mailing them to Xlibris Publishing to get the poems published under the name of Marie Maria.

Ma also was 5'4", blue eyed and had thin brown hair which she always tried to grow out but was never very successful at getting it past shoulder length. My entire childhood she struggled to lose the excess pounds which made her lap very soft and welcoming as she would welcome us to join her as she gladly would read us books. Ma's extra pounds came due to her love of food which often she would eat for comfort when she and her mother, my Grandma Nancy, would fight which was usually several times a day. Ma really wanted to please Grandma Nancy but Grandma Nancy always wanted things done exactly as requested with no variance whatsoever and on top of that she was such a perfectionist that Ma rarely could please. For example, when Grandma Nancy would send Ma to shop for her she expected Ma home right at the time she had calculated it would take Ma to find the items at the store and the drive time to and from the store. Also, Ma wasn't as bright as Grandma Nancy seemed to wish Ma was so that in many areas Ma struggled including confidence and managing her money which was just interest from her certificate of deposits she had in the bank from when she and her husband sold their farm often resulting in bounced checks which Grandma Nancy would agitatedly express her irritation over but would cover anyway. Ma also was never really good at figuring out just what people expected of her and doing so, but she loved being with people. She usually within minutes could be found deep in conversation with people she just met. A fact which I think Grandma Nancy did not like as Grandma Nancy was very private, preferring not to share conversations with others but would do so just to appear appropriately social. Also, I think Ma's conversational mannerisms bothered Grandma Nancy as she would have Ma's schedule worked for her down almost to the minute and so she would get worked up when Ma would be 10-60 minutes later than Grandma Nancy had planned on her being. Whenever Ma was late Grandma Nancy seemed to have imagined the worst thing possible as having happened.

Grandma Nancy also was 5'4" but started to shrink and stoop becoming increasingly frail looking while I grew up. It was not until I grew up that I realized her dark brown hair was actually maintained through her regular visits to a hairdresser which also helped keep curls in her hair. Once she decided to retire from teaching she then had Ma become her hairdresser which is when I first thought she turned gray. When Grandma Nancy smiled it would transform her otherwise very serious, often severe features.

Ma, whose name I first learned in my teenage years was Nora, married at age nineteen in 1971 as Grandma Nancy said she did not want Ma to marry younger than that. As teenagers my youngest sister, Abby, and I decided Ma probably had married in order to find love, which Grandma Nancy had rarely showed to her. Shortly after that time Ma mentioned to us how she also reached that conclusion.

While growing up I do not ever recall Grandma Nancy showing anybody physical affection in hugs, kisses, etc. This, in large part, was due to Grandma Nancy having a really bad back, which affected the way she interacted with people, and how she viewed them. Whenever interest would be expressed in giving her any physical affection she always was quick to remind us how bad her back was and how easily it was made worse. Throughout my childhood, I remember how her back would bother her and how it limited her in carrying things or moving things. Often, she would try carrying different things but would often have to ask for help or if she didn't Grandma Nancy would have to take it easy for days following it and would be found sitting a lot more praying, listening to a radio or reading a book. Her sitting instead of moving around became more and more pronounced in my later teen years up to when she passed away. Instead of affection, I remember Grandma Nancy's desire for perfection from all of us.

All through my childhood I remember how Ma never seemed good enough for her, resulting in Grandma Nancy sharing with my sisters and me numerous times about when Ma disappointed her in the past. One of Grandma Nancy's often repeated memory of when Ma disappointed her follows, "When your ma was two years old, she would always beg and beg to be carried until her dad would give your ma her way even though she knew how to walk." Ma would share with us later how when she was two she had had a "bubble in the leg" which made walking difficult which is why she would always want to be carried. Another memory of how Ma disappointed Grandma Nancy was in how Grandma Nancy "had informed Ma how she was not to marry before she turned 19 so right after she turned 19, your Ma had married, to a guy that your Grandpa Robert (Ma's dad) had repeatedly warned her could write any sort of nice things on paper as it would hold still for him to write anything your Pa would feel like writing."

So, Ma, hoping she could find love by getting away from Grandma Nancy, married my dad, Arthur, in 1971. Then sometime after 1976, when Grandma Nancy lost her youngest son and husband, she ended up moving in with Ma maybe around the time Ma and Pa moved to Echinacea City when I was one. It hadn't been immediately after her loved ones passed away though as I recently found a letter from Grandma Nancy to a family member sharing how it may have seemed like bad timing so soon after her loved ones had died for her to leave Wisteria City to go to college in Ranunculus City but it was what her deceased loved ones had wanted her to do, to finish her education and get a degree for teaching.

Ma's marriage got rocky less than ten years after she married and it fell apart after Grandma Nancy discovered how Pa was sexually abusing his two oldest daughters, Dora and Sandy, who were ages six and eight at the time. I was only two and my youngest sister, Abby, was just one at this time. So, the only details I know about the abuse are the ones Grandma Nancy told Abby and me. If Abby or I were ever abused neither of us ever remembered and Grandma Nancy had never seemed to suspect that either of us had been. Just how Grandma Nancy had discovered Dora and Sandy being abused I would learn as she would tell the stories only to Abby, me or Ma, as Grandma Nancy would always say, "I do not want your older sisters to have to remember any of these bad memories." Overall, other than when Grandma Nancy shared about the bad things Pa had done, we were discouraged from ever talking about Pa, meaning I never heard my sisters' side of the story and never really heard anything from Ma about Pa other than what Grandma Nancy already had told us. But Grandma Nancy wanted to make sure we "knew the bad things your Pa had done but your Ma would get in trouble with the courts if she shared any of these things, as the courts would look at it as if your Ma was trying to prevent you girls from wanting to have anything more to do with your Pa." Following are some of the details Grandma Nancy gave us.

"Your mom often woke up in the middle of the night to Dora and Sandy crying and only with a bath would they stop crying."

"At three Sandy used to chatter on like a normal three-year-old when I took her for car rides, but a few months later she had regressed to baby talk and never talked at a level normal for her age after that."

"Sandy used to fall asleep during kindergarten and when the teachers could not awaken her they would call your parents. When your mom came Sandy would be okay but when your dad would come to wake her Sandy would wake up screaming and run to hide from him."

"Dora and Sandy hate stuffed animals – especially bunnies – as that is what your dad claimed he was when he would visit them in the middle of the night."

Grandma Nancy also told of a much more sexual revelation my sister Dora had described which I feel better leaving out for my family's privacy and for the sake of potential younger readers.

Then apparently Pa also started to threaten to kidnap us children even before Ma left him and took us with her. Ma's divorce ultimately resulted in Ma being dependent upon living again with Grandma Nancy so she could help take care of my sisters and me, as Ma began battling depression. Ma and Grandma Nancy had at the time of the divorce then moved in with Ma's oldest brother, Larry. Uncle Larry was a few inches taller than Ma, quite tan and had startling blue eyes which had laugh lines permanently etched around his eyes. He usually was found in a t-shirt, blue jeans and a ball cap. When he wasn't wearing a hat, you noticed how his hair was receding which he tried to cover up by sweeping hair over the spot. He always had a ready smile and loved to joke around except when animals misbehaved, he was fighting with Grandma Nancy or some farm equipment was breaking down which caused his language to grow course and caused his temper to be displayed. One of his favorite jokes was when someone asked him what time it was as us kids weren't allowed to wear watches but he wore one. In reply, he would tell us that it was the same time as yesterday except twenty-four hours later.

When Grandma Nancy and Ma moved in with Uncle Larry they joined him at the farm he had moved to after leaving home in 1968 which was several hours away in the state I ended up growing up in from where he grew up in Wisteria City. Uncle Larry says it was because he wanted to be a religious farmer and he learned that the group of brothers he was working with in Wisteria City had a farm in Lilac City. Until I asked Uncle Larry why he had moved away, I had thought possibly it was to also get away from his mother, though Ma thought it was to show his dad's father, Pappy Archie R, that he could farm. Do not get me wrong. Ma and Uncle Larry both love Grandma Nancy very much, but not her frequent tendency to bring up past failures which is why I think they both were glad when they thought they had found an opportunity to have their own lives away from Grandma Nancy.

GRANDMA NANCY

It has just been in recent years that the Lord has helped me realize Grandma Nancy's tendency for perfection and control which kept most at odds with her were probably due in large part to several things in addition to her having what Florence Littauer in Personality Plus referred to as a phlegmatic personality. One reason was that she had had a very bad back since birth, which made her very sensitive. Grandma Nancy's back was so bad she would share the stories that follow:

"One day when I woke up from a nap at the age of two, I started crying as my diaper was wet. When my ma, your Nana Lilly M, who had other younger children to take care of, found my diaper wet, she gave my butt a swat and scolded me for making more work for her. That was all it took for Nana Lilly to potty train me as it caused my back to hurt."

"Also when I was years older, your Nana Lilly would send us kids out to play and ask us to watch our baby siblings. So I usually wound up carrying one or another of my younger siblings even though carrying my siblings around caused my back to hurt quite badly."

Also, when Grandma Nancy drove, a person could tell how badly her back hurt, as she would drive about five miles per hour down the gravel roads around the farm. Even when she did not drive but would ride, she always had to take a car seat, which was a lightweight frame that would fold up. But when it was unfolded and placed in the car, it would make for rigid right angles, as car seats tend to slope back toward the seat's back which itself would tend to curve. Both positions make for "comfortable" resting positions for most people but not for Grandma Nancy's already bad back. Instead, it was conducive for very bad posture that would hurt her back worse. Since I hurt my back in 2009 I also have discovered how bad "comfortable" things can be for ones back. There is a reason why teachers back in elementary school insisted that one's desk would allow for one's feet to rest comfortably, entirely on the floor yet have your leg between the hip and knee be parallel to the ground. Once I injured my back I discovered any position other than the one just described would make my back hurt worse including riding in the car with its sloping seats which is why a person will see I have a couch cushion on my car seat. It increases the height so that my legs are more parallel to the floor and maintains the height unlike bed pillows which go flat after a while which I tried first.

Another reason for Grandma Nancy's behaviors I believe was that she had a strong desire herself to be loved but she seemed to have more memories of how others had hurt her instead of how they had loved her. The stories she shared about her growing-up years makes me pretty sure this was also the case. Following are the ones I remember best.

"Since there were seven kids in my family growing up, I ended up having to share a bed with my sister, Rita. She would lay over half the bed and tell me that was her half and that I had 'better make sure you do not lay on my half.' If she would catch me lying on her half of the bed she would pinch me or kick me until I would move over. So usually I just lay as close as to the wall as I could to prevent laying on what she deemed her half of the bed."

"While growing up Nana Lilly M would have me go with my siblings to keep an eye on them when they went off the farm to play, to walk to school, or whatever it was they would do. During these excursions, I remember how there were times when my siblings would all choose to hold hands and not thinking anything of it, I would also take their hands. It seemed I was always on the one end, and the sibling on the other end would think it was quite funny to grab an electric fence. This always resulted in me getting shocked."

"Throughout our childhood growing up on a farm we never had much money. My six brothers and sisters and I would have to share a tube of toothpaste and make it last a month. This problem of never having much money was further compounded by my dad, your Papa Norb, who was an alcoholic. Nana Lilly was known to take the money earned and stash some of it for the essentials. Papa Norb though, would look through everything when the urge came to drink until he would find some of the stashed money. He would then leave the farm and drink. I especially remember how after having grown up and gone to college, one weekend I had come home and he had gone out drinking. I remember praying for him the whole time he was gone and when he came home I saw him puking beside the woodpile. This scene was what it took for me to decide that I really had no desire to return home again."

"When I went off to college I always would go to the sanctuary next door to my room which I shared with a roommate. She really did not like me. In fact, I remember one time as I was praying in the sanctuary I heard something break in our room, but I stayed where I was praying until when I planned to go to bed. When I finally went to our room, I found the lamp in our room had exploded with glass all over my things. I am sure that the time the lamp had exploded was after when I usually would go to bed, so that my roommate hoped that I would be in bed sleeping already when it exploded."

I believe that Grandma Nancy's desire for perfection and control also stemmed from her desire to be perfect in loving the Lord. I believe that her desire to be perfect in loving the Lord came because of her upbringing as a Catholic which had taught her that people need to be good enough to get to heaven, instead of being taught the truth of Ephesians 2:8-10 *For it is by grace you have been saved, through faith— and this is not from yourselves, it is the gift of God— not by works, so that no one can boast. For we are God's handiwork, created in Christ Jesus to do good works, which God prepared in advance for us to do.* This desire to always be good so she could get to heaven was then passed on to each of us as she stressed how important it was for each of us to be good or we would not get to see Grandpa Robert, Uncle Nekoda, or sister Nelly in heaven.

As Ma battled depression she relied heavily upon help from Uncle Larry and Grandma Nancy to help raise us kids. Throughout our childhoods my siblings and I would find her somewhere crying at least once a week if not more frequently. Of course, part of the reason for the crying was that Grandma Nancy reminded her frequently how she went against Grandma Nancy and Grandpa Robert by marrying Pa and now look what happened.

As Grandma Nancy was the oldest family member and as the Ten Commandments required one to "honor your parents," Grandma Nancy took this to mean complete obedience at all times. I remember how we were frequently reminded to honor our parents, meaning we needed to honor Grandma Nancy and her decisions. When we wouldn't Grandma Nancy would then remind us that the punishment for not following the ten commandments was not getting to go to heaven and seeing the loved ones who had passed on before us.

As Ma battled depression and Grandma Nancy was willing to raise us girls, Grandma Nancy then managed to take charge of all our lives. An example of how Grandma Nancy took charge of our lives was how one year she told us girls we were old enough to decide if we never wanted to see our father again. (He only had court-supervised visitation rights in Impatien City after the divorce, though I am told but do not remember how he still managed to get teachers and neighbors to feel sorry for him so that they would allow him to come see us.) I do not think I was even ten at the time Grandma Nancy told us we were old enough to decide if we never wanted to see our father again, but after that comment, I never heard from my dad again. Until just a few years ago I thought he never tried to see us again, but now, as I remember how my sisters and I were never allowed to answer or talk on the phone, and most phone calls were never talked about around us children, I think he may have tried to see us but was told that we never wanted to see him again.

The last time Abby and I did get to see him I believe was right around Easter. Grandma Nancy came up with the idea to dress us up as bunnies, including ears, nose and whiskers. To do this she marked nylons with a black nose and whiskers and stapled on paper ears. So as we are leaving home to go to the courthouse in no doubt the county seat, Grandma Nancy helped us apply our bunny faces and instructed us to stick together, and no matter what to keep on our bunny faces and like a bunny to not utter a single sound. So we climbed in the car with Ma and Uncle Larry. Uncle Larry would drive us and Abby and I would each have a magnetic board to draw on. After drawing for a bit we would then lift the top piece of plastic and our picture would disappear and we would begin again. The drive seemed to last forever and then Uncle Larry to make it a business trip would stop at a hardware store and pick up some nuts and bolts or any other item that he realized he needed. As he rang up his purchase he would see how they were giving away a little something for free like a little booklet with the Brewers schedule and containing some facts about several of the Brewer players, he would pick one up for each of us girls and then give them to us to look at and help us forget about how long and boring the ride was.

Finally we would arrive at the courthouse. About six to twelve months before this visit when Grandma Nancy had dressed us up like bunnies, Pa had become father to a son, Victor, whom he wanted us to meet. When we joined Pa and his family, I remember Abby and I huddled together in a corner away from Pa and his new family. Victor being fascinated with us came crawling over to us and then reached up trying to grab our paper ears. In the meantime Pa tried to coax Abby and me to take off the nylons but instead we followed Grandma Nancy's instructions by refusing to take off the nylons. Additionally Abby and I also followed Grandma Nancy's instruction of being like a bunny and remaining silent much to Pa's frustration as he tried to get us to interact with him and his family.

In addition, there were events that caused Grandma Nancy to feel the need to protect us from evil, which she would perceive from neighbors and such. One example is how at about the same time as we stopped seeing Pa, the various cars we had would break down when Ma tried taking us girls to church. As Grandma Nancy decided for one reason or another that she distrusted the priest serving the church in Lilac City, she would mix up which Catholic church we would go to. Depending on what she would decide, we might attend the church in Buttercup City, one of the three churches in Rose City or one of the churches in Snapdragon City.

The time I remember best was after we had gone to mass in what must have been Snapdragon City because it had been a long and unfamiliar drive. While we were on the way home all of a sudden we smelled something hot, and shortly afterwards the engine started steaming. We had blown the radiator. So while Grandma Nancy stayed with us children she had Ma walk about a mile to the closest farm to call Uncle Larry for help. It had taken her several calls before she finally got a hold of him as he had been out in the fields working to describe to him the trouble we were having. At that point we didn't have an answering machine yet and hadn't gotten one till many years later. In between calls out to Uncle Larry, the farmer offered to tow us to his farm to get us off the road. This is another reason why I think the church was in Snapdragon City as there is a farm along the highway between Buttercup City and Snapdragon City which seems vaguely familiar when I have driven past it in years since. While I don't think Grandma Nancy really wanted to have him tow us I think she wanted even less for us to be sitting on the side of the road so she let the farmer tow us to his place. The farmer then took a peek under the hood and helped us diagnose the blown radiator so when Ma finally was able to get a hold of Uncle Larry she was able to tell him how the farmer said it was a blown radiator. By the time my uncle finally arrived, the sun had already set as I remember seeing the lights come on in the farmer's barn as they started chores. The entire time we waited for Uncle Larry the only person whom Grandma Nancy allowed out of the car was Ma. Then after Uncle Larry finally arrived and it was too dark for him to see to fix the radiator he got permission from the farmer to leave the Blazer at the farm and all of us girls and women piled into Uncle Larry's two-door red Ford Nova and he drove us all home. When we finally got home, my mom still had to milk cows, so after changing out of our church clothes Grandma Nancy had us all headed out to the barn to help her take care of the cows.

Grandma Nancy interpreted this and several similar breakdowns of vehicles as the Lord's way of showing us he did not want us to go to church anymore. In addition to this, Grandma Nancy – who was raised Catholic and insisted to her death that she still was Catholic – decided she did not like where the church was headed in its teaching, so she started to hold church at home among family members instead of attending or letting us, other than Uncle Larry, attend any local church gatherings. The only time we would go to church was once a year, between Easter and the day representing the descent of the Holy Spirit, Pentecost, which is what Grandma Nancy said was all that was required of us to go to church to remain members of the Catholic church. Uncle Larry, though, she allowed to go every Sunday.

As Grandma Nancy taught catechism many years for the Catholic church in Lilac City, which was less than five miles away, she had lots of Catholic materials that she allowed my sisters and me to read. From the Catechism booklet, I remember reading in my teen years, I got the impression that in reality the Catholic church would not have actually considered us Catholic anymore, as I remember reading how the Catholic church requires weekly church attendance or for shut-ins at least a weekly visit from the priest to remain Catholic. Of course, other than Uncle Larry none of the rest of my family did either of these weekly attendance requirements, but instead, for most of the years growing up it was only just once a year between Easter and Pentecost.

With Grandma Nancy's strong Catholic beliefs and years studying Christianity at college (the college only had offered a course on Religions of the World but Grandma Nancy insisted she "would not study the beliefs of false gods but only Christianity," so the college had to make a special course just for her), everyone in my family had a sound grip on Bible stories and hymns. The hymns could be found in monthly mass booklets, which she knew were going to be tossed after the month was up so she would bring the booklets home for us. These booklets were what Grandma Nancy initially used to preach to us after discontinuing going to church. Over time though her sermons changed from what was in the booklets to long winded prayers about all her fears which easily lasted an hour. It was not until Abby started reading the Bible in her teens that I also started reading the Bible. I still never really grasped anything other than additional stories from the Bible until at least my late teenage years.

CATHOLIC DUTY TRIPS

The days when we went to fulfill our Catholic duty to remain Catholic usually tended to be fun for us girls. These were usually the only trips off the farm when Grandma Nancy joined us. The time at church we would struggle to remain focused on the readings in the booklet or the hymns that were being sung instead often we would find a young child or baby who would catch our attention. If we had gone to the one Catholic Church in Rose City, Grandma Nancy would usually choose to have all of us sit in the room meant for crying or disruptive children.

After church, I remember often going to Rose City's Catholic Second-Hand Retail Store where Grandma Nancy would usually have Ma lift us girls into their dumpster and we would scrounge through their "junk" to see if we could find something we would consider a treasure. As one never knew what one would find, it was a great thrill for us kids. I remember bringing home a toy barn which had a chalkboard built into it, a doll which my oldest sister got for Christmas one year, plastic stencils which had various multiple heads, bodies, and legs which could be pieced together with alternative pieces and when colored on, one could create a variety of paper dolls. I remember also getting many books and fabric scraps from our dumpster-diving days.

Now since I have worked in retail, I can see how I am sure that our dumpster diving did not endear us to the staff at the Catholic Second-Hand Retail Store. We finally ended up stopping dumpster diving after staff yelled at Grandma Nancy and accused her of stealing. While we frequently dumpster dived, there were some times when we would also do some shopping at the Catholic Second-Hand Retail Store. My favorite shopping that I remember doing at this Catholic Second-Hand Retail Store was when they held bag sales. Each of us kids was given a bag to fill, giving us a chance to get a great price on numerous treasures, and Ma could get us all lots of new clothes for not a lot of money. While I do not recall any specific treasures or anything we brought home I remember I also recall shopping there once and being told to help pick out four board games, which I remember then my sisters and I got for Christmas and our family sitting down to figure out how to play the game and then playing them in the pursuing days and years following. In fact, I still recall the games we got that year. Dora got Tic Tac Dough; Sandy got a farm matching game; Abby got Careers; and I got The Money Game of Junior Executive.

HOME SCHOOLING

In addition to now attending church at home, after fourth grade Grandma Nancy, who was also a teacher, decided to start home schooling Abby and me. I was told this was because the school was allowing my father to come see us periodically, though I do not remember seeing him. Maybe that was because I was so young.

However, I remember having a social worker come out to the farm a few times when I was young. Other than remembering seeing her, I do not recall actually doing anything with her. The one time when she came out I remember that Abby and I were in the library room off the kitchen working on a Lite Brite picture. Another time Abby and I were playing house under the pool table in the family room. On the underside of the pool table we had cut out pictures of windows and curtains from an old Montgomery Bay catalog to provide windows. Additionally we had cut out pictures of beds, people, toys, etc. to complete our house. So as the social worker talked with the adults Abby and I played with our paper dolls under the pool table converted to doll house.

So while I remember two times when I actually got to see the social worker, I do not remember seeing Pa at school. However, I suspect, that our being home schooled also might have had something to do with how the school tried to get me to see a counselor, since I spent the majority of my time (recess, bus rides, lunch breaks, etc.) with Abby instead of with other classmates. I was so dependent upon Abby for friendship that I was prone to make her choose between me and other students whom she tried to befriend. When I talked with Abby about it in the fall of 2012, she told me how she felt she always had to choose my friendship over the other students, as that is what Grandma Nancy required.

I remember how, during recess, Abby would be playing house with Tania where the Iris Elementary building overhung the doors leading out of the gym I believe it was. Seeing Abby I would ask to join her. Tania and Abby were always willing to let me play. Tania would then decide what role each of us should play and would object if she gave me the role of mother or baby and I did not play the role of mother or baby as she wanted me to. After redirecting me multiple times as to what her interpretation of how I was supposed to react, I would grow frustrated at Tania and leave the game trying to get Abby to join me in leaving it.

Another time I remember Abby playing with Cabbage Patch dolls with her classmate Rhea, who was also a farm girl but who always seemed to bear the smell of the farm on her, so I never really was all that interested in being a friend of Rhea's.

Then I remember how Abby befriended Sophie on the school bus. Sophie was just in kindergarten while Abby was in third grade and I in fourth. Eventually Sophie ended up sitting with us for a period of time. Often she would bring her Barbie dolls, which she let us play with if she was in the mood to share. One day I remember getting very upset with Sophie. I am not sure if she was not sharing or what, but I complained to Abby and got her to complain to the bus driver who was a substitute for the regular bus driver. Sophie then got up and also complained to the bus driver. I remember that this happened many times that day until finally the bus driver insisted we stay on the bus until all the other students got off at school and then he came back and told us he wanted no more of that type of behavior.

I only had a few friendships that weren't dependent upon Abby. One such friendship was with a boy, Reggie, who sat in front of us on the bus. Abby would bring scrap paper and pencils home from school each day. The scrap paper and pencils the teacher provided for students who needed them and Abby seeing what she saw was paper and pencils which she could take would take them. Ma said that the teachers never really appreciated Abby's willingness to help herself to these items. Meanwhile on the ride home on the bus Abby would crack out these papers she was bringing home and we would enjoy practicing third grade math tests. Then when we realized how Reggie Y had a watch we asked if he could time us and other times if we could time him. Reggie would then humor us by taking third-grade math tests and let us time him with his watch. (In Reggie's senior year I remember Uncle Larry pointing out how there was a fire on the highway which was about a mile from where we lived. Later we learned that a drunk driver had hit the car that Reggie was driving. Reggie's passengers were okay but Reggie died in the accident.)

Another friendship I had was with a classmate, Michael H, who struggled keeping his desk clean, and as I kept mine rather tidy, whenever the teacher would assign us to clean our desks I always had time to help him clean his desk. Often Michael would find a picture of one of his brothers in the desk and would show it to me. Also Michael's mom, Gayle, would volunteer to watch the playground, and when that happened Michael would take me over and introduce me to her.

Finally, the other friendship which I remember was when I once was told by a sixth grade boy how I was cute when I held the door to the playground open for him and other students behind me. This prompted me to try to get him to also call Abby cute, as I truly believed she was cuter than me with her curly hair and stronger-looking build.

Because of distrust, fear, and the hurts of my family, Abby and I were withdrawn from school and church around the age of ten and spent the majority of our childhood on a dairy farm, which is a place and a business that requires lots of time and attention. The farm allowed my family to keep Abby and me so busy that we were away from the farm for probably no more than seven hours a week if even that much.

These trips off the farm would usually include our going to the farm retail store to pick up at least one item for the farm so that the trip could be counted as a business trip. The stops at the farm retail store I fondly remember because of the many awesome smells there: rubber boots, calf feed, and milk replacer (a powdered milk substitute for baby farm animals), etc. and the wide selection of items to buy from candy, clothes, music, farm items, etc. Sometimes the trip would include a stop at the liquidator store in English Primrose City where we would find markers, yarn, records, school supplies, boots, food, etc. Usually the trip off the farm also would include a stop at a grocery store to pick up groceries for Grandma Nancy and where Ma would look for items that she felt the store was going to just throw out like bruised fruit or veggies, dented cans or expired products and she would ask for a discounted price which she would bring home for real cheap, though Grandma Nancy would often yell at her for not sticking to the grocery list and buying things which we did not need. Sometimes Ma also might buy a record book. Ma was a free spirit when it came to spending. She loved making special purchases for her girls but as she was not paid to help Uncle Larry with the farm – other than room and board for herself and us girls and Grandma Nancy prevented Ma from having any other job as she would comment that if Ma had another job then Pa would get some of her money plus Grandma Nancy would run down Ma's ability to work different places. So Ma only got interest checks from certificate of deposits she had in the bank. As Ma struggled with balancing her checkbook, she tended to bounce checks which Grandma Nancy would always cover for her then. One more reason Grandma Nancy found to yell at Ma about.

Then the trips off the farm often would also include a trip to the library where we developed our love for reading. Until the Rose City library started to charge out-of-county patrons, we would go there and attend their free movies and play with the toys they had, my exposure to the Fisher Price Little People. Meanwhile Ma would pick up books. Some of the books would include those which she would read to Abby and me. This is probably my favorite childhood memory of Ma, her reading to us! I can fondly remember curling up on her soft comfortable lap while Abby would curl up on the other side of her lap and she would read to us Little House on the Prairie, Boxcar Children, Black Stallion, Hardy Boys, The Hollisters, etc.

Those trips off the farm were about the extent of Abby's and my social life from the time I was ten until I turned twenty-one. After the Rose City library was no longer free for us, since we lived in another county, we bounced around from library to library until the Pine County Library started to have a bookmobile stop at Iris City Elementary

School. We went there for many years and the librarians there were our first friends since starting home schooling. Though about that time we also had started calling different country radio stations just to talk to their disc jockey and considered them friends too.

At the beginning I was excited about being home schooled. I loved change and for about a week to a month my sisters and I were not allowed into our home's library room as Grandma Nancy and Ma remodeled it into a schoolroom. When we finally were allowed back in we found it contained a couple desks, and a board which was to be used to showcase homework and put up articles that were meant to inspire improvement in our homework. Additionally, the room included a globe and numerous books that Grandma Nancy had used for teaching years past. That first year I remember Grandma Nancy working diligently at improving our handwriting and encouraging us to compare it to the Zoner-Bloser format which she had pinned up on the board. To do this Grandma Nancy had Abby and me trace the Zoner-Bloser letters daily for several weeks. Grandma Nancy also had Abby and me write book reports. The one time the book reports were to be on books we had gotten the prior Christmas. I remember my book had a collection of short stories in it and I had tried to write a report on a story other than the one she requested because I really disliked book reports as they required a certain format and length and as I really struggled with English writing so I had tried to rewrite one of the short stories as my book report. Grandma Nancy did not approve, which resulted in my having to write a second report, this time on the required reading.

Growing up we also had a talking typewriter that gave spelling quizzes that Grandma Nancy would encourage us to take in order to help us with our spelling. I remember for example how the typewriter would say when the spelling key was hit "Level One," then "Level Two," and "Level Three" in its deep electronic voice. For years, Abby and I would try to do "Level Three," which the typewriter for example would proceed to say at some point, "Now try 'conscientious.'" If we got it right it would say, "Very good, now try _____." If we got it wrong it would say, "That is incorrect, the correct spelling of conscientious is C-O-N-S-C-I-E-N-T-I-O-U-S, conscientious. Now try _____." I actually do not recall the other words it would try to get us to spell but because "conscientious" would almost always stump us I remember it. When we would finish spelling our ten words, the typewriter would play a little music and say, "Congratulations you got (say ten) out of ten right," then start the next quiz.

Another tool she used was spelling books, which gave a list of probably twenty-five words that she would quiz us on. The spelling books would also ask us to read a story with words misspelled and ask us to underline the incorrectly spelled words and then spell them correctly. Additionally, the spelling books would give a writing assignment. For example, once it shared a little bit about Don Quixote and then asked us to write a few paragraphs about Don Quixote using at least ten of our spelling words.

Grandma Nancy had Ma teach us some geography, reading, music, and physical education which was obtained through farm chores. I remember for geography one year, Ma took Abby and me up to our bedroom where she had the material which she would quiz us on like all the state capitals and she would give us clues. When helping us to remember the capital of North Dakota, Ma would say, "Think donut," as when she first told us each state's capital she had told us that "A bismark is a kind of donut." Other clues were "You know" for Alaska's capital, Juneau; "Well, it's not noisy," for Idaho's capital, Boise; and "It's a girl's name" for Montana's capital, Helena. She also used to break up the states into groups, although I am not sure if it was by territory or by location within the United States.

For music, I remember Ma always making sure Dora was never home first. (Dora hated singing due to her having to listen to it all the time during chorus and band, which she had taken in high school.) Then Ma would teach us new songs.

While initially Grandma Nancy always had us meet for class in the classroom, before she had us enroll in in Daffodil City, IL high school correspondence class at grade 9, she had started letting us do all our class work in our bedroom. On thinking back on this, the reasoning for her switching locations was probably because the farmhouse was so old and drafty that Grandma Nancy would have had extra expense trying to heat the classroom so she just chose to let us use the bedroom which she always tried to keep warm anyway. By warm I mean compared to the rest of the house which would be warmer than outdoors. Most of the house she tried to keep in the 50s to prevent frozen pipes while our bedroom was kept closer to mid-sixties with the help of a space heater. The only exceptions were over the holidays like Thanksgiving and Christmas when she would turn the furnace up to heat the whole house up to mid-sixties.

Another reason why Grandma Nancy might have switched locations was as Abby often felt poorly usually with a headache but sometimes also with an upset stomach. To ease Abby's headaches Grandma Nancy had found several pairs of old glasses she had and let Abby use whichever pair helped ease her headache the most. So apparently Grandma Nancy had suspicions that Abby needed glasses but from stubbornness and distrust of others chose not to have Abby get a prescription for glasses of her own. Though part probably was also due to the fact that the farm was more expense than income and she was having to use her social security income just to keep things from sinking financially.

1997 JOURNAL ENTRY CONFESSIONS

It was back in 1997, when I was eighteen that I have evidence of how Ma started to allow Abby and me to occasionally call country radio stations to talk to their disc jockeys so we could have friends. We always had to be real careful, though, because we did not have Grandma Nancy's approval to call the, disc jockeys and because our home had multiple phones. These multiple phones made it possible for Ma, Grandma Nancy, or Uncle Larry to pick up one of the other phones and overhear our conversations. Eavesdropping was something Grandma Nancy strongly disapproved of, although she did not seem to think twice about doing it herself. When she overheard us talking to disc jockeys, she wouldn't hold back from telling us that she didn't like what she had heard. Occasionally on our trips off the farm, Ma would take us to the radio station in Sunflower City to visit the disc jockeys.

The evidence I have of the phone calls comes through journals I kept. The journal entries mostly were about who was on the radio that day, farm happenings, or something about the animals, but occasionally I would write down my feelings I had that day for a family member or a conversation I had with a disc jockey or feelings that that disc jockey conversation stimulated. In this chapter I included a small sampling of my journal entries from back in 1997.

<u>August 14, 1997.</u> *My mind still thinks about what I said to Ryan R and how I might explain myself and how I could have said things otherwise (like usual). If he only knew that I really don't know or haven't talked that much to guys (the most being Ethan X and Uncle Larry) since fourth grade* when Abby and I became isolated from people except for family, so that basically I'm trying to feel more like I'm part of things again.

August 17, 1997. The last bull was sold for $1.55. I think he (Ethan) was surprised at the low price because he said that he always thought they went for more. Then I told him how my family had thought it bad to get only $56 for the previous bull.

August 21, 1997. Ethan sat on Dora's lap because she mentioned listening to a disc jockey on a rival station. Later I accused her of liking it since it put her at the center of attention. According to Ma, Dora then thought I had put Ethan up to it. Actually if I'd known all the trouble it would get me in, I doubt I would have mentioned it since Abby was also on my case about it.

August 22, 1997. Just a short while ago I got mad at Abby because she asked if I wanted to call Ethan. I asked her why my opinion counted. I told her I didn't want to call Ethan. I had homework to do, books I'd like to read (since she more than likely had already finished hers). Then I blew up at Ma when she asked me if I'd like to call Ethan. Shortly afterwards Ma called Ethan and we all got to talk with him a little while. Ethan was wondering if I'd be coming to Neal's show, to which I said I didn't think so. He then told me all I had to do was call and win. I told him we didn't have a key tag. He said that we could let it slip, to which I then responded that I doubt Grandma Nancy would like it if we just won a ticket, and anyway, the twins' birthday was that day. Ethan asked what I was going to buy her, to which I responded by asking, "What?" (I was thinking that maybe somehow he knew it was Grandma Nancy's birthday too). He corrected himself by then asking if I planned to make or buy something for them (the twins). I told him I basically planned just to spend more time with them than usual. I also asked him what days he was going to be at the fair and learned that he'd do his show out at the fair and introduce Neal.

August 26, 1997. Not much happened today. I lost my temper twice, once in the morning with Dora because of her complaining and the other time in the afternoon with Abby because she acted sorry for herself that she didn't get to talk to Ethan, by saying, "And who knows if I'll be able to Friday?" Well, I hadn't talked to him either, I told her.

August 28, 1997. This afternoon I told Abby and then Dora that *we should start cleaning up the house. I had enough of the cluttered "neat messes" here and there and if no action took place I'm moving out! I also made a list of objects I'd like to take (that are mine): Bible, the 96.7FM t-shirt, backing band notebook, this notebook, Doug tapes and blank tapes, school books and supplies, fresh clothes and other things.*

September 8, 1997. *This afternoon Ma called Ethan and started crying when she got off. Seems he told her that we (Abby and me) should have friends and to stand up to Grandma Nancy (easy for him to say). It also seems he got upset about her calling all the time (it's partly Abby's and my fault).*

September 9, 1997. *Ethan was wondering what I'd done today. (I told him about my walk out to the tree line.) He was wondering if it was muddy, my walk. (No, just wet.) Then we got to talking about the view of the farm, flowers, and how it would be pretty in winter. The last thing was brought up when I had told him I had started the walks in winter.*

September 10, 1997. *Abby and I were going to take a walk together but since Uncle Larry was out in his tractor, we decided not to until 1:30. So we hiked out and saw some small trees that were already turning red. (They weren't maple, either.) We took three different views of our farm from the tree line (actually I did). I suggested walking to the library but Abby thought we should have our homework done for the day (which we hadn't) while I thought we could take it along to do at the library. (We didn't go.)*

November 6, 1997. *Yesterday morning I couldn't get the algebra problems so I started out in a bad mood. Then Sandy (since it was her "pick of radio/tape day") made us listen to her favorite show, which hadn't helped.*

November 7, 1997. *This morning I got the algebra problem I couldn't get yesterday. This afternoon I talked to Ethan. "How you doing?" ("Fine.") "So what have you been doing today?" or "Anything happen today?" (Or something like that.) ("Well, we just moved about a half dozen cows.") "To keep them warm?" ("No. Actually, we have to sell one of them.") "How come?" ("Well, she was supposed to have a calf in August and we just found out her calf's dead.") Then I told him about how it would take a lot of drugs to get the calf out and if the drugs didn't work we'd have to try something else. So it might be two years before she has another calf. "I see. You looking forward to the big weekend?" ("The weekend? It's basically the same to* me.") "Oh, come on, the weekend is THE WEEKEND." ("Yeah, I guess it is different. You're not on.") "That's right. Thursday next week is my last day. How do you feel about that?" ("Well, I am going to miss you. You know you're the reason I started to listen to 96.7FM again.") "Oh really?" ("Yeah. Vanessa told us that the new guy was from Texas and I had something going for Texas.") Big laugh. "I'm sure they'll get someone you like in here." ("Yeah.") "Well, be sure you call early next week and Thursday." ("Okay.")

November 10, 1997. I had called Ethan before and he had asked me how I was. ("Fine.") "So what have you done today?" ("Well, we sold the heifer today.") "She's the one that had the dead calf inside." ("Yeah.") "You sound sad." ("I remember when she was born and I recently noticed that she had been born on your birthday.") "Really?" ("Yeah. I've had a bull born on mine, but Abby hasn't had any born on hers.") "So you and I are the lucky ones, huh?" ("Yeah. My grandmother has had three. The twins were actually the most recent.") "So do you know where the heifer is going?" ("The cattle auction in Morning Glory City. She should be sold by about 4:00.") "So do you have any idea if she'll be sold for meat or be used for dairy?" ("Probably meat. She was a hefty one.") "Bummer."

November 24, 1997. I had asked Riley if he liked the Packers. He said yes but not so that it sounded as if they are his favorite team. I asked him if he had worked on a radio station before. "Yes, why?" I told him that I thought he sounded familiar. "What stations do you listen to?" ("I've listened to quite a few country stations but Abby listens to other kinds of stations.") So he told me 95.5FM and 97.9FM. Since I hadn't understood him I said I didn't think it had been one of those two.) "It could be because I am sick that I sound familiar." ("I hope you feel better soon.") "I hope so too."

THE NEIGHBORS

Even though we had at least a dozen neighbors within a square-mile radius of our farm, my sisters and I never got to hang out with any of them because Grandma Nancy didn't trust them, for various reasons. We even had neighbors right across the road.

During our growing-up years, we had at least three families live in the house right across the road. The first family that lived across the street Grandma Nancy told lots of stories about why she never liked them. Grandma Nancy often reminded us how the mom, Amy G, practiced witchcraft, which she then taught her daughter, Natalie. As examples of Amy's practicing witchcraft, Grandma Nancy would tell us how "One day I smelled the perfume which Amy always wore. Shortly afterwards I heard what sounded like running water. Here it was the pipes that had broken which lead to the upstairs bathroom. We tried fixing the pipes but it happened again after I smelled Amy's perfume we found the pipes had rebroken. That is why I won't fix those pipes. Amy knows where the pipes in the house are and with her witchcraft she will break them again."

Needless to say, the water to those pipes Grandma Nancy has had turned off since that day. I remember that room as always having the door to it closed, even during the winter months, which I think may have been the actual cause of the broken pipes, as the heat was prevented from entering that room.

Grandma Nancy also would share how much Amy enjoyed the meat that Grandma Nancy would can with a bit of pepper on top. So

Grandma Nancy thought she would be kind and give Amy some of the jars of meat, which she so enjoyed before Grandma Nancy left town one weekend. When Grandma Nancy came back home she smelled something just awful. In tracking down the smell, she found a jar's worth of meat spoiling in the washer in the basement. Then, as if that was not enough, Grandma Nancy would always allow Amy's daughter, Natalie, to come over and play with us grandkids, but when my oldest sister, Dora, went over to Amy's place, Dora was told she could not play with Natalie over there.

Then Grandma Nancy would also share how "Natalie learned her mom's witchcraft. I remember having you children go fishing over the door for some ice cream bars. Right as the last of you girls went to fish for your ice cream bar, we ran short even though I knew I had counted the correct number. Natalie thought it very funny and kept calling out, 'Where did it go?' That is when I realized Natalie also was starting to practice witchcraft. Then there was the time, Renata, that you caught and killed a cricket. While I had gone to get a Kleenex or something to pick it up, the cricket ended up disappearing with Natalie again saying, 'Where did it go?'"

After Amy and her family moved out, in moved Ira and Rhonda N and their family whom Grandma Nancy said were worse than Amy's family. Ronda was an acupuncturist who held her business right there in the house right across the street. Grandma Nancy said she always knew before the next client would be coming, as she would feel the pins and needles pricking her. On top of that, she commented how once she saw Ira talking to his daughter after she had become a teenager. "He was talking about her needing to bring some boyfriends over and then made a gesture like the daughter was to become pregnant. I just knew he wanted her to become pregnant so that they would be able to claim money from welfare. Well, it was several months later and here came the daughter, pregnant."

Then there was the neighbor Ruby C who lived down the street a little way. She empathized with Pa not getting to see us girls so she would give him our phone number even after we changed it a few times. Additionally, she or one of her sons would often ask to borrow some farm equipment from Uncle Larry and he, being the generous man that he was, would lend it to them. Usually after Uncle Larry would lend them the farm equipment, he would never see it again or it would come back broken.

As these were Grandma Nancy's feelings toward our neighbors, she tried to protect us from them. This would result in her telling us that if the neighbors right across the street were home, us kids were to only play in the part of the back yard where we could not see their house. If they were not home, though, we were given permission to play on the front porch and in the front yard. On one summer day when the neighbors weren't home I remember Abby and I were playing on the front porch when Ruby walked down the road with her second husband. She called out a hello and waved. Later on, Grandma Nancy came out and asked us if we had said hello or waved back, which we could tell was something we should not do. So we probably said that no, we had not waved or said hello because we knew that pretending we did not see anyone or that they could not see us was what was expected of us. In fact, for a huge portion of our childhood I remember our quickly going to hide if we were playing in the front yard and saw even just the road maintenance man or another vehicle which we recognized as a neighbor's or a farm business persons.

The Lord has helped me to see today how Satan likes to use circumstances like the ones described above to cause friction between people. I would have to say that Satan did all he could in my growing-up years to manipulate certain events and people so that I would view them as enemies and be afraid of them, which seemed to include everyone not living on our farm. As I write this story, I also realize that Satan would love for this story to be interpreted as my unwillingness to forgive my family or others who have been the source of trials in my life since I was young, but this is not the case at all. I have forgiven them and I see how God can receive more glory from all the trials I have gone through, which he revealed to me in Romans 5. Instead of being afraid and hating our enemies, we are called to love our enemies and bless those who curse us. In this way, we demonstrate our love for God by following Jesus' example, who came to this earth and gave his life on the cross to die for all of us who were considered his enemies by the sin that separated us from him. Anyone can love those who love them, but God calls us to love those who hate us.

In addition to Grandma Nancy, Uncle Larry and Ma encouraging us to be invisible to neighbors and other personnel who they occasionally would have out to the farm, I recently ran across a letter Ma sent to one of her cousins which explains a bit about why Grandma Nancy and she discouraged interactions even from family members. The reasons listed were of how it was bad economy, bad world affairs and bad happenings in our country, etc. She concluded by commenting how maybe in 10 years things would be different.

Typical Day Growing Up

The typical day from 1989 until 2001 when I moved off the farm consisted of helping Ma and one or more of my sisters with chores twice a day. Ma would do chores three times a day until I turned eighteen and after what seemed like an hour or two of heated conversation with Grandma Nancy right before the two of us went to bed I managed to convince Grandma Nancy to let me take the evening milkings on myself instead of Ma having to do them. After I had that conversation I had crawled completely under the quilt on my bed and shook for many minutes as I worked on overcoming the intense emotions that had formed standing up to Grandma Nancy like one of the first times ever in my childhood.

For a period of a few years, Ma would wake me up to help her with the chores at 4:30 which later Sandy offered to assist with. While I never struggled waking up once the sun rose, 4:30 was a bit difficult for me to do. Upon rising I would go down to the bathroom off the entry room which we kept lit by a night light and a lamp in the entry room. In the bathroom, I would get changed into my chore clothes. In summer, I might take off my house clothes first but otherwise I usually just pulled my barn clothes over my house clothes. My barn clothes usually consisted of a well stained pair of pants and button down shirt plus a jacket and a pair of boots which could be pulled over my house shoes or a pair of knee high rubber rainboots. Upon getting dressed I would join Ma on walking out to the barn along the well-worn path through the backyard, past the post with the yard light and another post which held the power source which Uncle Larry would connect the tractor and generator to whenever the power went out for any extended length of time. Then we would go down a slight, steep hill and across the driveway to the barn.

Once we reached the barn Ma would go to the milkhouse. The milkhouse was a large room off the barn which contained a large stainless steel divided sink along the right wall as one opened the milkhouse door. Above the sink were three boxes one was to turn on the cooling system for the stainless-steel bulk tank which sat about a foot or two from the far wall and which was used to hold all the milk that the cows produced. Another box controlled the agitator on the bulk tank which was used to keep all areas of bulk tank with milk of the same temperature. The final box was the one the milk hauler used to cause his milk truck to have vacuum needed to siphon the milk out of the bulk tank and into his truck.

Just beyond the divided sink was a small hand washing sink also made of stainless steel. Then there was a large window facing the house and another window was on the opposite wall facing the silo. Under the window facing the house was a small metal box bridging the wall with an insulated door leading to the outdoors and a small door with a hole for the milk haulers hose to fit through. This was where the milk hauler would insert his trucks hose and attach the hose to the bulk tank when he would siphon all the milk out of the bulk tank and into his truck after he had recorded the readings from a metal stick which stuck down into the tank and recorded just how much milk was in the tank. When the milk hauler would take this reading he would record it on the sheet on the clipboard which hung on the other side of the window by the far corner and under a well-lit clock. The milkhauler would then also look at a chart under the sheet which he recorded his reading to convert the numbers he read into the hundred-pound weight those numbers corresponded to.

Then beyond the tank in the middle of the floor by the far wall was the milkhouse drain where fluids from the multiple sinks would escape out of the milkhouse. In the far corner furthest from the house was a wire basket where calf bottles and nipples were held. Coming back towards the milkhouse door along the wall farthest from the house and under the far window was the motor responsible for creating the vacuum used to draw and/or push milk or cleaning product through the pipelines and to make the pulsators fluctuate the vacuum from front to back of the milking machine's teat cups. Next to the motor then was the blue five-foot water heater. Next to it was the box which controlled the motor which had a switch that switched the motor from vacuum used for washing the pipelines to vacuum used with milking the cows and vice versa. The box also contained another switch which would pump the water or milk out of the collecting jar through the swinging set of pipelines which could swing between the washing station or the bulk tank sending the fluids from the collecting jar to the washing station or bulk tank depending on where the pipeline was at the time. Then between the box and the corner of the room was a storage cabinet above the motor used by the bulk tank to cool the milk. This motor ran a lot and during the winter months produced almost enough heat to keep the milk house at about forty degrees. Then along the wall next to the barn was where there were three sets of pipes which entered the milkhouse from the barn and attached to a large glass jar which had a motor attached to create vacuum to pump liquid out of the jar and through the pipelines when the jar's sensor, a stainless steel tube which lowered into the jar from the middle and which then looped back up and down to make a loop where a stainless steel tube would float within the loops according to how much fluid was in the jar. When the tube would float as far up as the loop would allow the motor would automatically send the liquid in the jar through the swinging pipeline. Two of the pipes entering the jar were for milk or water to enter the jar one on the right side and one on the left side. The other pipe entered the top of the jar and regulated the vacuum in the jar and through the pulsator pipeline. Finally along the wall leading to the milkhouse door was a box which was used to run the washing machine after one was finished milking the cows. First the washing machine would run a wash with plain water, to a detergent wash and then an acid rinse with a stop which one would progress to run the sanitizing wash right before one would start the next milking. This box had where two jars could be attached which after the machine finished with the plain wash we would have a jar filled with detergent and the other jar filled with acid. The machine would then have water cycle down into the jar depending on the cycle and the excess fluid would then join the water flowing out of the box through a tube into another stainless-steel sink which had a place where the milking machines could rest with their teat cups dangling down into the water. The milking machines also had to have their milk hose be attached to the pipeline above the washing station which then connected to the pipeline entering on the left side. During the wash cycle the plug at the end of this pipeline would have to be long enough to block off fluid from entering the jar on this side and to instead enter the pipeline circling around the barn between five and six feet in the air. When milking the cows the plug in this pipeline would be short so milk could enter the jar and not have to go all the way around the barn before entering the jar.

When Ma and I got to the barn and Ma entered the milkhouse, she would fill the jar on our milking machine flushing system with a chemical we called Sanitizer which was basically bleach and then start the machine. Meanwhile I would go and encourage all the cows to get up by giving them a quick kick. (Years later I opted to start whistling with an upraised arm and only if they refused to get up would I give them a sound slap. I doubt it hurt them any more than it made my hand sting but just the sound of it was enough to get them and several more cows who heard me trying to get everyone up, to get up.) Then I would borrow Mom's jackknife or a hacksaw blade to cut open a bale or two of hay or sometimes I would open them by pulling off the strings. Then I would load up my arms with half the bale inhaling the usually wonderful smell of dried grasses, dandelion, clover, or alfalfa. The smell of the dandelion usually had a sort of fermented smell which reminded me somewhat of the smell at the convenience store which smelled like yeast so it was one of my favorites. Then I would spread the bale out to all the cows on the north side of the barn then I would go get the other half of the bale and spread it out to all the cows on the south side of the barn. As I grew older I developed a love for the challenge of opening all bales by pulling off the strings. Very seldom did I choose to cut the strings.

After I had the hay fed I would go and scrape all the piles of manure or pee soaked bedding away from behind the cows into the gutter. While I really didn't mind the smell of the manure, I usually preferred not to be around the cows when they were actually peeing or pooping as the smell was very fragrant and overwhelming to both the nose and eyes.

Once I had the hay fed, Ma usually had completed all the milkhouse chores of getting a pail of sanitizer which she would dip the milking machines into between cows and a pail of dawn water containing the number of towels needed to wash each cow's teats clean of any straw or manure which might be clinging to the teats before attaching the milking machine. The towels were quarter of the original size. We then hung these pails up on strings hanging down from the barn's ceiling. She also would switch the swinging pipeline from the wash station to the bulk tank. Then taking a two-foot-long spring which she covered with a filter sock and secured the filter by pushing a hollowed-out rubber stopper up into the spring after the end of the filter was pushed up into the spring. Then taking a clamp, she would clamp the swinging pipeline onto a hollow stainless-steel pipe which was inserted into a hole in the bulk tank usually capped by a gray rubber cap. She then also disconnected the milking machines from the wash-line and hung up on the metal hangers which she then would carry out to the barn after turning all the motors on that were needed to milk the cows. She then would start to milk the cows which was the warmest job during the winter months and a very hot and sticky job in the summer. That was when having a cow vigorously lick your back would feel good. One it helped a person feel cooler and two it was as close to a massage any of us ever got.

Next, I would take a wheelbarrow filled with corn and pails of buffer (a product similar to baking soda), salt, and minerals and would feed the cows like five pounds of corn and an ounce apiece of the other three items. Sometimes we would also include a cup of grass pellets or ground soybeans. After feeding each of the cows their corn I again scraped behind the cows. Then I would quick feed the young stock a slab or two of hay per animal. I would also check to make sure they had a full container of clean water. If the water looked like one of them had pooped in the pail or stuck a foot in it I would then scold the calves as I dumped it out and then refilled the container with water. At one of the other two milkings I would also give the calves about a pound of Sweet Sixteen grain and five quarts of milk replacer. (I loved the smell of the grain with its molasses, corn and pellets as well as the milk replacer. They were a couple of favorite smells.) The older young stock I would just feed about a couple pounds of corn per animal. Then I would feed another bale or two of hay again to encourage the cows to remain standing until Ma finished getting all the cows milked. Then I would go around again with another round of corn. This time just feeding them corn. Finally, I would throw some lime under the cows to dry the floor and some bedding to provide some extra protection. Throughout the chore time Ma and I would also make time to hold some of our cats and give them some attention and the milk we collected into a cup which had a screen on its top as we made sure none of the cows udders were fighting an infection causing mastitis or chunky looking milk.

My favorite part of helping with the four o'clock milking would be on the walk out to the barn seeing all the stars and Ma would point out the large dipper and if she could find the small dipper she would point it out to me too. Another thing I would love would be when the sun rose I would actually be up and get to see all the color during the sunrise through the windows in the barn which faced the east.

Then after chores were done we would go back into the house and would change out of our barn clothes which we piled into a box containing all but Uncle Larry's barn clothes. He hung his up on the wall right behind the back door. Then I would wash up catching all the dirty water into a plastic bowl and using the mirror to check for any manure on my face. Once the bowl was filled it would be carried out to the entry room and dumped into a five-gallon container that was sitting out there where all the water from the house would end up being collected. Usually it was Uncle Larry's job to haul it out to the milkhouse drain off area and dump it. Sometimes Ma did it for him and when I got to my late teen, early twenties I started hauling it out sometimes too.

After washing up I would grab a plate from the kitchen. As Grandma Nancy had always felt so concerned about killing every germ she used to wash every dish and then dunk them in a pot of water she had boiling. When we grew old enough to wash our own dishes she let Ma and each of us girls have our own large plate, small plate, large bowl, small bowl, silverware and a cup which we were in charge of washing and in between uses we were to store under our own kitchen towel she gave to each of us to use.

So it would be out from under my towel that I would grab my small plate. Taking that plate to the table island set up in the kitchen I would then grab a couple pieces of bread from the loaf usually bought from the convenience store which smelled like yeast unless another store had sold a loaf of white bread cheaper than the convenience store which smelled like yeast as they sold their bread for 3/$1.00. I would then toast the bread and spread margarine on it and add a slice of American Singles sliced cheese to it unless it was Sunday in which case I would have peanut butter, preferably chunky, instead! Then after eating my sandwich(es) I would clean my plate usually just by wiping the crumbs off into the wash basin and then tuck the plate back under my kitchen towel. If we had a cow have a calf (another of my favorite smells-a newborn calf) one of the past few days I would also grab a glass of milk but if no calf had been born recently I just would have a glass of water to go with my sandwich(es).

Then I would either work on some homework, sit down with a book to read, or help Ma and my sisters unload one or more hay wagons until chore time at noon in which we would repeat the chores I mentioned earlier. This chore time Abby would join Ma and me and we would either feed haylege during the winter or green chop during the summer instead of hay. Abby and I would also help throw some hay down from the haymow and fill the bedding chute if needed. While in the haymow we would also goof around climbing up on the beams, stringing up some "ropes" we made and swing on them. Sometimes we would even see a cat who had recently had kittens and just watch her as she would go to feed her kittens and we would determine to find the kittens. We usually were successful at finding the kittens and would then set out to befriend the kittens and feed the kittens. Abby and I also would work with the young stock spending at least a little time with each of them leading them about or just giving them attention which helped keep them tame. Plus we would scrape out the calves pens daily unless we were just creating a manure pack, in which case we just threw more bedding where it was damp after removing manure piles.

After chores we would head in and find shrimp flavored Ramen Soup which I absolutely hated and would be bad and just go without eating. Additionally we would make up three tuna sandwiches apiece from a mixture made from half a jar of mayonnaise and a can of tuna for dinner. Whatever of this mixture was left would then have more mayonnaise added until that can of tuna lasted like a week. An exception to this meal would be when Grandma Nancy would plan on us getting some items from town in which case she would let us all split half a bag of cheese curls or corn chips and a couple hotdogs apiece or a slice of bologna with sauerkraut and we would head to town. But if it wasn't a day Grandma Nancy would send us to town I would resume reading, do some crafts or do my homework until Uncle Larry came home.

Once Uncle Larry would come home from working in town Ma and one of my sisters or I would usually help Uncle Larry fix the barn cleaner, farm equipment, or silo unloader if any of them needed repairs. Usually it seemed to be me who would be helping Uncle Larry as Dora would come down with colds so easily or she would become hurt some way or another and Ma did not want to take a chance on her getting sicker or hurt. Then it usually wasn't my other sisters as Sandy had some difficulty knowing what was being asked of her with her disability, and Abby battled headaches nearly every day and an upset stomach, often with vomiting, almost every month if not more often. (It was just frequently enough that I still cannot fathom getting drunk and purposely making oneself feel that way.) Once Abby finally got glasses in 1998, she experienced a lot fewer headaches and upset-stomach episodes, since she was so blind that she later said, "Descriptions in books did not make sense. I could not see leaves on trees, facial expressions, and spots on animals. That is why I would skim books and just read the conversations." Meanwhile Ma would usually either finally be getting some sleep between chore times or would be helping with field work.

In addition to reading or doing homework during our free time from chores my sisters and I would do crafts, or play with our toys or play outdoors during the summer. In the summer months, our free time would decrease, as we would have to help Uncle Larry unload as many wagons of hay each day as was needed to get the hay off all the fields. I always chose to work in the haymow as working under the sun in the heat of the day made me feel sick in less than half the time as when I would work in the haymow. The few times I didn't work in the haymow I would feel sick before we would finish the wagonload but despite how awful I felt I would make myself stick it out until the work was done or would ask to transfer into the haymow. In the haymow, I would throw the bales of hay which made it up the elevator and into the haymow and try to make sure the hay bales would go to the far wall of the barn instead of stacking up under the hay elevator. I always tried to imitate Uncle Larry, as he seemed so strong. This caused me to become the tomboy of the family.

During the summer, our dinner sandwiches would be complimented with tomato or cucumbers grown in our garden and the chips or cheese curls would be replaced by butternut squash. For supper we would have a bowl of boiled macaroni with a can of a gravy or cream soup, which later was replaced by margarine. Sometime during the day we would be allowed to have three cookies or bars if they had been made that day; otherwise we would only be allowed two. If we had a cow that had freshened, had a calf, recently we would be allowed as much milk to drink as we wanted, often with a scoop of chocolate if the milk lasted more than a day. But if no cow had freshened recently we were only allowed one glass of milk during that day.

Variance to these meals would, of course, occur during Lent where we would get three fish sticks for our sandwiches and Sunday meals. The Sunday meals would usually be special, as we would be allowed to have toast with peanut butter instead of margarine for breakfast.

Dinners would consist of three sandwiches of ham and French fries with a piece of cake and ice cream. Suppers would include a fraction of one Jack's pizza with cake and ice cream.

In the fall, Abby and I would sometimes get a break from our chores when Uncle Larry would decide he wanted to spread manure on the fields. Those days we would get to help in the tractor turning on the PTO, the metal shaft between the tractor and manure pump that ran gears which brought manure up from the pit dug in the ground behind the barn and would send it through a pipe into a tanker. When we did not have a tanker to fill, Abby and I would immerse ourselves in the books we had brought out to the tractor. From doing this with its change of pace for the day which was the closest to a vacation we got other than going to the local fairs occasionally, the smell of a freshly stirred manure pit and field freshly spread with manure were another of my favorite smells.

DISTRUST OF STRANGERS, ESPECIALLY MEN

As my family's distrust of people grew, we were only allowed to play in our front yard when the neighbors who lived right across the road from us were not home. When they were home, we were only allowed to play in the back yard making certain we could not see the neighboring house from where we played. Additionally, Grandma Nancy would scold us whenever we got too loud, as she did not want the neighbors to be able to hear us either. Ma and Uncle Larry would stand behind Grandma Nancy's decisions regarding this matter as well as almost every other decision Grandma Nancy made regarding us. This meant they also tried to keep us invisible from additional neighbors and most other people, including veterinarians and other farm businessmen who came to the farm. This also included Grandma Nancy's siblings when they would come calling, whom I never recall actually being invited into the house when they would come up from the state where Ma grew up to visit Grandma Nancy. In fact, I always got the impression after they left that Grandma Nancy felt they had only come to snoop and/or to pry. Since my family had stopped inviting anyone to the farm, since we never went visiting anyone, and since we were home schooled and home churched, this inevitably led to my leading a very sheltered life and resulted in my becoming wary of people, especially men and people in authority.

This wariness of men only grew as Grandma Nancy shared her experiences. I remember how she would tell us at the time, "It was after

Grandpa Robert died. I would be working in the garden and this guy would go driving down the road and he would always wave at me. I never thought anything of it and would wave back. One day when I was still in the house, he drove into the yard and came up to the house wanting to talk. I had not unlocked the door and he begged me to because he wanted to come in and talk. I told him that was far enough and that I was not interested in him and that he should leave. That is why you girls need to be careful not to wave to guys as you never know how they are going to interpret just a friendly gesture."

Then Grandma Nancy would share how Ma told her after she divorced that while Ma and Pa were still courting, Pa had taken Ma out to eat, and they were laughing and having a good time when Pa asked Ma, "When you laugh does that mean you would like to have sex?" So Grandma Nancy would tell us girls how "You need to be careful of laughing and smiling at guys as you do not know how men are going to misinterpret the gesture."

Also, throughout our childhood, Grandma Nancy always pointed out whenever she saw a woman dressed in a way to draw attention to herself and in a manner to turn men on. We would always know when she thought a dress was scandalously short, had a slit clean up to …, showed too much cleavage, or someone was wearing a scarf to draw attention to how low-cut her top was, etc. Additionally, Grandma Nancy was continually sharing with Abby and me how Pa had abused Dora and Sandy. Grandma Nancy tried never to bring up Pa around Dora and Sandy, as she did not want them to have to deal with remembering that time in their life.

Plus, Grandma Nancy discouraged physical affection or playfulness from my uncle, so that if Pa ever took us to court, my uncle could truthfully say he had never laid a hand on any of us or gave us any sort of physical affection, which the court or Pa might try to use to get us away from Ma, Uncle Larry, and Grandma Nancy. Also, because of how bad Grandma Nancy's back was, she refused to give or receive physical affection, and my older sisters didn't either because of the sexual abuse they had experienced, so my younger sister and I had been discouraged from showing any affection as well. The only exceptions were Ma, who was very affectionate and loved to give and receive hugs and between Abby and myself.

BENEFITS OF THE SHELTERED LIFE

The sheltered life did allow me to better develop my love of animals and taming and healing them. I remember as a real young kid being terrified of cats. I would often wake up clinging to Ma whom I shared the bed with after having nightmares of a cat sneaking into the barn. I slept with Ma until about the age of nine and then Abby slept with her and I would sleep with Grandma Nancy. Usually I'd dream the cat would be entering the barn from the haymow where there was a hole by the corn silo which is how in real life is where cats actually would enter the barn. The nightmares came about as my family for years had tried to keep cats out of the barn, but eventually I saw cats as something to tame and befriend. Throughout the rest of my childhood, that is what I did with many stray cats. It was always my greatest accomplishment when I was able to touch a cat successfully for the first time. Usually it would happen as I would put down some milk or cat food and then refuse to leave until the cat would come to eat. Initially I would have to ignore the cat as I sat down and waited. Then I would give it an "accidental" pet and go back to ignoring in when it ran off as if for its life. After petting it accidentally a few times, the cat would usually determine the food was worth the petting and the cat was on its way to being tamed!

I also remember we had a very ornery cow back in 1989 that would buck anyone trying to pet her. She was one of our blackest cows with four short white stockings, some white on the tip of her tail, a small white spot on her forehead and most of her udder was white. Pretty much the only competition she got for being the blackest was a grand calf born around 2001. Before Abby and I set to making friends with all the animals and giving them all names the cattle were just known by number and a letter. So this cow was known as 27A but as this cow was quite old and mother to a large portion of the herd she was the only one Ma and Uncle Larry gave a name to which was "Mama". I then became determined to break Mama of the habit of bucking. So every day I would pet her as I fed her as I was passing by her at arm's distance to avoid her bucking. After probably months of doing this, I was able to get closer and closer until one day I proudly showed off to Abby how the cow finally tolerated me and I was able to give her several minutes of attention. Enough time to turn her rather square-shaped white spot on her head into a more heart shaped spot.

Growing up on the farm, I also developed a love for trying to heal animals. One instance was in early 2001, about six months after Abby and I had convinced our family to let us work off the farm. We had a young bull calf, Nick (born on St. Nicholas's day), that I had bought from my uncle for $100. This bull calf would eat some grain but not as much as it should have at weaning age. So we tried to encourage Nick to eat better by putting him with older animals which was what we did with most of our young calves. Sure enough, Nick took off eating, but about a week or so later he went down and was unable to get up on his own. As Nick was my calf and I had no problem paying for a veterinarian, I called Tulip City Veterinary Clinic and Dr. Oliver Y came out. He noted how Nick had a swollen leg and said that he feared the infection was close to entering the bloodstream. He advised me to give Nick Nuflor and that I should put him back on milk replacer and add some milk replacer on his grain for extra nutrients. Additionally, I was to make sure to get Nick to his feet and make him walk if I did not want the infection to enter his bloodstream. So the first few days I would prop Nick up on some bales and massage his legs and move them about like he was walking as he was too weak to stand or do much more than eat and drink. This I did until Nick could again stand on his own. Once Nick was able to stand on his own again I would put the pail containing his milk-flavored grain a few steps away and, supporting him, I would move his legs forward until he got to the pail which he was then able to eat out of. As Nick grew stronger, I made the distance farther and farther away until his pen just wasn't far enough and I would walk and then run around the pen a few times to make him earn his treat since he was doing so much better.

Another time also around 2001, I was able to heal a wild male black and white kitten, EB, who must have tried nursing from one of our tame queens, otherwise known as a female cat, who must have been unaccepting (most of our queens nursed whichever kitten came to nurse whether it was hers or not). We always thought this was what happened, as his eyeball suddenly got this huge bubble in the middle, which just grew until he no longer was able to close his eye. Since he did not want to touch it, it started to get matted with all sorts of junk. So, as I had started to volunteer at Tulip City Veterinary Clinic, I had asked Dr. Oliver Y what I should do for EB and he sent me home some antibiotics and some eye drops. Well, as I stated earlier, EB was a wild kitten and I was not sure if I would be able to give him his treatment twice daily as I was told I should. I thought I would at least try, so I bought the medication and upon coming home went to the haystack where our cats would all lay and sure enough, he was there. As EB was so sick from the condition his eye was in I was able to catch him. So taking EB by the scruff of his neck I gave him a dropper of antibiotics orally (not an easy task for even tame cats) and applied some of the eye drops. After I gave the stuff to him, I thought for sure I would not be able to catch him again the next time he was due to get his medicine. The first few times it had been difficult catching EB since he was wild, but weirdly enough it was not long after I started treating him that he actually came to me when it was time for him to get his medicine. I have always wondered if that was because he recognized how very sick he was at the beginning of the treatment and as the medicine worked, he got to feeling better. If he recognized this improvement in his condition, maybe he actually wanted to get his medicine, or maybe he just realized he had just been a scaredy cat the whole time but with no reason to be scared. Either way, I fondly recall how I was able to tame him while giving him medicine!

As so much of our time on the farm was around the animals, we got to see and assist with many births and with treating sick animals.

One birth of significance which I remember seeing was by our first stray cat, Calico, which we had tamed. She was getting on in years by this time but she gave birth to four little kittens down inside the barn, even though Ma kept saying she thought something was wrong with Calico. Nevertheless, she successfully delivered the kittens and after nursing them a bit took each new kitten by the scruff of its neck and hauled them up to the haymow. About a week or so later we heard kittens in the haymow crying and crying. Ma kept telling us just to be patient that Calico would be back for them. But when hours had passed and those kittens were still crying, Ma joined us in removing a board from the haymow wall and calling for the kittens until they came where we could reach them. The next couple of months we used eyedroppers and a tiny bottle to feed the kittens. Sadly, two of the kittens ended up dying, but Abby and I were able to raise the other two. She claimed the orange and white tabby tom kitty for herself, which we named Toby, and I claimed the black and white queen kitty, which we called Ebony. As cats are supposed to be very agile we had the kittens learn to walk on a board only a couple inches wide (if even that) to work on their agility. We got them to do it but they were always so scared and cried and cried until finally they realized all they had to do was follow the finger that was crossing the board and then they would be helped off the board and given lots of praise, attention and a special treat. Then to work on their speed Abby and I would take them outside and walk backwards while they followed us. They were SO CUTE as they toddled after us as fast as their little legs could carry them!!!

Having all that time on the farm also developed my love of reading. Some of my favorite books during my earlier childhood years and into my teen years were the *Boxcar Children, The Happy Hollisters, Trixie Belden, Little House on the Prairie,* books by Gary Paulsen, and *The Hardy Boys* (until they started getting more violent and Grandma Nancy decided they accurately depicted the world and always wondered what the next evil was going to be depicted in their books.). Then in our teen years as we were told we were not supposed to read Harlequin books, I now regret to say how Abby and I started to read Silhouette books. I recently heard those types of books being accurately described as emotional pornography, as most if not all the books were rather pornographic in their descriptions and played on a person's emotions.

Another benefit of being on the farm so much was in our free time we got to learn and play a lot of card and board games plus some outdoor games, which I still love to do. Uncle Larry was very competitive with games, always seeking to win and if there was bidding (like Euchre or 500) he would always insist on having the top bid, sometimes even if his hand was not all that good. That sometimes really bothered us girls, in our inability to bid or win games, but those were the best memories we made as kids with Uncle Larry, playing games with him. He even tried to teach us how to play baseball, but we were never very good at that either.

Also while growing up we were able to learn quite a few crafts. Ma had paid for Dora and Sandy to receive a few lessons to learn how to knit, and by watching them Abby saw how it was done and helped me learn how to knit. Then we read somewhere about making looms out of a couple pieces of boards, a couple bolts and nuts, and several washers and brads. We made several items this way. Then when Ma ordered something once from a gift catalogue, she got a little metal loom free with her purchase and with that Abby and I have since made three to five full bedspreads over the past ten years.

I also recall doing some gardening. When we were little, I remember Uncle Larry plowing up a patch for us to plant a garden in next to George's House. As we were little, though, weeding wasn't something we did well, and, combined with lots of help from rabbits and slugs eating what we grew, our gardens did not fare too well. So for about the next ten years Ma got a bunch of the five-gallon pails, which initially contained the detergent or acid the farm used to clean pipelines between milkings, and she asked Uncle Larry to get us dirt to fill the pails. We then planted our gardens in the pails, which we put into the feed bin that had lost its roof. We never lost produce to rabbits and slugs there but it was a daily job to make sure what we planted got watered as container gardening lost its moisture more quickly than regular gardens. Then when Grandma Nancy decided to put up another feed bin to replace that one we started to plant gardens inside tires around the backyard and over the sewer tank. It was then that Abby and I heard how if a person plucked the ends of squash and cucumber runners toward the end of the growing season, it would encourage the plants to focus on the squash or cucumbers it already had, and we then did this every year. In my final years living there I remember how Ma enjoyed planting lots of flowers and how I found it to be relaxing to pull weeds from the flower gardens and to de-head old blooms to encourage additional blooming. I also took to pulling weeds from the flower garden area over by George's House to relax and loved to do it especially when the roses, honeysuckle, and peonies were blooming. The smell of them, apple blossoms, catalpa blossoms and lilac blossoms were additional favorite fragrances from my childhood.

These are just a few of the benefits that I got while living a sheltered life on the farm. I could tell more about how we gained the ability to lead all the cows and calves, tormented the calves trying to make them run like horses, tried to ride them or tried to treat them like bulls. Plus I could share how we made our own paper dolls, animals, and doll houses. I could also share how we got into painting shirts and sewing to make our own unique Packer and Badger shirts. Then I could share stories about catching grasshoppers and putting them in two litter bottles with several handfuls of mowed grass. From this we would see how the bigger ones would survive while occasionally we would only find a leg or other parts of the body of the smaller ones (same when we had too many tom cats and so many kittens or a starving mother cat). I could share the fun we had in George's House which was our playhouse where we pretended we each rented out a room, got mail at it (junk mail that Ma, Grandma Nancy, and Uncle Larry got), and used as a store (old food containers we taped shut and then bought with play money). Then there were our clubhouse days in the little woods next to George's house, or our trips into the field for apples or making mud pies with honeysuckle berries and mud in an old stove on our porch, which didn't actually work and was never plugged in, and the fun of drawing in the dirt, playing baseball, volleyball, and badminton.

DEPRESSION PERIOD

Despite all those fun things, in my pre-teen and teen years I suffered bouts of depression. The causes of the depression were threefold. One, I tried to be good enough to get to heaven and knew I fell short way too often, as was seen in my journal entries I included earlier.

Also in probably my pre-teen years Abby and I had read a book about a tragedy, which led to our making up our own similar stories. After months of telling these stories and Grandma Nancy's daily prayers for protection from that type of tragedy, I chose to look up the actual definition of the tragedy. I remember going to get dressed with Abby for chores afterward and asking her, "Do you know how in our stories we are having the tragedy Grandma Nancy daily prays for protection from occur in the stories?"

To which Abby calmly said, "Yes."

Her calmness, as if she did not care, made me mad and I told her, "Well I just realized it, and it makes me sick. I will not continue with such storytelling." As Abby still seemed indifferent, I told her, "Well as you do not care how sinful our story time characters are, I am not going to listen to the countdown tonight then." This countdown was a radio program with the twenty most popular songs of the week that Abby and I always listened to together.

Upon hearing that, Abby called out, "Ma, Grandma Nancy, Renata says she won't listen to the countdown with me tonight."

Ma or Grandma Nancy then reprimanded me. "You and Abby

always listen to the countdown every week. Don't be foolish and destroy this time together.

I remember thinking, *If Ma and Grandma Nancy only knew, surely, they would have sided with me in this.* But as I did not want to get Abby or I into trouble, I did as they asked but very unwillingly. For months after that, Abby and I would listen to the countdown together but that time together had been destroyed until Sammy Kershaw's song, "I Can't Reach Her Anymore" hit the top of the charts and we realized our friendship was more important than the fight. After my confronting Abby though, we never continued with making up stories though.

Another reason for my depression was because I seriously thought everyone in the world – except for probably my family – would be headed to hell, with the possible exception also of the Pope and Paul Harvey. This came as that was the impression Grandma Nancy would give and as she would always scold all of us kids and even Ma and Uncle Larry about not being able to make it to heaven where our deceased loved ones were, when we misbehaved or disobeyed her.

The third reason for my depression was due to seeing our farm falling apart due to financial strain and not being kept clean due to neglect. I remember how it started in the house with the entry room. Grandma Nancy put tape over the light switch as she had seen a spark from one of the lights so she did not want to take a chance on starting a fire. Then there were the pipes that burst, which Grandma Nancy refused to repair. Then she got tired of unclogging pipes so she started having us wash dishes and out hands in basins, which then would get carried outside and dumped which made washing anything lot less enjoyable so things like the bannister leading upstairs started to get black with caked dirt. Next, the fuses kept being blown upstairs so she ran an extension cord from downstairs to the upstairs so we could have light up there. (All our radios had to be run on batteries because she did not trust the electrical sockets. Plus, she wanted to save electricity.) Then as she wanted us to enjoy living at home, Grandma Nancy decided to put aside her desire for us to keep the place looking neat and instead let us collect projects all over the house which made dusting and vacuuming extra difficult. (This collecting of projects was probably the last straw for me as the untidiness just overwhelmed me causing me to feel claustrophobic. It also is why hoarders break my heart as that is what our pile collections turned into.)

Meanwhile the barn was not faring much better. One part of the roof rotted pretty badly, destroying a lot of hay. The stalls and the cement holding them together started to fall apart. The shed barn cleaner either always froze or broke down, which meant Uncle Larry had to use his tractor with a bucket to haul the manure out, maybe monthly, except in the winter when the manure froze solid. This would require my sisters and me to shovel or fork out the stalls the next spring. Usually it was just Abby and me though. That was hard, back-breaking work. What got me were the times when Uncle Larry almost finished, but because he had bowling or some other activity off the farm, he would choose to leave a big manure mess which he would cover with good hay or a board to be able to access the animals or bring in hay for the cows. That was one of the things that finally prompted me to move out, but I am getting ahead of myself here. I will have more on my moving out later.

During one of these periods of depression, I remember how I would wander over to where family member were playing badminton or volleyball and try to play with them, but my heart was not in it, as it just seemed like a waste of time. Other times I remember wandering over to where Ma was washing clothes and that really depressed me as I saw how vain it was trying to wash clothes which would just need cleaning again shortly, especially barn clothes. Plus there was the difficulty in removing stains in other clothes. Still other times I would accept an offer from Ma to read to Abby and me, and I remember feeling miserable but forced myself to stay as she read because I loved her and having her read to us. But I still felt that reading was meaningless (much like King Solomon felt about many things in life as seen in Ecclesiastes). Throughout that time I remember how I felt the need to constantly be praying the "Our Father," "Hail Mary's," and "Glory Be's" as a rosary as I sought a purpose for my life and felt despair over the thought of the world heading to hell. Those prayers I had heard were what many Catholics believed would wash away sins, so I tried to constantly pray them to guarantee my family, the world, and I could safely get to heaven.

For months to years, I brooded a lot over these things. When I became a born-again Christian, however, the Lord had me read in his Word – the Catholic version, in the book of Sirach 30:21 *Do not give yourself over to sorrow, and do not afflict yourself deliberately. Revised Standard Version Catholic Edition.*

THE PACKERS AND THE CHANGES THEY BROUGHT

In addition to being cut off from social activities with others off the farm, my sisters and I were not allowed for most of our childhood to watch TV. Real early in my childhood I faintly recall having gotten to watch some "Little House on the Prairie." One episode I seem to recall had a wolf that got in the house. The thought of the wolf being under the girls bed so freaked me out that I ran outdoors to seek comfort from Ma. She was picking raspberries in the patch next to Georges House. I did not leave her side until she was finished picking raspberries and she probably even let me very carefully help her pick raspberries too. The few times we picked raspberries as a family before my grandmother concluded they were the cause of hemorrhoids and discouraged us from eating any, I remember being encouraged to wear long sleeves and pants to protect us from the raspberry plants prickliness but more so the little rose plants which grew intermittently among them.

I also faintly remember getting to watch the news a few times with Uncle Larry and parts of an election. The only other memory that I remember with any sort of real clarity was watching "The Dukes of Hazard." The time we were watching the Dukes of Hazard happened to be during a real bad windstorm. I remember the entire family being in the living room with the TV on and praying for safety during the storm which was raging outside. Ma, Abby and I were sitting on the steps leading upstairs and looking out the window towards the north.

The rest of the family was in the middle of the room over by the TV. While Grandma Nancy prayed, as she was the one who led all prayers unless it was the rosary in which case she let everyone take turns leading the rosary, Ma, Abby and I saw the door from our machine shed came off in the wind. Boy did the prayers for safety intensify as we watched in horror as the wind blew the door toward the house. We then praised God when the wind lost the door and it fell on the driveway just feet from hitting the porch and the house. Sometime after this I believe Grandma Nancy heard Paul Harvey or someone talk about how people were able to use TV's to spy into people's houses so she took the TV out of the living room and hid it away so people couldn't use it to spy on our family anymore. Later Grandma Nancy heard how with modern technology that people were able to make cameras as small as a pinhead and she was fearful that somehow someone had or was going to get one lodged in our house so they could spy on us.

Through most of my childhood, though, I recall that while we weren't able to watch TV we were allowed to listen to the radio. Grandma Nancy had a phonograph player with a radio sitting in the library and she would daily be found listening to 1450AM's news and Paul Harvey on it around the noon hour. She would request that no one be in the room with the radio or she would have a collapsible carrying chalkboard which she would set up in front of the radio so that nobody could somehow spy on us using our radios. Uncle Larry and Dora would also turn on another little radio Grandma Nancy had sitting in the entry room to listen to evening news and sports programs. Only Uncle Larry, Dora and sometimes Ma were allowed to touch the radios as the rest of us Grandma Nancy would accuse as being the cause of thing getting broken. On occasion Dora or Uncle Larry would additionally listen to 104.5FM for the weather forecast and then listen to the country music they played. 1450AM and 104.5FM for the longest times were all that we were allowed to listen to.

A few years into being homeschooled Abby and I protested to earn rights to listen to music too as Dora could turn the music on when she desired and sometimes she would choose to turn the music off when it was a song Abby and I were enjoying because she did not like the song.

Grandma Nancy obliged us and found us a little radio which we could move between our bedroom to Uncle Larry's bedroom where we would use one of the looms we had made to work on making a yarn throw for a family member for Christmas after we completed our homework as by then our school room had gotten moved to Uncle Larry's room for our school room as it was warmer than the library. The one thing she requested was that when we listened we were to have the radio in a drawer and close the drawer after we turned on the radio. Initially they required that we listen only to 104.5FM but eventually they okayed us to listen to other stations as long as they were just country music stations as the rest of the stations played evil music.

In the course of listening to country music, the Lord led Abby and me to 92.3FM, a station that also aired Green Bay Packer football games. I remember Abby listening to the whole season leading up to the Packers' first Super Bowl under Coach Mike Holmgren in the 1990s, while we did crafts or played Monopoly or Payday together. As Dora seemed to be a sports person, I never cared to share her passion for it and so for the longest time resisted becoming interested in the Packers as Abby obviously had. It was not until the excitement of the Super Bowl, though, that I really paid any attention and became very interested in football.

Abby and I were in what was the school room making some homemade cards using glue to make designs on construction paper as she listened to the Super Bowl game. Initially I paid very little attention to the game but when Desmond Howard made a record breaking ninety-nine-yard runback I started to catch a bit of Abby's excitement as well as the radio announcers Jim Irwin, Max McGee and Larry McCarren's excitement. Then a bit later Chris Jacke made a record breaking fifty-three-yard field goal. The Lord used my excitement over these two plays and the Green Bay Packers' Super Bowl win to change my life.

The excitement from the Packers winning the Super Bowl prompted Grandma Nancy to dig out the TV which we used to watch when really little and she started letting us watch the Packer games the next season out in the summerhouse the family had built the one summer. At first, mostly we just watched games and player interviews before and after the games and during the news. As we started to watch the games I started to see Christian messages like John 3:16 (*For God so loved the world that he gave his one and only Son that whoever believes in him shall not perish but have eternal life*) in the crowds and I also started to hear them as there were a lot of outspoken Christian players on the Packers' team.

Then Abby and I would coax Grandma Nancy to allow us to watch a few more shows on TV. Initially it was the Seinfeld show which played right after the news which I actually found dumb but Abby enjoyed so I watched it to spend time with her. Then we started to watch the movies which played after Seinfeld and then we started checking out what other channels also carried. It was several months later that we found the local CBS station in Snapdragon City that aired programs like Touched by an Angel, Promised Land and Billy Graham crusades. From all these Christian messages that I began hearing and seeing, I learned that Jesus Christ died for everyone, including me. So by deciding to live for him in all that I do and by telling him I am sorry for my sins (my self-centered living, which includes anger, which Christ regards as murder, and lust, which Christ considers as adultery, and lies; etc.), I became a born-again Christian. The day I made that decision Ma, Grandma Nancy, Abby and I were all watching a Billy Graham Crusade and he gave his alter call. While I was watching, I was working on my journal entries which is when I normally worked on my journal entries, during TV shows. I remember wanting to go upstairs or out to the barn and calling the number which ran across the screen during Billy Graham's alter call but fearing Grandma Nancy would pick up and never let me forget how she disapproved of the decision I never did make the call. I was sure Grandma Nancy would disapprove as she was quite vocal about how she did not believe in the "born again" messages she would hear and let us know that that was her only reason for disliking the messages. Then as there were multiple times Grandma Nancy would find something one of us had done which she disagreed with the entire family would hear of it for weeks to months later.

Through all my bouts of depression in feeling like I could never be good enough to get to heaven, I now knew that I am a new creation who really never could be good enough to earn this gift of his, which is eternal life in heaven with him. All I needed to do and all I could ever do was simply accept his gift of salvation by believing in the work that Jesus did for me on the cross, repenting of my sin, and living for him. I still struggle with sin, but I know God loves me, which is why Christ died. His death was for people like me, who too often are more like the Pharisees in the parable in Luke 18:9-14 than the tax collector in our thoughts, thinking we are better than we really are.

The Luke 18 passage reads: *"To some who were confident of their own righteousness and looked down on everyone else, Jesus told this parable: "Two men went up to the temple to pray, one a Pharisee and the other a tax collector. The Pharisee stood by himself and prayed: 'God, I thank you that I am not like other people—robbers, evildoers, adulterers—or even like this tax collector. I fast twice a week and give a tenth of all I get.' "But the tax collector stood at a distance. He would not even look up to heaven, but beat his breast and said, 'God, have mercy on me, a sinner.' "I tell you that this man, rather than the other, went home justified before God. For all those who exalt themselves will be humbled, and those who humble themselves will be exalted."*

As I got hooked on football, and after becoming a Christian, I started watching every game and interview that I could. This means that I would start with the pregame shows on Sunday to both ball games and then Monday Night Football plus The Mike Holmgren Show, sports news interviews, etc. I also started reading all I could find about the Packers which was how I ran across books written by Steve Rose, a Christian disc jockey who interviewed Christian Packers on his radio program. His books prompted me to try to find the station he wrote about. Instead, I ended up finding 88.5 FM in Peony City. I especially had wanted to find his station as he recalled how Reggie White (who was still playing at that time and was a favorite of mine) while listening to Christian music felt that the Lord had healed him. That season Reggie came back from a season-ending injury of a torn hamstring with the hamstring still torn, but he was able to make plays happen even with the hamstring still being torn.

I thought surely my family would be okay with my listening to

Christian music, as the music and programming would surely meet with their approval and not be overly sexual or evil in their eyes like possibly other forms of music. Additionally, now that I knew that there was Christian music I asked the local bookmobile librarians if they could bring me some Christian music. It had only been after the bookmobile brought me a cassette including the song by Carmen, "We Need God in America Again," that my family finally was supportive of my listening to Christian music. In fact, I remember how Grandma Nancy agreed so much with the song that she had written Carmen about getting a copy of the lyrics to the song. That Christmas she had given each of us a copy of the lyrics while she informed us how Carmen had sent her lyrics to all his songs on that album too.

88.5FM, the radio station I found, advocated Hebrews 10:25: *not giving up meeting together, as some are in the habit of doing, but encouraging one another—and all the more as you see the Day approaching,* so I informed my family that I would completely stop watching sports if I was not allowed to go to church. By this time, I was watching each week at least three NFL games, Packer interviews, occasionally some college football, and Indy races. Surprisingly, Grandma Nancy agreed. "Okay, you can go to church, but you won't find any sermons like what you hear on the radio. Also, I would prefer if Abby goes with you. Until you turn twenty-one you need to go to the Catholic church as you do not want your Ma or Uncle Larry to get in trouble for not making sure you were raised Catholic." At this point, I believe I already was twenty-one but Abby was not.

My feeling like I finally could get to go to church had become a possibility when in September 1999 Grandma Nancy and Ma thought it might be a good idea to let Abby and me learn to drive. After all, one would hardly know if both Ma and Uncle Larry might both be busy in the field when gas would need to be gotten for the tractors. Whatever the reason, Abby and I were ecstatic about the prospect of learning to drive.

Our learning to drive then prompted us to beg to find work off the farm. So in January 2000, after much persuasion, Grandma Nancy decided to let Abby and me get jobs. Her stipulation, though, was that it would be at a cheese factory where Uncle Larry worked and that Abby and I would take turns every other day working off the farm.

The experience was quite an eye opener as I could see why Grandma Nancy probably was as offended by people as she was as it seemed over half the coworkers tended to swear unnecessarily, talk about their alcohol intake and their sex lives more than I cared to hear about.

At the cheese factory which was about five miles from home we would run cheese through machines which had a button which would propel the cheese through multiple wires which was used to cut the blocks of cheese into smaller pieces. First we would start with a five pound block of cheese which would get cut into like five one pound blocks. These blocks would then be sent through a machine which would cut it horizontally into like five slabs. Next the slabs would be moved to a machine which would cut the slabs vertically into like 10-15 sticks of cheese. The first two machines only needed one person per machine but the last one needed one to push the button and the other to catch the cheese as it came up through the wires to keep the cheese from scattering all over and to take the cut product over to the conveyer belt. Along the conveyer belt there usually was two to three people pulling out the obvious broken pieces of cheese and sending them on to be further processed while the intact pieces would be boxed up at the end of the conveyer belt. Then the next person would put the box on the scale and weigh it to the desired five pounds adding a few sticks of cheese to it if needed or removing a few sticks of cheese. Then the box would be taped shut and stacked on a gaylord to send to the company who hired the cheese factory to cut up these blocks of cheese. The cheese factory also had where they actually processed cheese but I never really worked there. Plus they would cut into 2 pound blocks or 5 pound blocks of cheese and then packaged for the IGA store or for Kraft just changing the label according to what the order requested to be sent to the store. Then we would pack them into boxes, label the boxes and stack the boxes on a pallet.

Needless to say, the other employees were a bit confused for several days after Abby and I started about it being two different people working and about who was who. Meanwhile, I decided that since I now knew how to drive and was making money, I wanted to volunteer at Tulip City Veterinary Clinic's branch in Lilac City, which I started doing in May 2000. There I got to help Dr. Oliver Y, Dr. Tim J, and Stacie Y with cleaning and some small animal care.

For years, Abby always dreamed of having dogs and horses, much as I dreamed of getting off the farm. So once Abby finally got a job and was making money, she convinced the family to let her finally have a dog. So in April 2000, Abby got her first dog, Two Tone, and in June 2000, she got Two Tone a companion, her second dog, Dolly. In December 2000, I talked with my family about buying Abby a horse. She wanted a regular-sized horse but the North Central Free Newspaper or Free Mailed Newspaper also had listed a miniature horse that had been born on Abby's birthday. (Abby was the only one who never had any of our animals or ever learned of any former classmates or anybody else who had been born on her birthday.) I ended up getting permission to buy her the miniature horse, Cinnamon, which shared her birthday and later another miniature horse, Spice, in April or May 2001.

When I was given permission to go to church, it felt like an answer to prayer, as I had dreamed of getting away from my anti-social life and the rundown conditions on the farm since the age of seventeen. In fact, I remember in my teen years thinking how I would love to run away but knew I couldn't because I knew that to do so would terrify Ma and Abby, who I felt were the only ones who took the time to know and love me. Additionally, since my family never gave my sisters or me any allowance or paid us for any of the chores we did (as they did not want to take a chance at being accused by the courts or by Pa of paying us off for preferring them over Pa if Pa ever chose to try to press to get custody of any of us girls), I knew I had no money to leave and survive on my own. (Once we all turned eighteen, the legal age to be on our own, Grandma Nancy encouraged Uncle Larry to give us $20 a month. Before we turned eighteen the only time we got any money was for our birthdays and Christmas (which would just be $5), or a shopping spree like the $5 bag sales at Catholic Second-Hand Retail Store or when coupons specified one item per customer). Also, I only knew how to do farm work, and I also knew I lacked social connections and skills needed to make it off the farm. Finally, I knew that I was not yet at the legal age to be on my own yet, so I told myself I had to wait until I was at least eighteen.

Once I turned eighteen, though, I told myself I couldn't really leave yet because I still had to graduate from the correspondence classes Grandma Nancy had signed Abby and me up to take years earlier, since she only had a license to teach up to eighth grade. Then after I graduated from high school, I talked about how I wanted to go to college to become a veterinarian. Grandma Nancy opposed the idea because she had gotten a flyer from a career institute that provided correspondence classes for various programs, including becoming a veterinary assistant. So she insisted on this instead, by telling me: "You should take this veterinary assistant course via correspondence until veterinary courses themselves became available for correspondence." So from February until probably May of 2000 I had taken these correspondence veterinary assistant courses. Of course, I ultimately was interested in becoming a veterinarian as I wanted to do something helpful for the farm, but I also wanted to get my schooling off the farm where I could make social connections. So getting to attend church was an answer to prayer toward my goal of making social connections.

GOING TO CHURCH

Sadly, I have to say that at the Catholic church I went to for a period of time I never came closer to making social connections there (other than meeting God there) than the *peace-be-with-you* that Catholics say during their church services. During those many weeks Abby and I would go to the Catholic Church in Buttercup City. The church was quite impressive looking with their many pews, the stained glass windows and the alters and statues in the front of the church. The organ also was quite impressive as it resounded through the church. When we would enter the church we would enter quite obscurely and secure a church bulletin and dip our fingers into the holy water inside the door and make the sign of the cross, touch our forehead, our chest right where our ribcage ends, our left shoulder and then our right shoulder. Then we would find an empty pew and sit down. We would then follow along in the missalette which had several songs and several weeks' worth of readings that the congregation would recite or read along with the priest. During one part of the mass the congregation would be asked to welcome those around them and the congregation would then shake hands with those around them and offer the blessing of *"Peace be with you."* This was the part of the service which Grandma Nancy had always hated. I know this as Grandma Nancy would share how she felt like people would actually use that time to wish opposite of peace for her when they shook her hand, often much too firmly.

After the mass I would go out into the foyer and make Abby wait with me as I would hopefully wait to be approached by someone so that I could finally meet someone other than family. Abby and I never were approached by anyone. Probably my never getting to actually meet anybody was due in large part to my not approaching any of the church members myself. Still, I would push Abby's patience at times when I would insist on lingering as long as possible as the congregation broke up, hoping someone would notice that I was a new face in their church. I know the reason I never approached people was that subconsciously I knew how distrustful and vexed Grandma Nancy was when people would approach her. So after all those years that I lived to please Grandma Nancy and my family, I continued to do what I thought would please them as I started spreading my wings. Even today I still find myself doing this – living as if to please my family – in many areas of my life.

It was shortly before Abby and I started going to the Catholic church that she and I convinced our family to let us learn to drive and to get jobs off the farm. Our family managed to work it out so that my sister and I would work at the place where my uncle worked and initially Uncle Larry would always drive us to work with him to the cheese factory. Together Abby and I would work every day but would work alternative days of one another. Once I was able to start saving some money and felt like I had gas money I managed to convince my family to let me start to volunteer one to two days each week at Tulip City Veterinary Service's Lilac City location when they would hold small animal clinic hours.

When I worked at Tulip City Veterinary Clinic, the staff would let me spray down the table between clients and then wipe it down. Eventually they taught me how to hold the animals so that the animals head would be turned away from the veterinarian and hold the leg so the vein would be occluded and the veterinarian could draw blood or give the animal a shot. Most days I got to work alongside Stacie Y and Dr. Oliver Y who helped me to learn a lot as they shared about what they had all done in the past appointment and why and then shared with me what various medications they had on hand were for and such. Additionally they had a lot of old looking veterinary manuals which I would try to read in between patient visits when Stacie and Dr. Oliver weren't sharing their wealth of knowledge with me. All these things that they taught me just continued to develop my interest in becoming a veterinarian.

Then as I was frustrated about not meeting anyone at the Catholic church, I convinced Abby to help me as I wanted to try finding a church with hours which were not on Sunday morning so that I, at twenty-one years old now, could go there and hopefully grow in my newfound faith while meeting people. If we were successful in finding such a church we planned to ask to go shopping during their service hours. I then planned to have Abby drop me off at that church while she shopped.

This search for another church happened as Grandma Nancy let us help her with her shopping or if we were able to convince her to let us go do some shopping of our own. Occasionally we would offer to buy farm supplies for Uncle Larry also. After looking at several churches between Lilac City and Rose City and not finding any with Saturday hours, God caused Abby and me to spot a little church called Buttercup City Bible Church which was a block east of Buttercup City's Ice Cream Store. As the church hours weren't posted on the sign by the road, as Abby was driving she suggested that we see if the hours were posted on the church's door so she drove in. When I saw a couple guys working in the garden in front of the church, I told Abby, "You know, let's forget about checking the hours until later when the guys have gone home." But Abby insisted we check then, so she drove up to the Buttercup City Bible Church to see if their hours were posted on the church door. Ned F, whom I later learned was an elder at the church, was one of the guys working in the flower garden when we pulled into the church drive. Ned stopped what he was doing and came over to our vehicle. He then asked us, "Is there anything I can help you with?"

Abby responded by saying, "We wanted to see what hours your church is held." Ned said, "Oh, the church meets at 10:00 a.m. on Sundays." This was just an hour earlier than Buttercup City's Catholic Church's hours. Then Ned said, "Would you like to go inside and check it out? The church is open if you want to do so." So I went inside by myself as Abby still was not twenty-one (Grandma Nancy had said we couldn't attend another church until we turned twenty-one), but I was, so I checked out the church. It was because of how the elder approached us and welcomed us, in addition to seeing how much smaller the church was compared to the Catholic churches Abby and I had been attending, that kept the church's hours in the back of my mind and put the desire in me to check it out at a later date.

Several months later, Abby got a new job that would train her to become a Certified Nursing Assistant (CNA). However, her first day of training landed on the same Sunday that Buttercup City's Catholic Church had their festival which I initially really wanted to attend as I felt maybe the festival would finally help me meet some people. The week of the festival Buttercup City's Catholic Church had moved their church service up an hour. That Sunday, I realized this synchronizing of church service hours would give me a chance to check out Buttercup City Bible Church. First, though, I had chores to do before I could go to church, which ended up making me cut it very close to ten o'clock after I got cleaned up and dressed. So I debated whether I should take the chance that if I was late I would attract everyone's attention, seeing how small the church was, or if I should just go to the Catholic church as I was curious about their festival, which maybe would help me meet people finally.

BUTTERCUP CITY BIBLE CHURCH

I ended up taking a chance and went to the Bible church that October day back in 2000, and the congregation was in the middle of greeting each other after singing. This meant that the congregation was milling around shaking hands and sharing bits of friendly conversations with each other so I was able to come in without being an obvious distraction like I could have if they were preaching or going through a missalette program. As it was the sermon had not yet started when I got there and some of the congregation noticed when I got there and made a point to come over and say hi and introduce themselves. The very day that I attended the church for the first time the congregation was having a bonfire at parishioners Dave and Trish N's farm after the service. Also, in the church bulletin I saw that there were a few more events scheduled in the upcoming months: a couple potlucks to be held at the church, caroling, a potluck at Pastor Martin S's for Christmas, and another event at Dave and Trish's farm for New Year's Eve. Additionally, after the service most of the rest of the parishioners who hadn't introduced themselves to me earlier swung by and said hi. Before attending this church, I remember having been told by Grandma Nancy that I would never find sermons like the ones I heard on the radio, and while Pastor Martin's sermon wasn't the same, it was close enough for me. I liked how most if not all in the congregation had their own Bible and how the sermon came from the Bible. This prompted me to go to the Christian Bookstore which had been in Buttercup City looking for a Bible and a Bible cover. The Bible was the hard decision and I am not sure why

I picked the one I did, as for the Bible cover as soon as I saw one in my favorite color of blue which allowed for a picture to be inserted in the front I knew that that was the cover for me. When I went to purchase the Bible and cover the clerk informed me that they had covers which would fit my Bible lots better than the one I had picked out. Embarrassedly and shyly I just shook my head and insisted that those were the items I wanted and paid for them.

After that first service at the Buttercup City Bible Church on the first day I attended one of the parishioners named Roger X came up to me and asked, "You planning to come to the bonfire?"

I said, "No." Mentally reviewing how late I already was returning home and wondering how my family would take the news I went to Buttercup City Bible Church instead of Buttercup City's Catholic Church.

Roger said, "You really ought to consider it as you will really get to know people as most of the congregation will be going." I continued trying to say no while Roger continued to share why it would be a good idea for me to go. He even went so far as to say, "You can follow Ned and me as we drive out there."

As I feared I would be in trouble if I did go, I still hesitated but was getting in my car to follow them out to Dave and Trish's farm when, luckily, Pastor Martin came over and introduced himself and we got to talking. As we were talking Pastor Martin noticed how Ned and Roger were parked at the edge of the driveway right before pulling into the street and said, "I wondering why they are just sitting there."

I told him, "Oh, Roger really wants to make sure I am able to go to the bonfire but I do not think I should as I do not think my family would be okay with my doing so."

"Okay, I'll tell them they should just go ahead then," said Pastor Martin, which gave me a chance to get out of going to the bonfire that time but hoped that I would get to go the next time one was held. After Pastor Martin convinced them to go without me, I remember how he and I talked for a while longer before I decided I really needed to get home.

When I arrived home, Ma asked me where I had been, so I hold her that I had gone to the Buttercup City Bible Church and she told me in no uncertain terms how I had to go talk with Grandma Nancy. In other words, she let me know how she would not intercede for me to Grandma Nancy, as she frequently had done when my sisters and I were younger. Back then, when we wanted something which we were not sure Grandma Nancy would approve of but we knew she needed to approve in order for it to happen, Ma would step in to ask Grandma Nancy for us. This time I think mom feared somehow that she would be the one getting in trouble, which very likely may have been the case, and that is why she insisted I go talk to Grandma Nancy.

I realize now how frequently I had Ma intercede for me, and how, as children, my sisters and I were not encouraged to speak out by asking questions, explaining ourselves, or engaging in many other normal types of conversations. In fact, in my late teen years, conversations got to the point where if something was not "necessary, helpful, or important," Grandma Nancy would tell us, "don't say anything at all." Then when Grandma Nancy would ask us questions she got to the point of asking them in such a way that just a strict *yes* or *no* answer could be used and she would strictly request that her questions were not to be given anything more than a simple *yes* or *no*. If more than a yes or no was given Grandma Nancy would vent for several minutes about how all she wanted was a simple yes or no to her question. As a result of growing up talking these ways, I find that frequently I am much more comfortable speaking just to one person rather than to larger groups of people, and I become very self-conscious when other people are around me while I am speaking.

This self-consciousness in speaking around others I realized back in 2006 was due to mainly having had conversations *only* with Ma and Abby when I was growing up. Often our conversations were about things we felt others in the family (particularly Uncle Larry and Grandma Nancy) disagreed with, or we were just venting about another family member, which resulted in many conversations being dropped suddenly when another family member entered the room where we were talking.

So when Ma told me to tell Grandma Nancy about my having gone to the Buttercup City Bible Church, I nervously went upstairs to

Grandma Nancy's prayer chair in her room which was in front of the window facing west overlooking the neighbors' place where she was listening to a NASCAR race. Shaking a bit internally I said, "Grandma Nancy, as I am now twenty-one, you said it would be okay if I went to a church other than a Catholic church, right?"

Grandma Nancy said, "Yes."

I told her, "That's what I thought, so I went to Buttercup City Bible Church today since Abby had to work."

"That's fine," Grandma Nancy said and so I went back downstairs to eat, feeling thankful that Grandma Nancy was okay with my going to the Bible church. I then also shared with Ma how Grandma Nancy just said it was okay that I go to Buttercup City Bible Church since I was twenty-one.

When Abby got home, I shared with her my excitement about Buttercup City Bible Church but I told her I would wait until she turned twenty-one before going back again. But Abby insisted that if I liked the church so much I should just keep going to it instead of the Catholic church and not wait until she turned twenty-one to go back. So I continued to go to Buttercup City Bible Church weekly after that and that was the last time Abby regularly attended church with me. In the following years, I have been able to talk her into joining me a few times a year.

It was through Buttercup City Bible Church that I received lots of encouragement towards gaining independence something which I struggled to gain from my family other than Abby. A few months after I started attending I got an invitation from Erma X (Roger's wife) to move in with her and her family after I expressed a desire to move off the farm. Additionally, Pastor Martin offered to see once if Robin M, who also grew up on a farm but was now allergic to cows, would be willing to let me stay with her and her husband, Louis. Pastor Martin also gave me the name of a friend of his who was a veterinarian, Dr. Kurt Y, who he thought might be able to help me find a place to keep my pet steers, Nick, Ezekiel (Zeke), and Joshua (Josh).

Dr. Kurt went to the church Pastor Martin would occasionally swap pulpits at. Pastor Martin would occasionally preach at Buttercup

City Evangelical Free Church, while the Evangelical Free Church's Pastor Ulysses P would occasionally preach at Buttercup City Bible Church. My desire to meet Dr. Kurt, along with my friendship with April X and Luke and Betsy S who would come with Pastor Ulysses when he preached at the Bible church, convinced me to check out the Buttercup City Evangelical Free Church. At Buttercup City Evangelical Free Church they had a youth group which Pastor Ulysses, April, Luke, and Betsy encouraged me to be a part of even though I was older than most of the other youth. This is how I first really got to know Luke and Betsy, who co-led the group with Dr. Kurt. Luke and Betsy were instrumental in helping me grow socially. Luke was just enough like my Uncle Larry with his constant teasing that he put me at ease while Betsy always made you feel like she really wanted to hear what you had to say and that it was very important to her for you to share. It was during one of the youth group meetings that I first heard of how Jesus was either a liar, a lunatic, or Lord, which C.S. Lewis had written about in one of his works. I still remember the persuasiveness of his writing in showing how it could be reliably proved that Jesus was neither a liar nor a lunatic, which meant he had to be Lord.

After checking out the Buttercup City Evangelical Free Church events a few times, I would often go to the Bible church and after their church service when everyone had dispersed, I would then head over to Buttercup City Evangelical Free Church. While I did not catch the entire service at Buttercup City Evangelical Free Church, I would usually catch most of the sermon, the closing song, and the fellowship that followed as they dispersed. It was several months after I started doing this that Tina P, Pastor Ulysses' wife, encouraged me to read the Bible in a year. Their church used to provide a reading plan for doing this, so for several months I used their plan along with the one I found in *Our Daily Bread* booklets. But once I started college, I would not always be able to pick up their Bible-in-a-year plan so I started just using the one in the *Our Daily Bread* booklets, which I still use to this day. Through *Our Daily Bread*, I have found many devotions and Bible passages which have been really encouraging and just what I needed to read at certain times in my life.

ASH-PINE VETERINARY CLINIC AND DR. REUBEN F

Upon Pastor Martin's recommendation, I called Ash-Pine Veterinary Clinic (APVC) where Dr. Kurt worked. My family used the veterinary services of Tulip City Veterinary Clinic instead at this time because Grandma Nancy had heard a report about how a passenger Dr. Kurt had riding with him one time was homosexual and she did not want to take the chance of having that passenger out at the farm. As I had already been interested for several years in becoming a large-animal veterinarian, I asked the APVC receptionist if it would be possible for me to ride with Dr. Kurt, whom I figured had to be an okay person if Pastor Martin approved of him. So we set up three days for me to ride with Dr. Kurt. During one of the three days, I mentioned how I was looking for a place to keep my steers for when I moved off the farm and how Pastor Martin had mentioned maybe Dr. Kurt could help me. He and the other veterinarians at APVC had not able to help me with finding a place off Uncle Larry's farm for the steers, though. As Dr. Kurt usually ran several minutes late each day, Dr. Reuben, another veterinarian at APVC, would always come in to the clinic and to the receptionist desk a bit early and upon seeing me would energetically ask very hopefully, "So, you want to ride with me?"

After I rode with Dr. Kurt on the days I had set up to do so, I then decided to start riding with Dr. Reuben, since he always seemed so eager for me to do so. Dr. Reuben was about my age and very handsome, but married, so I considered him a brother as I always wanted a brother and he seemed like what I thought was the brotherly type. About a month after I started riding with Dr. Rueben, I ended up quitting my job where my uncle worked, since over time many of my favorite coworkers who did not swear or tell drunken or sexual stories had also quit. During this newly gained free time I then chose to ride daily with Dr. Reuben for a few months.

While I rode with Dr. Reuben he did his best to try to draw me out of my quiet shell, often by sharing personal stories or at other times by asking out of the blue, "What are you thinking?"

This usually made me stop at whatever my current thought was and silently start to backtrack on my thoughts to what led me to my current thoughts so that I could answer his question. For example, I may have seen a hole in the road, which Dr. Reuben pointed out which made me think of something I saw at a recent farm we visited which led me to think of some scenery we passed, or something along those lines of thought. As my mental backtracking seemed so long and complicated, I would usually just give Dr. Reuben a shy, contented smile, thinking how much more fun it was riding with him and helping with his farm call than it was doing chores all the time with only my family's company.

I remember how much I enjoyed riding with Dr. Reuben because I got to meet a lot of local farmers during our farm calls which the majority were "herd health" which consisted of checking cows to see if she was pregnant. After all dairy farms cannot remain successful without the cows remaining pregnant as much as possible so as to keep them producing milk but could include injuries or sicknesses or calving issues. On occasion we also helped with other than dairy farms but probably 90% of the business that APVC did was with dairy farms. I also enjoyed the opportunity to be driven down roads I had never been down before, seeing all the local rolling hills of various shades of green. Since it was not me driving, I have to admit that I am thankful I never was asked to give directions, as sometimes I got confused if the road we were driving down went north and south or east and west.

During that time, because of all the help I gave him by roping cow's heads, fetching and filling his pail with soapy water, etc., Dr. Reuben would occasionally provide some extra help and advice on our farm when I mentioned a problem we were having with one of our animals. I specifically recall him checking on one of my favorite cows, Yippy Daisy.

Yippy Daisy was the great grand heifer of Heify, a cow which I claimed as a replacement for a heifer that Ma had bought for me. Ma had bought herself and each of us girls a springing (pregnant) heifer. Except a few of the springing heifers apparently lost their calves and so Uncle Dale choose to sell the heifer when he couldn't get her pregnant again. When that happened Ma had us choose one of the heifer calves born on the farm to replace the heifer. That is how I came to choose Heify who was the first cow named as I would always go up to her to give her attention and ask her, "How is my Heify?" Ma and Abby then started to refer to her as Heify, too.

Anyway, Yippy Daisy's udder became very inflamed and when we had a veterinarian from Tulip City Veterinary Clinic come out he had diagnosed it as the start of gangrene. As I hoped we could save Yippy Daisy, I had convinced my family we should give her the antibiotics the veterinarian recommended. When I mentioned Yippy's case to Dr. Reuben he came out and checked on her a couple times as Yippy Daisy lost a good chunk of her udder to the gangrene and then stopped producing milk and became skin and bones. Dr. Rueben then recommended taking her off the antibiotic and switching her to aspirin as he feared she would die despite being on antibiotics and so he then gave me some tablets of aspirin to hold her over for a few days. Additionally, at times he would also provide me with some anti-diarrhea pills for other cows and check some of our farm's cows for pregnancy from time to time. He also began training me to check cows for pregnancy both at home and on other farms if the farmer was okay with my doing so.

While we were at various farms, he also liked to let me halter the cows for him, tie their heads off to the side, and pop the needle into their jugular vein. (It had to be done quite forcefully in order to get the needle through the cows' thick hide and allow it to bleed a bit before the IV was started to make sure we were actually in the vein. Before I had been given a chance to try IVing a cow I always thought the vets were popping the cows unnecessarily hard in the vein and then making them bleed unnecessarily for a while before IVing them. Once I started to IV the cows myself, however, I realized my misunderstanding as the cow hides are really thick and a person wanted to make sure they were actually in the vein.) Dr. Reuben, though, would not let me IV the calcium solution which we gave cows diagnosed with milk fever. Cows contracted milk fever when they pulled excess calcium out of their system after calving to produce milk for their newborn calf. This excess removal of calcium from the cow's system then prevented the cow's muscles to contract fully in order for the cow to get on its feet making the cow unable to stand. The reason he would not let me give the calcium was that if too much calcium was given too fast the cow's heart which is a major muscle could have a major contraction which could make her just as easily die as be able to get back on her feet. Since Dr. Rueben was the veterinarian, he had insurance that would back him if a farmer would sue him, but since I was just volunteering, I did not have insurance, so he could not risk my treating other farmers' animals, even though he would let me treat the family's milk fever cases.

At farm calls, Dr. Reuben would also let me use his stethoscope to listen to the cow's hearts, lungs and stomachs by which I sometimes would inform him and the farmer when the cow had a displaced abomasum (DA). I usually struggled to hear anything unusual when it came to the lungs or heart. A DA though could be heard through the stethoscope when you snapped the cow's stomach right behind her ribs. It sounded like you were snapping a basketball. If the DA was on the cow's left side, Dr. Reuben usually operated and would let me scrub in so that I could feel the stomach which was ballooned as it twisted on itself and felt like a ball. Then after Dr. Reuben would untwist the stomach and sew it down so that it couldn't twist again, he would close up the under layers of the stomach wall and muscles and then would often let me sew the outermost layer of skin closed if we did not have a lot of calls to do yet.

I have to admit that Dr. Reuben spoiled me because he would usually end up taking me to fast food store, a gas station, or to his place to eat lunch. Whenever we went to his place I always felt a bit uncomfortable as I could just hear Grandma Nancy saying how improper that looked and wondering what rumors his neighbors would start about us. So I would usually eat what he offered and tried to play with his mostly white border collie outside whenever possible. Then usually once a week all the veterinarians at APVC would get together and have a business meeting at a restaurant. Sometimes I was allowed to come; other times I was not. When I was not I usually caught up with Naomi, the veterinary technician, or whichever receptionist was working that day.

The reason I say that Dr. Reuben spoiled me was because while growing up my family seldom ate out. Through my entire childhood, I can remember eating at Old West Steakhouse maybe two or three times, getting an occasional hamburger from a fast food store, which my sisters and I usually had to share, getting a milkshake, burger, and fries at Golden Arches Fast Food Shop, pizza from Farmer's Convenience Store, or ice cream in June when businesses offered them at a special price or gave it out free. But my sisters and I got to eat at these places maybe only monthly if we were lucky. When Uncle Larry started delivering the North Central Free Newspaper, our chances of getting any of these types of fast food grew to sometimes weekly if we chose to go with Ma while we helped Uncle Larry with the many routes he signed up to deliver.

FIRST MOVE OFF THE FARM

After I had been going to Buttercup City Bible Church for a while I had started to have hope that I finally found a way off the farm as one lady, Erma Y, welcomed me to move in with her family and Pastor Martin had gotten the okay from another parishioner, Robin M, for me to move in with her family. But my family weren't ready to have me leave the farm yet but after four months of terrible tension within my family, I moved in with my friend from church, Robin M, and her husband, Louis. I am ashamed to admit, however, that especially during the last two months of tension-filled times with my family, I acted not Christ-like at all but instead was very, very angry. It was after all the extra help Dr. Reuben provided my family and I had moved in with Louis and Robin that my family finally started to become open to the idea of my leaving the farm to go to college to become a veterinarian.

This is how I remember it coming about. As you saw back in 1997 in my journal entries, I had been preparing to move out eventually. Ultimately I was holding out, hoping to get my family's blessing to move out. When my golden birthday, my 22nd, rolled around in January, I really had high hopes that I would finally get their blessing, but it never came. Meanwhile I kept waiting week after week, while my disappointment was mounting, for my family to tell me I could move off the farm. While I waited, I began to condense my belongings more and more as my family's possessions took up more and more space at home. Then one-day (by this time Abby and I had our driver's license and I had gotten Abby and me cell phones), we told the family we were going to go do laundry, which we did, but we had also packed all my things in the truck as I planned to take Erma Y up on her offer of letting me move in with her family. As I talked with Erma, I decided I really wanted Ma's blessing so I took my cell phone and called home. When Ma answered I told her, "Hi Ma. I am at Erma's as she offered to let me stay with her family for a while. I am planning to take Erma up on her offer but first I wanted to get your blessing."

After a moment of silence on Ma's end, she finally said in a hurt and angry voice, "You get home right now."

As I refused to think Ma was unwilling to give her blessing for the move, I was sure she had answered that way because Grandma Nancy was standing over her shoulder, furious that I would even try to move out without her approval. So I told Erma, "Ma says I need to go home right now, so I guess I won't be moving in today."

So Abby and I went home where Ma greeted me very upset at the door. She started by saying, "I took Dora and Sandy to Nashville to give them a vacation and then I took you to the North Central Christian Festival for a vacation. In June I plan to take Abby on her vacation; can't you wait till then?"

Abby, in my defense, said, "It should be fine if she moves out before my vacation."

But Ma insisted on my waiting until after Abby had her vacation in June. After many moments of my glaring, angry refusals to wait that long, Ma started to say, "Well, since it is the beginning of Lent, at least wait until after Lent" and "Erma's husband, Roger, has come here accusing your Uncle Larry of having an affair with a married woman, so I refuse to let you move in with him."

I then told her how I also had an offer from Robin M, which she was not as upset by but still disapproved of. Meanwhile, I still angrily refused to consider waiting even until after Lent until Ma tried to switch back to me waiting until June, at which point I declared, "Fine, I will wait until Lent but no longer." During the whole conversation, I was still sure it was because of pressure from Grandma Nancy that Ma persisted for so long and so hard and so angrily that I not move off the farm.

Of course, neither of us thought to write down what we had agreed to, so when Easter came, I fearfully went to Grandma Nancy as she sat in her prayer chair and asked her, "Grandma Nancy, it is now after Lent, which is how long I promised I would stay. Is it okay with you if I move off the farm now?"

I was pleasantly surprised when she said, "If that is what you agreed to with your Ma, then yes, you may leave."

So I went downstairs to where Ma sat reading and said, "It is now after Lent, which I agreed to stay till. I still want to move and Grandma Nancy said it is okay with her."

Ma then said, "You agreed to stay until June. You better keep your word."

Back and forth we went disputing when it was that I agreed to wait until. Finally, Grandma Nancy came downstairs and said, "If your Ma says that you cannot move out until June, then you wait until June." At this point I gave Ma the most angry glare I recall ever giving anyone or anything and angrily left the room, feeling betrayed by one whom up to that point I had always thought was my second best friend after Abby and whom I thought supported me in my dreams. After that I have wondered how many times Grandma Nancy would have let us do things if we went first to her instead of Ma, and how many times did Ma convince Grandma Nancy she did not want us to do those things. Ultimately, now, it really does not make much of a difference, but if Grandma Nancy was not always the bad guy saying no, then she unfairly became the bad guy in our eyes, ruining the relationship which I might have tried to have with her while my relationship with Ma grew, seeing how she always seemed to approve but would later tell us Grandma Nancy said no.

So I ended up living at the farm for another two months. One day during this time, however, I became pretty depressed. It began the day before while cleaning the cattle shed when Uncle Larry had gotten the manure to come right up to the barn door. Then, since he had to leave to go bowling, he just left the manure there, which meant Abby and I had to re-fix the pens and move the heifers back to their pens. This resulted in Dora sprinkling good hay over the manure in an attempt to keep the manure off her boots as she went into the cattle shed to get hay. Later Uncle Larry decided to take a good chipboard and lay it down over the manure so we could keep the manure off our boots. That was better than the hay but was still a waste of a good board. On top of that, the little shed Abby and I had made was starting to come apart in the wind. We had made the little shed to house Cinnamon and Spice, a couple of miniature horses I had bought. Abby had always dreamed of having horses. Then I decided I had to help her get Cinnamon especially since we saw an ad in the paper saying Cinnamon was born on Abby's birthday and Abby had yet to have anything on the farm to be born on her birthday while I already had calves born on my birthday.

So feeling despair over how maintaining the farm just felt useless and impossible, I asked to go for groceries just to get away from the farm, and I ended up about five miles north on the same road at Robin's place and just sat and cried for a while as I shared with Robin my feelings of despair. Robin encouraged me to stay with her at her place since it was, by now, after Lent. So I called Abby and asked her if she would let Ma and the others know I was staying at Robin's.

My staying at Robin's created very negative feelings at home, which my family expressed through a letter they wrote to me and delivered to Robin when they came to pick up their red Chevrolet pickup which I had used to go to Robin's. Robin had considered not sharing the letter with me as she had read it and felt I did not need the additional hurt, which I was sure to feel from reading it, but she ended up giving it to me just so that I could say I had received it. Robin was right; I had not wanted to read the note. Overall, it reinforced my desire to get away, but a day or two later while Louis and Robin were working I did end up walking the five miles home to do some chores. After all, I still had a few pets on the farm to look after and I wanted to do a share of the work for their room and board.

So I walked home and hoped none of the family saw me as I went straight to the haymow. While trying to get hay ready to be thrown down without letting Uncle Larry and Dora who were in the cattle shed know I was home, I overheard a conversation between them as they worked on attaching a hose to a drinking cup for the cattle in the shed so that we would be able to stop running water out via the hose and filling a barrel which the animals weekly if not more often would poop in or otherwise soil. Abby and I would then take the effort to dump out the soiled water but Dora and Sandy just tended to ignore.

On this day as Uncle Larry grew tired of having so much water get wasted and was attempting to provide water using a hose and attaching it to a drinking cup, Dora had been venting about how unfair it was for me to leave home and make everyone else pick up my chores, especially making them take care of my pet steers. After overhearing the comments about their displeasure at my staying at Robin's, I came back home until the additional two months were up, for fear my family would sell my pets without my approval.

ABBY'S MOVE

About the same time as I finally moved in with Louis and Robin the end of June 2001, Abby headed to Training Center for Troubled Young Adults in Lily City. She had seen an advertisement in a local free paper where Training Center for Troubled Young Adults advertised they provided free education to low-income people between the ages of sixteen and twenty-four to learn a career in the fields of carpentry, masonry, automotive and machine repair, finance and business, hospitality, health care, information technology, etc. When she expressed an interest in going for this training, Grandma Nancy said Abby would need to be twenty-one first. So Abby registered to go shortly after her twenty-first birthday. Abby tried to convince me to go also, but I wanted to be a vet, which this program did not offer, and by then I was twenty-two and it did not seem a long enough time for me to be there. Additionally, when the woman from Training Center for Troubled Young Adults came to talk to Abby, she mentioned how Abby did not fit the picture of the typical person they accepted into their program, as many were kids who had gotten themselves into some form of trouble with drugs or gangs, and Training Center for Troubled Young Adults provided them with an option to avoid juvenile detention or jail time. As a new Christian, and being raised as a goody two-shoes, I was not interested in surrounding myself with these types of people.

When Abby attended Training Center for Troubled Young Adults, she was told she could not bring a cell phone so she gave hers to Ma. Also Training Center for Troubled Young Adults only gave a ride to students as far as Snapdragon City every other weekend and after each trip off campus, every student's luggage was checked for weapons, drugs, alcohol, and other prohibited items. While at Training Center for Troubled Young Adults Abby met lots of people and whenever she came home she always had lots of stories to tell while I felt like I lived a boring life comparatively, even though I never really wanted to exchange it. Though if I would have ever felt Abby or Ma was interested, I probably could have come up with stories too, though I'm not quite the storyteller like them.

The days Abby would come home Ma, Abby and I would sleep in the old 1979 tan Transvan Camper which Ma had convinced Uncle Larry to get. Ma always dreamed of living in a camper and traveling. As we would lay down to sleep Abby would share all her stories about her time at Training Center for Troubled Young Adults and her interactions with all the people she met there. Meanwhile I'd think of some of the things I was doing as I had entered college at this point but felt like compared to Abby's stories mine were boring plus neither of them seemed particularly interested in what was going on with me as they never asked me and I never felt brave enough to share.

So Abby would tell us occasionally about boys she met and if any had expressed interest in her plus her regular activity learning carpentry and the many gals she shared a dorm with. This was how she ended up meeting Nathan S whom she ended up marrying less than a year after meeting him. I remember in my freshman year Abby shared how she had broken up with a guy who then began treating her like she was invisible whenever she was around him. He would come over to where she was and strike up a conversation with a friend of hers whom she was sitting with and act like she was not there or totally ignore her if she came in the area where he was. Occasionally he would say mean things about her while she was right there, too.

It was less than a month later when she met a guy but said she was not sure she wanted to become his girlfriend. She was afraid that if for some reason she decided later on she did not want to continue to be his girlfriend that she would break his heart. This guy was Nathan Y. By that summer, she graduated from Training Center for Troubled

Young Adults with a degree in carpentry and had found an apartment in Buttercup City, where she went back to working as a CNA for the summer.

I chose to live with her that summer after I completed my final exam for the semester and Uncle Larry and Ma came and picked me up and took me over to Abby's new apartment in Buttercup City. That summer while I really didn't care to actually milk cows but that was the only type of job I had been able to find in the area, I ended up working at a large dairy farm in the Spring Beauty City area. The family had given me the 1979 Transvan to drive which I drove as minimally as I could as it only got 7 miles to a gallon while one of Abby's instructors had helped her get a 1980 Crown Victoria.

Multiple times throughout that summer, Abby drove to Snapdragon City to pick up Nathan as he had come over for the weekend to spend time with Abby. It was during that summer Abby learned to cook a wide assortment of foods as Nathan taught her how. Otherwise Abby and I tended to buy lunch meat and other "prepared" foods.

In the fall of 2002, Nathan returned to his home in Daisy City and Abby chose to join him after he proposed to her. Abby started making plans for a wedding. The family told her they would not be able to make it to Daisy City as it was too far from the farm that required around-the-clock care. Also I told her I was not sure if I could financially afford going and that I was not sure when I would be able to go as I was then in the midst of my second year of college and the family took back the Transvan after the summer so I didn't have any personal transportation of my own. So Abby ended up deciding to go to a justice of the peace in Daisy City to get married. She chose to get married on Grandpa Robert's birthday December 10, 2002.

COLLEGE AT CATALPA CITY

Strangely enough, after Dr. Reuben started helping my family and I finally moved off the farm with Louis and Robin in June, my family went from being against my going to college to helping me all they could so I could go to college. While out of pride and anger at my family I wanted to do the contacting and everything for college all on my own, I did allow Grandma Nancy to place a few calls for me as by that time I was enjoying riding with Dr. Reuben daily during the weekdays from 8:00 to 5:00. Since I was too uncomfortable making calls in front of Dr. Reuben or others, this made calling any college impossible for me. Grandma Nancy had no problem sharing with College at Catalpa City (CCC), how I got all A's and B's while being home schooled in addition to getting a "with honors" diploma from the veterinary assistant course I had taken. If I had not swallowed my pride and allowed Grandma Nancy to make these calls, I probably would not have been accepted into CCC in the fall of 2001.

Additionally, Grandma Nancy had put $500 aside into Saving Bonds for each of us girls and she decided that this would be a good use for that money. So, I accepted the money from her to buy some things she and Ma thought were essentials once I got accepted into CCC. Ma then took me shopping and we got an extra-long twin set of bedding as that was what the college had for beds, a lamp, pencils, pens, bath towels, notebooks, etc. It was a good thing I finally swallowed my pride, as otherwise I would not have had most of the items I needed for my classes though I tended to look for the cheapest items instead of accepting Ma's suggestions of bigger, more practical towels and such.

Once Pastor Martin heard I got in at CCC, he told me, "You know there are Christian organizations similar to churches on colleges. Why don't I look into what they have at Catalpa City so you can continue to grow in your faith and have Christian fellowship while you are there?" CCC was one of three colleges in the state I grew up in with a large-animal pre-vet program. It was also the college Dr. Reuben went to, which is why I focused on going there.

Pastor Martin ended up telling me about CODCL, which he told me was directed at that time by a guy named Samuel N. Pastor Martin gave me Samuel's email. I was told I also needed to take college placement exams once the check-in day arrived, just a week before classes started.

So, Ma drove me the two hours to CCC. As we entered the town of Catalpa City we had already started to drive past the College when I realized the big brick buildings which we had been passing were part of the CCC campus. So Ma ended up turning around and we drove around for several minutes longer trying to find Ravens Commons and the Science Hall where the testing and signing up was to occur. Finally, we found Ravens Commons, and I signed in and got CCC's welcoming package including a t-shirt. (By the time I signed in the smallest t-shirt they had was a size XL which was quite large on me. That was okay for me as at that time I rarely cared about how big and lose my clothes were. It was not until eight years later that I stopped wearing anything much bigger than a size small.) After I signed up, Ma helped me find the Science Hall where I took the placement exams. After that I went back to Ravens Commons to connect with the advisor assigned to me, a biology advisor. When the advisor heard I had been home schooled, she decided twelve credits (chemistry with a lab, English, algebra, and biology) were enough for me to sign up for. Once I was done taking the test and was signed up for classes, I was allowed to move my things into a temporary dorm room in Hummingbird Hall, the dorm in the center of campus, as all the permanent housing had already been filled. Mom stuck around until she helped me move my things into my dorm room which was in the east wing and contained three sets of bunk beds.

Most of the beds had already had peoples things on them other than one of the upper bunks so I set up that upper bunk for my own and a desk which didn't look anyone had chosen. After all my things were in the dorm room Ma then left as she had to get back to the farm.

It was later that day when I went to eat at Ravens Commons that I first saw the poster advertising a picnic that CODCL was going to host on Labor Day, the day before classes actually started, with games and food at a local park. For the longest time, I hadn't realized that there was more than just the west side of Ravens Commons available to eat at or that the sub-station in the entrance also accepted a student's card for meal payments. The week before classes officially started the new students were assigned an orientation group and told where to meet them later that day and every day for the upcoming week. The leaders of these groups helped orient the new students to the campus and help them meet other new students by doing a bunch of ice-breaker games and taking them to activities being held on campus throughout that week. I only recall a few events from that first week, one being a few groups of new students and orientation leaders hanging out together on the lawn in front of Hummingbird Hall for a period doing icebreaking games and another of walking to the Kingfisher Center about a fifteen-minute walk for a hypnotist and then back to our dorms afterwards. They would also take us to eat every day at Ravens Commons and it was while dining that I really met Rachael, one of the orientation leaders. She wasn't my orientation leader but she was the leader whom seemed determined to make sure I felt comfortable and connected at CCC.

When I would go to Ravens Commons to eat it seemed that she would notice me enter the dining room look around at all the people dining and feeling out of my comfort zone, unsure if anyone would welcome me at their table and not brave enough to ask, I would choose a table away from everyone and sit to eat. Rachael would then either come over, asking if she could join me or she would invite me to join her and her friends. Whichever offer Rachael gave me I would gladly accept as ultimately, I really did not want to be alone but didn't want to impose or assume I'd be welcome.

When Rachael learned I was interested in becoming a part of

CODCL she told me about her roommate, Lena U, who was part of CODCL. One of the activities the orientation leaders were required to take us freshmen to was a carnival-like event which was being held in the Student Center. The event had lots of various games, popcorn, slushies, and other activities one could do. It was here that Rachael introduced me to Lena, who actually was several years older than me while most of the others who were my age were graduating that year. Lena though remained at CCC yet another year. Lena at the carnival like event in turn introduced me to Ronald S, who also went to CODCL and who was a resident assistant (RA) in Chickadee Hall. I remember that Ronald sang "Ice, Ice Baby" with several friends during the karaoke activity that was being held at the event.

During that first week that I had been in Catalpa City I had also seen a flyer about how there was a Christian band going to be playing in a small park in the down-town area so I had walked over to that. I had wandered around Catalpa City' main street until I found the park and stayed for the concert. It was attended by about a handful or two of hippie looking folk with their dreads and flowing outfits. Most of them smoked and apparently one of the gals who didn't smoke started smoking that day which I learned as her boyfriend shared with the others how he caught her sneaking a cigarette. After the concert, the people who had attended made plans to go to a pizza shop and invited me so I had joined them. It turned out they were a Christian group also on campus who were part of a local church in Catalpa City. Due to the way they dressed and smoked I hadn't been entirely comfortable with them and so I continued to plan on getting involved with CODCL over this group.

When classes started, I had forgotten that my first day of classes was on a Tuesday as Monday had been Labor Day, so I initially went to the classroom of my Monday class which was held in the Science Hall just west of Ravens Commons where Dr. Alan I was teaching psychology. When he first entered the classroom he started off sharing his name and by doing some joking around. Then he asked people to raise their hands if they weren't there to study psychology. Several other students and I all raised our hands. I thought he was joking around at this point but then he reminded us how it was Tuesday not Monday. Dr. Alan then helped each of us figure out where we were actually supposed to be. I was actually supposed to be in the chemistry lab, which was right across the hall. Of course, since I did not know the layout of the building I didn't realize the lab was across the hall and spent some time looking for the room before I found it. When I finally found the room, the lab instructor seemed quite put out about my interrupting her class and as she then had to find someone for me to work with. Then she informed us how each student needed to record their own results even though they worked on the experiment in pairs. As I had never had a lab class before, I was quite confused about what the experiment was asking for, so I was just trying to comprehend what we were doing when my lab partner walked out of the lab with the results of the experiment and never returned. So I finished the best I could, taking notes the rest of the way. For the next three weeks I ended up getting a new lab partner each week. The second week they assigned me a guy from a threesome group who did not show up the third week. The third week they assigned me a girl from a different threesome group. I got the impression throughout the remainder of the semester that the girl always resented my having taken her away from her other two friends who were in the other group, even though I really hadn't meant to break her away from her friends by the re-assignment.

A few hours after chemistry lab, I then had algebra which was held in the Flycatcher Building, just a building west of the Science Hall. On the first day, the algebra professor went over his expectations of the class and reviewed the first several chapters of pre-algebra material. He then told us how the next time we met we would begin on chapter one but that we should read the pre-algebra chapters and do the problems which he had listed for those chapters. So I went back to my dorm room which I had been told was just a temporary room feeling swamped with how much I needed to do on just this first day of classes and settled in to work on my studies for the two classes I had that day. I managed to finish recording my chemistry lab notes in the appropriate book which I had to buy from the bookstore. I then had read over the lab for the next week and completed writing up an overview of the lab that I had done earlier to turn in the following week; and I was starting to work on doing the problems assigned for the chapters of pre-algebra materials after having read the chapters when Nina, one of my four roommates, started to invite friends and other students she had met to the dorm room so she could get to know her dorm residents better.

After a time, the noise just got to be too much and hindered my finishing the algebra homework I felt I needed to do before I met again for the class in a couple days so I left the room. As I left I met one of the students who I had met the week before at the Christian concert who was posting flyers for their Christian group with his girlfriend. When they heard of my problem, he told me how his girlfriend's roommate had just left so maybe I should see if I could room with his girlfriend in Starling Hall. So I talked with my RA and Hummingbird's Hall manager and they both took down my request. Then I found a quiet place in the dorm and sat down with my algebra and completed the assigned problems.

On my second day of classes, my first class was chemistry again in the Science Hall west of Ravens Commons taught by Dr. Ralph V. He started his lecture by listing the prerequisites for the class, which was the beginner's chemistry which the college offered or high school chemistry. He then said that if anyone had any questions we should swing by his office and talk with him. So after his class I swung by his office to talk as I had never taken any chemistry classes prior to his class. When I voiced this concern to him he told me, "I am required to tell my class those are the prerequisites but seriously, even those who have taken chemistry classes in high school do not always remember what they have been taught. So as long as you do the studying I have down in the syllabus you should be fine. If you have questions I am usually here so you can always come and ask me. If you need more help, there is the chemistry help room next door you can go to or I can help you get a personal tutor if you continue to struggle. Currently the beginner's chemistry class is filled but if they have an opening I could get you a transfer into that class if you prefer." I chose to stick with his class, however, because he had just spent about a half hour trying to reassure me that I would be fine. (With his help, I got an A in his class at the end of the semester!)

It was also in my freshman year that the September 11 attacks occurred. In fact, I remember how I was supposed to have an English class that morning, but when I got to the room there had been a note posted saying the class was cancelled for the day. So as I had some time to kill I thought I would wander the hallways where the professors had their offices. Seeing comics on the doors, I went from door to door reading the comics and happened to overhear a couple English professors talking about the destruction but did not know what they were talking about. It was not until later that day when my other class had been cancelled and I went back to Hummingbird Hall that I passed the hall manager's room where the TV was on replaying the attacks. Then I understood what the English professors had been talking about when I overheard them and why classes had been cancelled. The September 11 attacks increased my bumbling attempts to share my faith with my family and only created more tension between us. In fact, Grandma Nancy would remind me that she had taken classes on studying the Bible and had a degree in Christianity so she knew more than I did about being a Christian.

Since I was very concerned about the world ending and my family not having the same faith that I had recently found, I am thankful that before college I had lived for a few months just a few miles away from the farm at Louis and Robin's. I am also thankful that I had support from veterinarians and from my church family. Otherwise, I probably would have moved home again as I struggled with the transition of being home schooled to attending college classes and living two hours away from home with no transportation of my own to be able to get back to the farm to help my family.

Then sometime about a month after classes had started as I tried to sleep, I overheard Nina complaining to Reba, another roommate, about how she had gotten a letter saying she was being transferred to Starling Hall but how it was actually me who wanted to move to Starling, not her. A couple days after that my RA informed me that I was being transferred to Starling Hall but not with the guy's girlfriend.

Starling Hall was on the west end of the campus several blocks west of the Science Hall and Ravens Commons but across the street from the Ag Science Hall where most of the agricultural classes were held.

The following weekend Ma and Uncle Larry came up to help me move to Starling Hall. They were not too happy when they found out Starling Hall consisted of boys and girls in about every other dorm room. In fact, my RA was a guy – Levi. His room was located just one doorway east of my room. He was very friendly, and his door was almost always open and he was willing to listen whenever I just needed someone to talk to which was several times a week and overall I just felt comfortable hanging out with him for a while when I just wanted a break from studying. He had been so excited when he heard that I was a science major as he said there was only one other person besides him and me on our wing who was. He usually was always studying, too and sometimes his girlfriend also was hanging out with him and studying.

Later in the year, Kurt Y, who helped hire resident assistants and desk assistants, called me to ask if I would meet with him. When I met with him, Kurt said someone had recommended me to him and I always wondered if it was Levi, though it may have been a friend from CODCL. When Kurt asked if there was anything he could help me with, I admitted I was lonely. Then I shared with him how I had discovered that five of my friends who went to CODCL lived in the neighboring dorm, Plovers Hall. As I knew that visitors after ten o'clock were supposed to register at the front desk, I always felt guilty if I visited with them and stayed past 10:00, as I never registered as a guest. So I asked if it would be possible to move over there. Kurt looked into it and found me a spot the next semester.

I always felt bad after I moved that next semester, as I feared I hurt Levi by moving as I didn't share with him the reasons why I had but had just moved without much if any warning. The one reason had been how uncomfortable it was for me to be living in a dorm where the door across the hall was resided in by guys as well as knowing that half of the rooms were especially when I would go for a shower or to use the bathroom. Also at that point I had been struggling with my roommate as she watched TV all the time and rarely did I find her doing any studying. I think the one or two times I had, she admitted to having an exam later in the day. The fact that the TV was always on was a distraction for me which kept me from studying and for that first year I had almost always tried to do most if not all my studying in my dorm room. I remember that I lived with her in Starling Hall during the time leading up to Halloween and that there were horror movies on which she would choose to watch usually on a daily basis. Occasionally she would otherwise choose to watch baseball game. No matter what I did to try to prevent my watching the TV constantly even if it was a horror movie which I absolutely could not stand as they were too real and it took several years before I was able to tell myself that the movies weren't real so that I could stop looking over my shoulder for fear something evil would get into my dorm room. It was only right before I moved to Plovers Hall that I had found the most successful method which worked for me which was to put my dresser between the end of my bed and the TV so that when I sat on my bed to study I was not able to see the TV. If I was standing though the TV continued to trap my attention and occasionally it would when I craned my neck to look around the dresser. In fact, this frustration over roommates watching TV was how my sophomore roommate, Debbie I, and I decided to room together. I had shared with her when she swung by my room after going to a Bible study that was held in Starling's basement, how I was frustrated with my roommate watching TV all the time and being distracted. Debbie had then shared how she also had a roommate who watched TV all the time and Debbie found it distracting as well.

COLLEGE ORGANIZATION DEVELOPING CHRISTIAN LEADERS CODCL AT COLLEGE AT CATALPA CITY

On the day before college classes were to start, Labor Day of my freshman year, I had gone to the Student Center as that is where I saw the poster had said the group from CODCL was going to meet students in order to walk over to the picnic at Grouse Park together. Lena U was one of the students there and she helped introduce me to many of the other CODCL students, like Melinda N who usually carried a pretty large backpack which looked like it always contained 3-5 large textbooks, Michael V whom was a friend to most people which is why I'm sure he made a great CODCL staff person several years later, and Curt X who loved to tease. That was also when I met Samuel N, the CODCL campus staff director. At that time I hadn't know that this was the Samuel that was the leader for CODCL though and hadn't until several days or weeks later. Then after a couple handful more students joined us, we had walked the few blocks over to Grouse Park where several other students were already gathered and were starting to barbeque hamburgers, brats and hotdogs while others were starting to play games. While we waited for the food to finish cooking, Samuel and quite a few other students started a game of Ultimate Frisbee which I had never played but chose to play after hearing how it was played as I thought it sounded a bit like football and as I was invited to join

102

them. My favorite role to play was on defense as I tried to intimidate the person who had the Frisbee and try to keep them from getting it to a teammate. I remember often choosing the smallest guy on the other team to try to keep him from receiving the Frisbee or to intimidate him when he tried to throw the Frisbee. Without knowing it, I had chosen Samuel, the CODCL campus staff director, who after the game said I made an intimidating defensive player.

In addition to thinking it was a bit like football, while on defense it took me back to working on the farm and trying to outsmart the cattle when they were loose and trying to present myself as more intimidating so that the animal would not try to charge my way in their excitement. When a cow got loose she would get so excited as we always kept them tied up around the clock in their stalls but after time the twine string which we used to keep cows tied with would wear out and the cow would get loose. Either that or the swivel, which we used between the twines to tie her to the stall as it kept her from twisting the twines eventually to the point of twisting her collar and starting to choke her, would instead break. Once she got loose often it was while nobody was in the barn and once it was discovered, Abby, Ma and I would get called out to the barn. One of us would set to working on getting new twine strings tied to her stall ready for once we got her back in her stall to tie her up. One of the other remaining people would use their hand or ball cap to slap her face to get her to back out of wherever she currently had herself and to get her to head back toward her stall. The remaining person would stand on the other side of the stall which she was to head toward and would be holding twine, their cap, or a shovel to encourage her to not run over them as she came racing up the aisle toward them. They would use one of these items to smack her one if she was not slowing down and showed no sign of wanting to respect them. The cow if she was too excited might then duck into another stall or turn and race the other way again. The person who initially sent her back toward her stall would then be trying to intimidate her with her cap, or would have grabbed another shovel or some twine and then try to send her back toward her stall. Sometimes this back and forth happened about a dozen times before she finally was ready to settle down and go into her stall where one of us would quickly tie her with the twine we had made ready. The more excited the people were who were trying to shoo her back to her stall, seemed to feed into the cow's excitement and make her less likely to want to go into her stall. Towards the end of Abby and my teen years we started to try to get a halter on her wherever it was that we first found her and then try to calmly lead her back to her stall. When that did not work we would revert to using shovels or twine to intimidate the cow. So I was used to intimidating things multiple times my size so Ultimate Frisbee defense was a breeze.

Throughout the following weeks of my freshman year, the friends I made through CODCL helped me when I needed help and as I battled loneliness. I remember how Lena or Melinda had shown me the area upstairs in the library that had several tables and was off the hallway where she and a few other CODCL students liked to study. So usually between classes I would head to that area in the library and join anyone who was there. When there was no one in that area I would head back down toward the entrance of the library. The library had two entrances to the library, one which was to the basement area which contained many computer rooms and then another entrance in between the basement and the first floor. Often I would choose the in between area and would sit by a window and work on my homework. In order for me to concentrate, I strangely enough needed just enough distraction by being able to look out the window or by seeing the people who were entering or leaving the library. One time I remember sitting in this in between area while working on my Algebra. I had gotten all but like two of the problems and no matter what I did I couldn't seem to figure out what I was doing wrong so that I was not getting the same answer as the back of the book had. So I started to feel miserable and discouraged. (My discouragement had gotten to the point where I was questioning being in college. Since math was my favorite subject, if I was having troubles with it now, then how could I expect to be able to finish the semester or get through any other subject? Overall, I was just feeling sorry for myself as I missed the friends I had started to make back in Buttercup City and even missed my family and the farm. On top of this, I had still yet to hear if I would get any financial assistance so was feeling stressed because of that as I knew neither my family or myself had any money to put me through even a semester of college.) As I was feeling sorry for myself Michael V, a friend from CODCL, came up from the basement and upon noticing me, he swung by and asked me how I was. I shared some of my frustration and while he said he really had to get somewhere, Michael sat down with me and using his calculator he started checking my work. In a matter of minutes, Michael noticed how I forgot to carry a number, and several other similar small problems. Once I corrected those things I got the correct answers and felt foolish over my bout of self-pity, and quite grateful for Michael's taking time to help me.

Another time, Melinda N, also with CODCL, showed me the downstairs of the library where all the computer labs were and taught me how to read the schedules posted outside the door to see when the labs were open. There were many days when I had an assignment I had to do on the computer that I then would head to the computer labs and look for an open room and would specifically look for one of my friends from CODCL, if I didn't see any of them I would choose a room where I would be least likely to have to leave for a class before I would have to leave myself. One time I remember how I had found my friend Melinda in a computer and showed off my keyboarding skills as I would type for minutes without looking at the computer screen but instead would look to the side. These keyboarding skills I had gained thanks to my having taken my keyboarding class on a typewriter while being home schooled. The class had encouraged students to not look at the printed results but to focus on what one was trying to copy so as to be more productive with one's typing by decreasing how often one would have to find where they left off and pick up again from there when they would keep switching their focus while typing.

Another time I remember being in one of the computer labs one Friday night and feeling very lonely. Rose N, another CODCL friend who had a horse that she would barrel race at college rodeos, saw me and after hearing about my loneliness invited me over to the Catholic Nuthatcher Center where she was headed, where we played games and watched a movie. On a different day when I was lonely, Nicole Q, another CODCL friend who had dark red brown hair and an infectious smile and laugh, had seen me and upon hearing how I was lonely, invited me to join her for a birthday party she was throwing for her friend Shannon N at her apartment just north of campus. While I was there I learned how Nicole had been a Resident Assistant in the dorm where Debbie currently lived and the dorm Debbie had invited me to live with her as her roommate during my sophomore year.

In my freshman year I used a lot of the CODCL activities to help me get to know my fellow CODCL students better in addition to the CODCL meetings which were held weekly, I think it was on Wednesdays. The CODCL meetings would be held in a room in the student center right at the top of the stairs leading to a couple upper rooms. As every week the CODCL leadership would have to set out chairs for students to sit in for the meeting and then pick it all up again afterwards. I quickly realized that if I got to the meeting early I could help set up and then if I stayed late I could help clean up. Lots of the students on leadership was quite appreciative of my help and I enjoyed the chance to linger and that way get to know a few extra CODCL students.

There were a lot of the CODCL activities which I missed though as they were held on weekends as half the time my freshman year I was usually trying to make it home to coincide with the weekends Abby was coming home. Some of the activities I missed included going to join fellow CODCL groups at Carnation City and again at Easter Lily City campuses. Events which I had gone to though included invitations to go to watch CCC football games in which CODCL students' Curt X and Randall Y were playing. Lena was real good friends with Curt and her excitement made me enthusiastic about joining her at the games which with my CCC ID were free to attend. Other events were when Melinda N and her roommates would hold their monthly game or movie nights at their apartment. Those nights a group of students would meet at the Student Center and as the time when their game or movie night was about to begin, the students would walk over to Melinda's apartment. Another time, CODCL had an event which involved singing Karaoke that I had gone to and I managed to find the courage to sing

"Heartland" by George Strait, my first-time singing Karaoke which I actually enjoyed. They also had a group one weekend that went skating at a local roller rink. I needed to hold onto someone all night to skate due to my inexperience, and by the end of the night I was so sore that the next day I could barely climb my dorm stairs. I hadn't enjoyed it that much so I have never felt inclined to try again even though my niece has since tried to convince me but since I've injured my back in 2009 it has also played a role in keeping me from ever trying again. It was while roller-skating that freshman year that my sophomore roommate, Debbie I, said she first met me, but as the night was such a blur with all the new faces while I was also trying to focus on staying upright on skates, I hardly remember meeting her or anybody else from CODCL who was there.

CODCL also offered a conference event down closer to the Magnolia City area with a bunch of other colleges across the state. When I talked with my church friends in Buttercup City about going to it they gladly raised some money to help me be able to afford going. CODCL had the students who signed up to go to the event make note if they would be able to provide a ride or if they would need a ride. From that, CODCL then assigned various students who said they could drive with students who said they needed rides so that all the students would be able to make it down to the conference. I ended up being assigned to ride to the conference with Rose N, whom I already knew somewhat from the CODCL meetings which were held weekly I think on Wednesday nights and when she had invited me to join her at the Catholic Nuthatcher Center, and with Irene S, whom I met for the first time on the drive. As Rose drove us in her pickup, it was cozy in the cab so I really got to know both her and Irene a lot more. It was from here that I learned how Rose also was involved in the Rodeo that CCC held and had a horse she barrel-raced. Irene I learned was a local Catalpa City resident who chose to live in a dorm rather than at home which she could have. At that conference, I remember meeting Samuel's brother-in-law who was leading my track for freshmen and one of the messages being about needing to be purposeful about getting to know people whom God put beside you which is the only reason I ended up connecting with Ian C who was Debbie I's friend so she had chosen to sit next to him when we met in a large group. Due to that message I forced myself out of my comfort zone so that I made eye contact with him and joined him and Debbie in conversation. Then I spent a good chunk of time the rest of that weekend with him during free times at the conference and we shared addresses before the end of the conference and kept in touch for the rest of the school year and the following summer. He was the closest I feel I came to a boyfriend until in 2010 when my coworker Matthew M expressed an interest.

It was a few days after the conference that I saw Irene again and after she asked me how I was doing, I expressed my frustration about not being able to study in my dorm because my roommate was always watching TV. And even though there were rooms meant for studying, these almost always had their doors shut, and I did not feel comfortable opening them because I didn't know if I should as I feared some of the rooms were still being used for temporary housing or who knows what else might be happening behind the closed door. Irene then invited me over to her dorm where, "The door of the study room on her floor was always open." Also, she said I could always find her or other CODCL students like Nadine Z, Iris J, Rhea N, and Isabelle T. So for the rest of the semester that is what I did; I went over to Plovers Hall and hung out in Plovers' study room until I'd get an invite to hang out at Irene and Rhea's room, or the room next door where Iris and Nadine lived. I spent a lot of time over there the rest of that semester and the next of my freshman year. It was by joining them that I first started to get meals at either their fast food location in the main level or a meal from their cafeteria in the lower level of the Student Center. Afterwards they would often join a group of students from CODCL which would be eating at one of the tables on the main level. Prior to their inviting me to join them, I had used to see the CODCL students eating together but had never had the courage to join them as I never knew that there were a few meal options available at both food locations which came with a student's meal plan and always felt it might be an exclusive meeting of students. From these meals, is where I really connected even more with CODCL students especially those who lived off campus who didn't invest in a meal plan as anyone could eat there or a person could pay for meals to eat there.

Then as the second semester of my freshman year started, I decided I wanted to throw myself a birthday party as my birthday was right after classes resumed following winter break. I talked to my family about it and they sent me back to campus with a bunch of Little Debbie snacks and a big can of hot chocolate mix. I remember being touched by their generosity but feeling guilty, too, as they always seemed so strapped for money. Then I also talked to Nadine about my plan for throwing myself a birthday party and asked her if she could help me invite people to the party, which I decided to hold in Plovers Hall's basement as unlike Nadine, I didn't know a lot of people nor very outgoing, so I struggled with invites especially when it involved any of the guys which I really wanted to be invited so I could maybe meet someone like Abby apparently had. I remember having lots of fun and that Curt from CODCL and an CCC football player had come and been amazed at the spread my family had sent with me for my party.

For the remainder of my first year I hung out a lot with Iris, Nadine, Irene, Rhea, and Isabelle. I remember how Irene's grandmother had entered her into a sweepstakes, which resulted in Irene winning a Volkswagen Bug that was decaled to look like a pair of blue jeans. Until she hit a deer with it my sophomore year when she ended up painting it white as it would cost her too much to get the decal work touched back up. During my freshman year, Irene had lots of fun driving us around in her new car often with lots of goofiness going on. They would also often go over to Baltimore Oriole College to participate in their vesper event (an hour dedicated to singing worship songs to God) which I would also join them at if I hadn't gone home of the weekend. Other times they had Steven M, a freshman football player probably over six feet tall, squeeze himself in the back seat as one of her other friends refused to give up the shotgun position preferring instead to see Steven squeeze himself into the back.

I'm not sure how long it was before someone finally pointed out to me how in Ravens Commons they had a board where a person could put requests to find a ride home on a weekend on the left side of the board or on the right side if someone was going home on a weekend and would be willing to provide a ride home for other students they could put down what city they were headed to. That is what enabled me to be able to go home almost every other weekend my first semester and is how I first met Michael V's roommate, Stuart, as Michael V shared how Stuart lived in my hometown. This knowledge resulted in my asking Stuart for numerous rides home until I'd graduated. Both of us were really quiet people so there wasn't much if any conversation the entire two hours of driving so frequently I would end up dozing off a good chunk of the two hours to or from campus. Inactivity has a way of doing that to me. I often would doze off as I'd try to study if there wasn't enough stimulation around me to help keep me awake which was why I rarely would stay in the study area that Lena or Miranda had shown me as if no CODCL student was there I would be dozing off most of my time instead of studying if I stayed there. This rider board is how I met several other non-CODCL students who lived in the Lilac City/Buttercup City area though if I could find a CODCL student who would be driving around that area I usually chose to go that way rather than going with a non-CODCL student. In fact once I remember having Iris a very outgoing CODCL student popular with most of the CODCL guys and several CODCL gals, take me home as she took her roommate home with her over in Lavender City. As I didn't want to make her go out of her way and I knew my family didn't want me to bring any friends home to the farm, I had asked her to drop me off at the Lilac City/Buttercup City exit off the Highway separating Buttercup City and Lilac City.

Another time I remember hanging around Iris and heard about a Packer/Viking game that was being held at Rob M's house. Rob also went to CODCL and lived in Starling Hall. He was a Viking fan while the majority of the others of us who ended up joining him and watching the game were Packer fans. Iris reminded me throughout the following years how she had almost forgotten I was along until I let out an excited yell when a Packer player made a spectacular play. Then another memory I have was when the school year was almost over and Isabelle was transferring to another college. Iris started planning an event for Isabelle. Isabelle knew about it and invited me to come, but when I asked Iris for details, she said it was just for the five of them. I remember how I went back to my room, ducked down in the corner behind the desk CCC supplied and cried, thinking I had overstepped my friendship boundaries in the past year with that group of women.

Even as the years have gone on I still struggle to get past old habits and actually succeed with feeling part of most groups to the point of actually being a friend whom someone will take time to contact in order to set up time to spend time together, with a few exceptions. I'm not sure if it is because I am not very outgoing or because I'm not usually very good at being vulnerable or if when I am vulnerable that I fail to be a good listener or confused on what I can or should do to build better friendships. Something tends to make me feel like I am not a good friend of others. Maybe it is because I come across as being busy volunteering all the time, so they don't even try setting up time together. Maybe I don't try hard enough or maybe I come across as too desperate that people don't try. I am not sure but if I were to choose which "Love Language" of Gary Chapman's that I have it probably would be Quality Time and so it's when I feel people give me some of their valuable time that is when I feel the most appreciated and loved.

Anyway, while going to CCC there was also a family in Honeysuckle whom befriended some CODCL friends. That family then would yearly invite CODCL to come over to their farm for a bonfire, 4-wheeling, horse riding, games, sports, etc. One time during the bonfire Curt, the football player who loved teasing, which reminded me of Uncle Larry, repeatedly gave my friends, Iris and Nadine a hard time. So as I tagged along with them, I eventually decided to tackle Curt and after several minutes managed to take him down. After we both got back up he then took me down, initially I had resisted but then decided to just give in and let him take me down. Afterwards Curt offered to help me back up but I had refused and got up on my own. Several years later, Carrie whom I had befriended in Ravens Commons and later became my roommate had I believe been climbing trees and slipped and landed wrong. She was helped into the living room where she sat with ice on her foot the rest of the evening. She felt certain it wasn't broke as she was able to move it, but a few days later when she finally got it looked at was proven wrong as it turned out it was broken. This led to her friends coming down to the first floor in Tree Sparrow Hall and spending a fair amount of time with her and was where I got my first exposure to video games which I have yet to get into video games unless you count games played on a smart phone like One Draw, Cookie Crush and Words with Friends.

STRETCHING MY COMFORT ZONE

During my freshman year, I tried to convince Debbie I we should live in Plovers the next year so we could remain close to Irene and Nadine who signed up to keep a room in Plovers my sophomore year. But Debbie insisted on staying in Tree Sparrow Hall all the way on the other side, the east side of campus. So that is where I lived my sophomore to senior years of college. As my freshman year ended I decided I wanted to be like the upperclassmen who had befriended me. But I realized I needed to stretch my comfort zone if I was ever going to be like them. This prompted me to volunteer to help with CODCL's Outreach from my sophomore to my senior year, to apply for the desk assistant job my sophomore and junior years, to host my own game and movie nights, and to befriend people I saw that were eating alone in Ravens Commons until I graduated.

CODCL's initial event for Outreach was to set up a table the first week of classes at Ravens Commons, the main food joint on the east side of campus. Here, CODCL students would stand behind a table containing survey cards, candy and some handouts. The CODCL students manning the table would encourage students coming to eat to fill out a survey card with their name, address, and phone number in order to get a piece of candy and to enter a drawing for a prize. CODCL then needed additional students already involved in CODCL to help follow up with these students unless the student marked the line saying, "Do not contact." If that were the case, then we were just supposed to pray for them. Otherwise if the student had not marked the "Do not contact" CODCL had their current CODCL students follow up on students in an assigned area (dorm or region off campus). When I expressed interest in helping with the follow up I was assigned Tree Sparrow Hall as that is where I was living my sophomore year and then Meadowlark Hall my junior year as there were lots of current CODCL students living that year in Tree Sparrow Hall but none currently living in Meadowlark. To follow up with a student required me to knock on their dorm room door and if after several tries I would try to call the student. Initially that first year, my following up with these students was very hard and awkward for me as I had never been encouraged to call people or go visiting while growing up, but following up got easier the more I did it.

It was through the following up of surveys filled out during Outreach that I got to know Rebecca S, Leah M, and Caroline M. They had all marked their card saying they were interested in learning more about CODCL. So, I went to their dorm rooms, knocked on their doors, and shared with them about CODCL including when and where the CODCL group met. I also told them I would be willing to go with them to CODCL and/or Ravens Commons if they would like me to. It was as I continued to follow up with Rebecca and Caroline that I found out both were unhappy with their roommates. Caroline was a big brown eyed, brown haired city girl who loved to make people laugh. She shared how her roommate was into witchcraft and she had overheard her roommate saying she was putting a spell on Caroline. Meanwhile, Rebecca was a big blond farm girl who had transferred to Catalpa City her sophomore year who shared how her roommate had disturbing gory posters and sayings up in the room. A few weeks after I first met them and was joining with them to go to lunch together at Ravens, Rebecca mentioned to me how her roommate was considering moving off campus and how Rebecca was considering requesting a single room. Since I noticed that Rebecca and Caroline had started to hit it off together when we went to lunch together, I decided to ask Rebecca if maybe she would like to room with Caroline as I told her Caroline was unhappy with her roommate as well. Since we were heading to meet Caroline for lunch, I brought up the question of whether they would like to be roommates and both of them were quite excited about the idea. After Rebecca's roommate moved out, Caroline moved in.

Leah M though enjoyed her roommate and became quick friends with Rebecca and Caroline. She had a disability which caused her to walk with a severe limp which prompted the dorm to build a storage place to put her motorized scooter she needed to decrease further injury of her hip and leg. She, Rebecca and Caroline seemed to constantly be doing things together and occasionally I would join them especially on the walk to the CODCL meetings which now were being held in Quail Hall auditorium as CODCL had doubled since my freshman year and had outgrown the room in the Student Center. Quail Hall was probably one of the oldest buildings on campus. It sure smelled like it as it had an old musty smell. The auditorium involved less set up and take down as it had its own seats. Since it had so many seats though, CODCL students in charge of set up would take some twine string and rope off the back half of the seating areas to encourage people to sit together and they would also set up a table outside which contained nametags and CODCL student directory, etc. It was here that Emory C, a tall, muscular guy whom I met during a sophomore Bible study whom was in a military training program also started to pick on my sophomore chemistry lab partner and friend, Norma J. One time I tried to come to her defense and grappled with him but with his size and training I was unable to stop him and barely even slowed him down as I hung on him. Several years later these two ended up getting married.

As I also was working as a desk assistant in Tree Sparrow Hall my sophomore and junior years, I got to connect with a lot of people in the dorm like Caroline, Rebecca, Leah, and a few other students too. As a desk assistant, I was required to check to see if the mail had come in and if it had, I was to sort it. I also would rent out equipment (pots and pans, games, movies, etc.) to the residents of the hall. The "fee" for the rental was just to give us the resident's ID card until they returned the item. As most used their ID card for meals, usually we had no problem getting the item back but Leah's roommate usually made her own meals so she tended to rent out the cookware the dorm had and not return it for days or even weeks later. At the desk we also would sell stamps and exchange quarters for cash so residents could do laundry. My sophomore year I just did the job as was required of me, but in my junior year I chose to do a bit more. When students would come to check their mail I would hear how disappointed students were if they did not get personal mail or frustration over a mass mailing. So in my junior year I would ask the residents what their favorite flower, animal, sport, etc. was. Then I would go to a campus computer in the library, dorm's computer room or in the student center and get pictures of what the residents said were their favorites. Once I had the picture of their favorite item I would then write them a little note on the backside of the picture and put it in their mailbox. It really seemed to make the residents days. I had also brought a Lite Brite from home and would let the residents decorate it if they expressed interest in doing so. Additionally, I would provide crayons and pictures for the residents to color which I would then hang up on the wall around the desk. The end of my junior year I was invited to a party for the desk assistants, resident assistants, etc. where I found out I was nominated for Desk Assistant of the Year. After the meal and as they were handing out the prizes I learned that I was the winner of the Desk Assistant of the Year.

In addition to working as a desk assistant my sophomore and junior years, I also had worked at CCC's dairy farm. The dairy farm was a bit more than a mile if a person walked the sidewalks along the road leading out there but under a mile if one took the paths winding through the woods and over the South Fork Kinglets River, which ran just south of the campus, to the farm. There I usually helped by feeding calves and occasionally helping with milking. I really disliked milking as I found it tedious and particular, so only if they were in a pinch did I offer to help with the milking. The part I found tedious is that milking never really required interaction with the cow. The lab farm had a couple stalls per side in their parlor which you would fill with a couple cows and then you just made sure to clean her udder so that a milking machine could be attached without getting bacteria into the milk which was then routed through the milking machine's claw, through a pipeline, to the bulk tank where the milk was held until a milk truck would come and haul it to a cheese factory. The entire milking would require a person to just go from one cow to the next and without getting to interact with the cow it just became quite repetitive. The part that I found particular was while you didn't get to interact with the cow you had to know just enough about her to know if she was one who tended to have an infection in her udder, called mastitis, and if so to watch out for it and milk that quarter differently while keeping that milk from entering a regular milking machine, pipeline and bulk tank by instead using a special milking machine which would direct the milk into a bucket which would get dumped out. A person also had to be attentive enough to notice if a cow who wasn't on the "to watch" list flared up with mastitis as mastitis was caused by several different types of bacteria which made the milk less desirable. But if the mastitis was being treated with an antibiotic, the milk was even less desirable for several reasons including that the antibiotic would keep cheese from forming and the milk would be unsellable to humans due to allergies to antibiotics.

Feeding the calves, though, I loved. I took great care in making sure all my bottles and pails were cleaned well after I fed the calves. I would feed all the calves their milk in either the bottles for the calves who hadn't been pail trained yet which usually were less than a few days old or pails to those who were pail trained. Then I would take their milk pails back to the shed where the milk replacer, calf feed and hay was stored and I would scrub each bottle and pail after every use in soapy water and then sanitized them with bleach water. I would also make sure to switch out and clean the grain buckets in a similar fashion on a daily basis. I would give what the youngest calves, under a month, choose not to eat to the ones who were between two months to a year old whom were housed together in a couple groups in an overhanging shed. I also would provide hay whenever I saw any of the calves from a week old to a year old whose hay was gone. The lab farm manager seemed quite impressed with my work, but by my senior year I decided I needed to work more on my social skills versus my farm skills, so I discontinued working at the lab farm and applied instead to help tutor chemistry, biology, and math.

As I continued to try to stretch my comfort zone, I also did it by trying to befriend people who sat alone which came about because of

Rachael, the orientation leader. It seemed that whenever she had come to Ravens Commons and saw me eating alone during my freshman year she would invite me to join her and her friends or she would join me after asking if she could do so. As I always appreciated her attempts to befriend me like that, I decided that in my successive years of college I wanted to try that too. This is how I got to know Gena N, Carrie N, Kendall V, Brenda, and Steven. While I probably did not make a major difference in some of these lower classmen's lives, I am certain that the friendships created through these outreaches did make a difference in each of our lives.

One time I had joined a group of fellow students some of which went to CODCL as they went, to eat at Ravens Commons when I saw Carrie, a blue eyed golden brown-haired freshman eating alone. I went over to her and invited her to join us. She declined, but partway into eating my meal I glanced in the direction where she had been eating and saw she was no longer there but rather was at a table right behind where I was sitting with another group of students. When she saw that I saw her with the other group she got embarrassed and looked away and so did I. Several more times through the meal we caught each other's glances before looking away in embarrassment each time. After the meal, I noticed that Carrie's RA had provided her residents with a bag that people could leave notes in, so I wrote a note to Carrie apologizing for all the embarrassment and explained why I kept trying to invite her to join me. I included my phone number in the note. Later that night Carrie called me to explain how she had been struggling since the prior fall when one of her hometown classmates had committed suicide. After we talked, laughed, and cried for a half-hour we became friends, good-enough friends that she and I became roommates in Chickadee Hall my final semester of college.

With Gena, a very skinny freshman about 5'6" with brown eyes, glasses and short dark brown hair, I usually had a very difficult time getting more than the briefest of answers to my questions out of her. She continued to allow me to sit with her, however, whenever I saw her eating alone. I always hoped I was not annoying her, but sensing that she was just shy and needed encouragement, I kept asking to sit with her. Since she lived on the same wing as Caroline and Rebecca, they eventually connected and together we got her started in attending CODCL where she connected with other CODCL students, particularly Iris J and Rachael F, Gena's future roommate. Then between Caroline and Rebecca's zaniness and Iris's outgoingness we started to draw Gena out of her shell. Later when Iris was graduating Gena gave credit to Iris for befriending her, which she said kept her from taking action on the suicidal thoughts she had struggled with her freshman year.

Another incident with Gena was one time when I knew her birthday was coming up. Since I knew how much she liked squirrels, I bought a sweatshirt, paint, and brushes and painted a squirrel on the sweatshirt and asked others to decorate it too. I remember how Caroline had drawn swiggle lines around the tail to make it look like the squirrel was wagging its tail and then she drew a balloon with a rhyme about how much it would wag its tail upon hearing her name.

Then as I wanted to continue Melinda's hosting of game and movie nights, I told my friends Dave and Trish N from Buttercup City Bible Church that I wanted to do this. They told me how they had an extra TV and some games and movies I could have. That was the start of my game and movie collection. Some of the movies no one had heard of but at least four of them became favorites of mine. They included *Swept from the Sea*, *Dear God*, *While You Were Sleeping*, and *Renaissance Man*. Each of them have a very realistic storyline where the changes in characters was seen developing and while I usually do not cry at movies *Swept from the Sea* was about the closest as I ever came as my heart felt the main characters loneliness and rejection by most of the other characters and then once I learned the cause of the rejection. As for the games Dave and Trish had given me they were Battleship, Monopoly, and Payday as well as several containers of Play-Doh,. The Play-Doh and Payday became favorites among my friends. In fact, Debbie told me once that she had invited a group over one weekend when I was gone and our friend Eric N had made the golden Play-Doh into tiny squares, put in toothpicks, and then went around the dorm offering people cheese. Initially Eric was Debbie's friend, as she was very popular with everyone but especially the guys. But even though Eric was initially

Debbie's friend he became my friend too as he was the only one of Debbie's guy friends who would take time to talk to me if I answered the phone when he called or if I was also in the room when he called. Eric would also go to the same church, Church Sweeping the Area with the Gospel, that I went to and as I had decided I wanted to get involved in the church, I would help serve the juice and cookies. Eric would tell all our friends whenever he saw me serving the cookies how I had made the cookie, which I would always shake my head to as I had been raised not to lie and protested him telling people that as it was not true. He loved to tease like that which was what both made me uncomfortable yet comfortable with him.

Then almost every time I had people over to play games I remember playing Payday. There were two memorable times of playing this game. One time was when I was graduating and a group got together to celebrate and we played it then which probably is memorable mostly due to the fact I have a picture of a group of us playing the game while some of the students also decorated some turtleneck shirts I brought for them to paint. The other memorable time playing Payday was when I was mingling with a group I had met through CODCL's Outreach that lived in Meadowlark Hall my junior year which consisted of a group of gals and one guy. The guy, Dan R, a tall skinny blond freshman and brother to Nick R, who lived in Violet City whom I had started to regularly catch rides home with even though Nick was about as quiet as I was. Nick I had a crush on as I found him handsome, knew he lived by my family, and as I knew he loved farming as much as I loved my cows. Ultimately though Nick found another farm girl, Rachael F who had an outgoing, bubbly personality who was happy about leaving the farm which he fell in love with and married. Anyway Dan had once during that game landed on a mail slot with one of the bills resulting from "having a boyfriend who was in town." Dan had gotten really red and embarrassed as we continually teased him for the rest of the game about having a boyfriend. We knew that wasn't really real as in real life. Dan was always hanging out with a group of fellow freshman girls who lived in his dorm.

Between being involved with CODCL, working as a desk assistant, and trying to befriend loners I grew a lot socially. Still, during my senior year Carrie N accused me of hovering around people. My hovering was a result of my wanting to be included in things but not being brave enough to ask if it was okay for me to be a part of the group or of not feeling like I had anything to add to the conversations. To this day, I still struggle with starting conversations and in knowing if I am welcome to stay or if people would prefer if I left. This reflects my sensitivity toward Grandma Nancy who always seemed to prefer being left alone but who never actually told a person to their face that was how she felt.

My college years, being part of CODCL, and having the desk assistant job were God sends as they gave me a chance to push my comfort zone and grow socially and spiritually, and I am very thankful to the Lord for making these things possible. My social struggles, which I have struggled with since childhood, seem due to doubting myself. I often realize how many of my hobbies can be done at home where I don't have to spend money and be by myself without having to go and be with people, and that makes me wonder if anyone would notice if I cut myself off from people, which would be very easy for me to do. Sometimes I wonder if I am struggling because I have not given these social struggles over fully to the Lord or recognized that his grace is sufficient for me. At other times, I think maybe I have given this over to God but that God plans to use this struggle to create ministry opportunities for me similar to like how the apostle Paul in the Bible put it in 2 Corinthians 12:7, *"Therefore, in order to keep me from becoming conceited, I was given a thorn in my flesh, a messenger of Satan, to torment me."* So maybe this area is meant to be a thorn in my flesh.

SUMMER JOBS WHILE AT CCC

The summer following my freshman year at CCC of 2002, I was undecided about what I wanted to do. I knew I needed to find a job and a place to live as I didn't want to move back home. As Abby had graduated from her trade school, she had found an upstairs one bedroom apartment in Buttercup City to live. So I moved in with her, and looked for a job. Ma told me how she saw in the local paper a help wanted ad for a large dairy farm of around 500 cows, run by Ace V, a few towns north of Buttercup City in Morning Glory City that was looking for someone to help milk cows. I continued to look for a job for another couple weeks though, hoping to find something else as I really disliked milking cows. But then when I talked with Dr. Rueben about how Ma was trying to get me to apply at that dairy farm, he shared how he did herd health at that farm (Herd health is mostly checking cows for pregnancies or where in their monthly cycle they are as farmers want to keep their cows pregnant as much as they can as it is by her having calves that allows the farmer to have peak production of milk to sell.) After words of encouragement from Dr. Rueben, I was finally prompted to apply for the job. I got the job and initially only milked one of the three milkings but after a few weeks, I sometimes got scheduled to milk a couple times a day.

When Ace discovered how I aspired to be a veterinarian, he then also asked me to start checking the cows looking for lameness, other injuries, heat (time of month most likely to become pregnant), ketosis (a disease caused by her using more energy to produce milk than she was consuming—which I could smell but many other people never develop the ability to smell), etc. which could affect the cow's ability to produce milk. I gladly started to help Ace with this. There were a few times I felt like I must not have done as good as I should have when I would learn he had a cow go down and was unable to get her to stand again. Also Ace had three bulls running with the herd. Occasionally he would let one or another of the bulls run with the cows in the one pen which was the only one that had access to pasture and was where he housed the cows whom had been treated with antibiotics for mastitis or another infection, just had a calf within the past week or so, was lame, etc., I stopped going out in the pasture as the one bull would start bellowing at me when he would see me which made me nervous as I had heard stories about bulls killing people. When Ace put that bull back into another pen a few weeks later, he continued his bellowing with me in that pen so I took to avoiding the bull. Ace discovered how that bull had taken up bellowing at people and he told how I needed to take some string or something with me and instead of avoiding him should come up on the bull and attack him with the string or whatever I was carrying and make him run from me as I needed to remind the bull I was boss otherwise Ace said the bull would attack someday if the bull would get the message that he was the boss by my avoiding him.

The summer of 2002, I had continued to ride with Dr. Rueben as much as I could around my schedule milking. Also I would hang out with Abby. Prior to that summer I had never microwaved but Ma had given Abby a microwave that we had out at the farm. Early into that summer I learned how microwaving metal was a no-no. I hadn't destroyed the microwave but had created quite an electrical storm within the microwave. Then as Abby loved watching movies it seemed that every night we would be watching one.

The one night as we were watching a movie we had both fallen asleep and as it had been very hot and muggy with no air conditioner, we had all our windows wide open. Suddenly I had woken with a start as I realized how a very strong wind had come up, I woke Abby asking her to help me get all the windows closed. As we finished closing up the windows, the electricity went out and the storm siren went off. Abby quickly got our battery powered radio and turned it on and then she and I lay down in the hallway. That morning I was scheduled to work at 2AM and there were a few detours due to down trees and powerlines but for the most part, I was able to take my usual route to work in the 1979 Transvan that Ma had bought and offered to let me drive for the summer. Later that day, the city unofficially declared that a small tornado had touched down about half a mile east of us.

Driving the Transvan was quite the experience. Dr. Rueben liked joking about my looking like a hippie driving it. I quickly determined I did not want to drive it any more than I had to though as it only got about seven miles per gallon which got quite expensive. It hadn't been until one night after someone flashed their headlights at me that I learned how it's button for the high beams was built into the floor, resulting in my driving around with my high beams on for a while until Grandma Nancy thought to ask me if I had looked for the button on the floor. Once she asked me, I discovered that that was where the button was so that I discontinued driving around with my high beams on. Another experience I had with the Transvan was my inability to accurately gauge it's back end which resulted in my backing it into ditches a couple times when I tried to do three point turns. While it was old, the Transvan was able to go over 55 miles per hour and a few times I even discovered that I had managed to hit like 70MPH when I drove home after I got quite worked up at work and thankfully I always succeeded in slowing back to the proper speed of 55MPH before a police officer saw me to give me a ticket. Though an officer had come to my aid the one time when I had backed into a ditch at night and was waiting for Uncle Larry to arrive with a tractor to pull it out. Uncle Larry was quite upset about having had to come help me even if I had thought I had seen some cows out and had wanted to let the farmer know. Uncle Larry informed me that the next time I was to just keep driving.

The 2002 summer was also the summer following when Abby had met Nathan. I remember her saying the beginning of 2002 how she felt he was very sensitive so she would not become his girlfriend unless she was sure she would never break up with him. Obviously by that summer she had determined she wanted to commit to a long-term relationship with Nathan as one or two times a month Nathan would come over to Buttercup City and hang out with Abby. By the end of the summer, Nathan decided that he was finished with the trade school and invited Abby down to his mom's place in Daisy City. They lived together with her that entire fall before he proposed and Abby accepted. Abby and Nathan chose Grandpa Robert's birthdate to get married. As I was back in college and broke and my family was broke and had the farm to tend, Nathan and Abby ended up just getting married by a justice of the peace in Daisy City.

Then in 2003, the summer following my sophomore year, I worked at CCC's dairy farm. I was mostly in charge of the heifer calves from newborn to one year old. That summer I lived in the apartment complex that one arrived at by entering a shed south of the dairy barn which on the east end contained a school room area while the west end of the shed was an area one could use as a show ring. On the east end of the show ring were bathrooms and or changing rooms for both men and women which I was always using when I worked out there. On the south side of the school room was a door which led to the apartment complex. It contained a stove and a few cupboards and drawers and a bathroom on its west side. That summer I also took some four-week summer classes of Spanish I and II, and Speech 101 so the fact the bathroom contained a shower was much appreciated as otherwise I would have smelled like a cow which I was okay with but most of my classmates would not have been okay with. The apartment ran on the cool side so I kept the window on the south side of the building cracked which warmed the apartment by about ten degrees which was a more desirable temperature for me. The window overlooked the huge garden of the on-site farm manager. At one point that summer, the farm manager told me that I would be welcome to help myself to any of the produce in his garden. I hadn't taken advantage of his offer as much as I could have as I just felt weird about it and just didn't feel experienced enough to pick appropriately ripe produce from the garden.

So each morning, before school, I would start out by feeding each of the calves. I would go to a shed west of the building where I was living. There I would mix up milk replacer for the number of calves I had in hutches, and a pail of grain for each of them. Then I would take out their old pail of grain while giving them their milk. Once they finished their milk, I would give them their fresh pail of grain. The old pail of grain I would then mix in with the corn and oat combination I was to feed the calves which had outgrown the hutches and the oldest pen of calves I gave the straight corn, oat mix. Next I would feed all of them the amount of hay which would tide them over till I came back that afternoon and would feed them again like I had that morning. After both feedings I was then required to help the person milking cows by starting to scrape down the holding pen and then hosing down the milking parlor area after the cows were all milked. Thankfully, the person hired to milk the cows usually worked so that I was not asked to milk them. Once the parlor was washed down, I would head back to my apartment, shower and bike over to campus for my class. Usually I liked to bike the trails through the woods as I felt very vulnerable biking on the roads. The one morning I biked to class along the road though as it had stormed all night and parts of the trails had flooded along the riverbank.

That entire summer I continued going every week to Church Sweeping the Area with the Gospel church in Catalpa City. Church Sweeping the Area with the Gospel met weekly at the elementary school about seven blocks north of CCC, so every week "the church" would have to get unpacked out of a trailer before service and then repacked back into the trailer after the service. So usually on Sundays I choose to go to church early to help Church Sweeping the Area with the Gospel with set up and at least one weekend a month helped serve coffee and a desert and then after service I would also help pack everything up and carry it over to the trailer to be packed up. (I also continued into the fall every Sunday while I lived there and whenever I hadn't gone home for the weekend which became more frequent after Abby stopped coming home bi-weekly and when Dr. Rueben moved from practicing at Ash-Pine Veterinary Clinic to a clinic closer to where his wife grew up.) That summer, I really got to know some of the congregation better, including making friends with a couple who ended up becoming my college "parents," Brad and Raine R. I actually got to know Raine really well that summer when I saw that Church Sweeping the Area with the Gospel was planning an activity where whomever of the congregation brought vehicles and bikes would meet at the school's parking lot to carpool down to the Cardinal River State Trail. We started at the point where we were 10 miles into the forty-mile trail. As I had an old bike without any speed or brake lines on the handle bars and the most I had biked was the daily trips to and from CCC and the dairy lab farm which was maybe around a mile, I wasn't as fit as many of the others so Raine slowed her pace to stay with me. After we had biked fifteen miles and were biking through a town, she saw an ice cream store and offered to stop and buy us some ice cream. Together we hung out for a while sharing personal stories before we biked back to where we had started. As Raine had two bikes back in Catalpa City, she offered me the three speed she had. I used it a lot until somebody decided to bend the rim of its back tire. A few semesters later when Church Sweeping the Area with the Gospel developed an "Adopt a College Student Program" Brad and Raine R officially adopted me as their college student. That summer I got around to exploring Catalpa City and found several parks including one with trails up a hill which overlooked all of Catalpa City which was one of my favorite places to go. That summer, I would also use my bike a lot even to get groceries which I would hang on the handle bars or stuff into a back pack.

The summer following my junior year, I worked at the Training Camp for CODCL which I share more about in a following chapter. My final full year at Catalpa City, the summer of my senior year, I decided I wanted to try making myself a better looking dairy farm candidate for veterinary school. So, as I saw that there were a variety of dairy internships offered throughout the state I grew up in I talked with Dr. Eric N who was in charge of overseeing the Dairy Club about doing one of the numerous internships that I saw posted. That was how I come to work at a dairy farm in Begonia City.

When I called Archie E, the farm owner, to ask about working there, he asked me a handful or two of questions before telling me that he was interested in hiring me for the summer. That summer I mostly helped feed animals, cleaned stalls and the barn, unloaded hay, and trimmed weeds. One job also had included going around and trying to pull a weed which spread like crazy and just wasn't palatable for the cows to eat. Archie was quite a story teller and I always learned a lot from him while his wife, Andrea liked to keep moving. She could always be seen doing something whether it was laundry, cooking, chores, etc. When I first came out to the farm she told me how she would be willing to provide meals and she'd be willing to include my laundry with her family's as long as I had it down in the laundry room when she started doing the laundry. As I hated doing laundry, I really appreciated her offer and I know that with her cooking, I definitely ate better than I would have if I had fixed my own meals. While Andrea wasn't quite as talkative as her husband, she also was a wealth of information especially if it involved any family member. So by the end of the summer I felt I kind of knew each of their three kids even the one who I never had the opportunity to meet as he was the only one living over an hour away. Ishmael and Raya though lived and worked in nearby towns so they usually came out at least once a week to help out, sometimes bringing Ishmael's two kids also.

By the end of the summer I came to realize that Archie had actually put out the internship position as he had hoped to find someone willing to take over the family farm as his kids weren't planning to. He had built a quite solid dairy herd with some top purebred cows which some people were willing to pay top dollar for some of his cows. For my internship, I had been required to do a research type of paper so I had done it on genetics and with the handful or two of bulls, Archie used I determined which bull I would have breed which cow to hopefully improve upon feet, udder, etc. while trying to keep from inbreeding the herd. Archie and Dr. Eric both approved of my matches. But that summer reemphasized my feelings that I did not want to milk cows and probably would not actually want to work full time on a farm with limited social opportunities. So Archie was unsuccessful at getting me to take over his herd for him. It also did not help that his farm was in an area that was rather sparse population wise with the whole county it was in containing less than the city of Rose City or Cherry Blossom City contained.

FUN WITH TREE SPARROW HALL FRIENDS

Caroline and Rebecca were a hoot together. Both Debbie and I spent a lot of time on the second floor up in their room. In fact, once Debbie was studying in the study lounge next door to their room when she realized it was time for our first floor east wing's meeting with our RA. As she was gathering her things, Caroline had grabbed Debbie's keys which were lying on the table next to Debbie. As Debbie was in a hurry Debbie left her keys with Caroline so that she would not be late for the meeting. Upon returning to our dorm room, Debbie discovered that Caroline had taken things from my side of the room and put them on Debbie's side and vice versa. After taking a picture of the mess, Debbie went to Caroline's room and demanded her keys back. It took some doing but she finally got her keys back. Debbie and I then worked on straightening our room back to the way it was before Caroline came and rearranged it.

A few weeks later both Debbie and I were up studying in Caroline and Rebecca's room when we realized how both Caroline and Rebecca had left their room but had left their keys behind. When I pointed it out to Debbie we decided we were going to return the favor, so we took their keys and were about to lock the door when Rebecca came back to the room. I took off immediately but Debbie didn't and Rebecca caught her. Debbie came to our room begging me to help her so I opened the door and Rebecca came in with Debbie. Immediately she released Debbie and blocked the door. Both Debbie and I tried to pull her away from the door but we were not able to get her far enough away for us to open the door. As that did not work Debbie tried using some of her perfume to gas her but Rebecca just grabbed a towel from a towel bar beside her while Debbie had to go over to the window for fresh air as she had gassed herself out. Then Caroline called us on the phone, telling us how hungry she was, and said she would help us get out of the room if we would just return her keys as they were attached to her ID card that she needed in order to get lunch. Then she wanted to talk to Rebecca as she pretended that she was siding with Rebecca. When Caroline came down, Rebecca realized she had been duped as Debbie and I burst out of the room with Caroline's help. So we all headed to lunch while Rebecca continued to insist on getting her keys back. We made her wait until after lunch though.

A couple years later, Rebecca moved to Hummingbird Hall, Caroline moved off campus into an apartment with her cousin and his girlfriend to cut costs, and Gena was living in Plovers with Rachael. As for me, I was still in Tree Sparrow Hall living with Kendall V, a tall honey blond gal I had met as she had sat alone a few times at Ravens Commons who loved to skate. Kendall and I got along fine; we just did not have a lot in common other than some friends. Meanwhile I continued to hang out with my friends who also used to live in Tree Sparrow Hall. One night in particular I remember how Gena N and Rachael F had come home to find their dorm room door papered shut by Nick R and Evan H who also lived in Plovers. So, a week later when we learned how Nick and Evan had both gone home for the weekend we decided to return the favor. Together Rebecca, Caroline, Gena, and I gathered in Rebecca's room as I came up with a plan to shred some newspaper to put behind the paper in hopes of making a bigger mess. While we were shredding the paper, Gena and Caroline started to read the articles in a funny way, by either putting the end of each word at the end or adding, for example, the letter "g" to the end of each word. We were all having a blast, laughing like crazy, when a freshman in Hummingbird Hall who was always looking for someone to have a good time with came by to ask if he could join us. We said sure and continued what we were doing. I am sure he must have thought we had taken something or been drinking but we had not, and of course we did not do so for the rest of the evening while he was with us either. After we had shredded several newspapers we took more papers and some tape the couple blocks west to Plovers Hall and taped the papers in front of their door and stuffed the shredded papers behind it. Then Caroline called their room and left a message about how we had come to visit them but when we saw they weren't that we had a bit of an accident. When Nick and Eric returned that weekend they claimed how they actually really appreciated the shredded paper being included in the papering of their door as they said it made it more fun.

TRAINING CAMP FOR COLLEGE ORGANIZATION DEVELOPING CHRISTIAN LEADERS CODCL

The first day of my junior year in the fall of 2003 my roommate, Debbie I, came back to college very excited about the job she had that summer working at a summer camp. Rebecca S and Caroline M, our Tree Sparrow Hall friends, whom had also worked at summer camps also shared their excitement and enjoyment over their summer camp experiences as they all swapped stories. This prompted me to ask Ruth B, one of our two CCC CODCL campus staff workers, about her summer camp recommendations for me to work during the summer of 2004.

Ruth ended up recommending the Training Camp for CODCL in Trillium City as she knew that periodically throughout the summer she and others from CCC's CODCL would be there. The thought of going all the way to the northeast side of the state east of where I grew up was very intimidating for me though, as Training Camp for CODCL was the farthest distance from family I would ever have been (eight to nine hours away versus the two and a half hours away which Catalpa City was), especially as Interstate Bus System was my only method of transportation. (I did not get a car of my own until 2006.) As it was the camp Ruth recommended, I decided I would apply there anyway. Shortly afterwards I was interviewed and at the end of the interview I was told that they were willing to hire me for the summer. They also shared how they were accustomed to picking up their employees from the Interstate Bus System station or airports down in Azalea City, I decided that I would work there. I also learned that they were willing to pay the travel expense which a person incurred to come work for them.

The thought of working at Training Camp for CODCL probably would have been harder still, though, for me if Abby had still been living within the state we grew up, but she had gotten married in December 2002 to Nathan Y, the son of an US islander who loved to make jokes and was over 6 feet tall, by a justice of the peace. Nathan and Abby lived in Daisy City with his mom for a while before they were married and continued to for the next two years, rarely ever making it back home. Having my best friend over seven hours from where we grew up, made my working so far from family a bit easier. While my family and I still drive each other crazy sometimes, I recognize that they are the family the Lord gave me and I love and care for them. I still struggled being so far away from them though. Nevertheless, the summer I spent at Training Camp for CODCL ended up being a very good summer for me as I saw hospitality at its best in a wonderful, Christ following environment.

So once I completed my junior year, I spent a couple weeks with my family before they took me to the Interstate Bus System station in Snapdragon City at like 4PM for my fourteen hour trip to work at the Training Camp for CODCL. It was a long drive and I tried to catch some sleep on the way over but as I kept fearing I would oversleep and not get off at the right place I slept in short stretches throughout the night. I think the whole night on the bus I never really had anybody sit in the seat right next to me and definitely didn't have any conversations with any of those I rode with. Upon arriving at Azalea City the closest Interstate Bus System bus station to The Training Camp for CODCL at about 7 the next morning, I met Raymond Y a middle-aged man a few inches taller than me with fine brown hair blue eyes behind glasses and a ready smile. Raymond was going to be my supervisor that summer as I worked on the maintenance crew. As Raymond drove me up to The Training Camp for CODCL which was a few miles north of Trillium

City he shared many stories about the camp and the work which he oversaw. I learned that The Training Camp for CODCL had two sites: Gander Point and Mockingbirds Cove which were based on two spots along Puffins Bay. He shared how I would be living on the southern site, Gander Point. Gander Point was set off the highway leading to the Training Camp for CODCL along a private winding, tree and boulder lined road which was about a mile long. From about a half mile in to the mile in there were about a half dozen wood cabins and the sauna scattered mostly along the northern side of the road set several feet off the shore of Puffins Bay. Then at a mile in was the Gander Point site scattered with multiple other cabins, the lodge, The Training Camp for CODCL's main office, the laundry cabin, a recreation hall and a meeting hall all made of wood. It was at Gander Point that I was assigned to live that summer in a cabin with several other women whom had also been hired to work as crew over the summer. The cabin which I was assigned to live in was called Duck Cabin which only female crew was allowed to be in. If a guy was found there, he risked being kicked off the camp and the same was true for Cormorant Cabin where the male crew members lived which no gal was to enter without risking being kicked off the camp.

When a person entered Duck Cabin you saw that its interior also was made entirely of wood (as were all The Training Camp for CODCL's buildings) and as you entered, you stepped into a hallway which had a door immediately to the right which contained two toilet stalls. Off of this room was a door leading to a couple shower stalls which were usually stained yellow as the water contained lots of sulfur in that area so only the water which was filtered didn't have a sulfuric taste and tended to leave sinks and showers yellow. The shower room was poorly lit and dark as it didn't have any natural lighting and only a single light bulb. Off the room with the toilet stalls was another room which had two sinks on either side of the doorway. At the end of the hallway which a person found themselves in when they entered Duck Cabin there was a closet and three doorways. The farthest two were a couple bedrooms. The one on the right contained a bunk bed, closet and a dresser. The one on the left contained two bunk beds, a couple dressers, a desk and a closet. The third doorway led to a living area which contained a table, a couch, a few chairs, a closet and a bookshelf with several books. Off from the living area was another bedroom with three more bunk beds, three dressers, a desk and a couple closets. That summer I lived in the bedroom on the far-left with Ivanna, a young blond blue-eyed lady from Europe and Louisa a young dark skinned, dark haired and dark eyed gal from the state south of where we grew up. My bed was the top bunk and Ivanna had the lower. Louisa had the other lower and over the summer various other crew would use the top bunk.

My first morning at The Training Camp for CODCL after Raymond dropped me off at Duck Cabin and I had taken my things in to my room, I then headed to Swan Lodge which was where the meals were served for some breakfast. Swan Lodge was a two-story building which stretched at least a hundred feet East to West with fireplaces on both ends. On the West end was more of a meeting area with a piano and several chairs and couches, stairs leading upstairs, a library, a couple restrooms and an office. On the south side of the building was the kitchen with an office, a walk-in freezer and refrigerator and industrial sized ovens, stoves, dishwasher and sinks. The rest of the downstairs portion of the lodge was taken up by a huge dining area with around twenty-five tables which had eight chairs around each one. The entire dining hall was lined with huge windows overlooking Puffins Bay. The upper part of the building contained rooms for lodging with each room containing two bunk beds.

After I had grabbed some fruit and some juice from the dining hall that first morning at The Training Camp for CODCL I then headed to the Goose Yard to meet the rest of the building and grounds crew that I would be working with. That was when I first met Matthew S and Noah N who were additional camp staff as well as Radulf and Adrian, fellow crew member.

It was during this first meeting with the maintenance crew that I learned how every member of the crew would typically get only a day or a day and a half off each week and we were to meet every morning we worked starting at nine at the Goose Yard and then work until five in the afternoon. For most of the crew, Sundays were the day we got off. The crew members who wouldn't get off Sundays were the kitchen crew as everyone still needed to eat on Sundays. Every day that the maintenance crew would meet we were expected to meet at the Goose Yard. All except Saturdays, that is, as on Saturdays all the crew and staff would meet in the Swan Lodge by the West side fireplace to receive our assignment of what part of The Training Camp for CODCL we were to clean. When we cleaned we would make sure all linens and towels left in the cabin or room in a lodge were removed to be taken to the laundry building. Also we would then wipe down surfaces to remove dust, vacuum, clean the bathroom and if it had a kitchen to clean the kitchen and it's appliances.

For most of that summer, I had been the only female on the maintenance crew. Most days we split and stacked wood and cleaned the dining room after the one hundred to three hundred guests finished eating their midday meal as well as mopped the kitchen floor and cleaned the bathrooms. For most of the summer I worked with Radulf a blond haired blue eyed young man from an European country and Adrian an middle-aged darker complexioned brown eyed and brown haired guy from another European country. I remember having to dig a ditch with Radulf and Adrian to lay a drainage pipe for a cabin, the cabin which crew lived over on the Mockingbird Cove side and how impressed Radulf and Adrian were that I was able to work as hard as them. Additional maintenance jobs would include restocking firewood, kindling, paper, and matches at all the cabins that had fireplaces or mow the lawns.

After breakfast each morning the maintenance crew would have a meeting out in an old wood shed which was split into two large rooms, contained a restroom, and many tools. The old wood shed also had a doorway which led to a stairway leading to a couple lofts above it in which a couple staff families lived. It was at this wood shed where we would get our days assignment and learn which day we would have off that week. One morning, the day after Raymond, the camp's lead staff person for the maintenance crew, had directed me on how to fire the sauna I had given him a paper where I had written down the steps he had given me to fire a sauna which he had been very proud of and would talk about that list I made periodically throughout the rest of that summer. As I had never made a fire prior to that day which Raymond had assigned me and told me how it was done, my first attempt at firing a sauna was a disappointment to the campers and the crew because it never got as hot as they wanted it to be. It took me firing the sauna periodically throughout the summer before I ever really started to get the hang of getting the heat to the desired temperature by the time the campers came to the sauna. Once the crew talked me into joining them in the sauna and I was miserable. I felt like my skin was burning hot and I hated being so sweaty and dressed so scantily even though my swim suit was a one piece. Also I feared that I would get a headache.

Since when I was younger working on the farm unloading hay, I became prone to headaches whenever I'd get too hot which happened especially when doing hard work in the sun versus the shade. No matter how cool I tried to dress or how much water I tried to drink, when I learned that my job was to mow lawn I would end up getting too hot. Lawn mowing at The Training Camp for CODCL was mostly done by a push mower and after pushing the mower usually within an hour the blood would start pounding at the base of my neck and temples, and then a headache would set in. While I knew, I had these tendencies to get headaches if I overheated I never shared it with Raymond or anyone that entire summer, choosing instead to suffer through the headaches as I didn't want to come across as trying to get out of doing jobs assigned to me even if some of the jobs I knew were very likely to cause me to get headaches.

Every week every crew member was required to go to a crew Bible study held by a The Training Camp for CODCL staff family. I always enjoyed the Bible study as it allowed me to get to know other crew members whom I otherwise only got to know if they happened to sit at the same table as me. As there was only eight chairs at the table which was reserved for the crew which usually was more like triple that number, I seemed to end up eating about half of the meals at another table with some of the campers. Usually I would look for a table with another displaced crew member or one of the staff. The Bible study group that I was assigned to meet with that summer was being held at the cabin of the head chef, Daniel S and his wife Yvonne would host the study in their family cabin which was tucked in between Duck and Cormorant Cabin.

Daniel and Yvonne were a middle-aged couple with three young sons and a young daughter. Daniel was about my height, whose hairline was starting to recede and black beard was starting to gray. He would always try to make a person feel welcome by asking them questions and always had a ready smile. Yvonne was also around my height, was a reddish brown haired woman who loved to tell stories and laugh. There was one week that summer, on the day the Bible study was being held, I had mowed lawns around several cabins so I was struggling with a headache. Since I had a headache, I had curled up in bed after supper to take a nap till it was time for the Bible study. I hadn't thought I would truly fall asleep or I must have thought that if I did that my roommates would wake me so that I would attend but they hadn't so I had ended up sleeping through the Bible study.

Another time Matthew, another maintenance staff person about my age, slightly taller, with light brown hair and blue eyes which seemed to always sparkle with laughter, whom was dating and later married one of my cabin mates, had decided that because there was a continual need for firewood due to campfires and fireplaces, he had noted several trees which were dead which he determined to be cut down to make firewood. He then would cut down these tree and cut it into lengths that would be easier to carry. He then assigned me to help him transport the cut logs to the waiting vehicle. After doing that for an entire afternoon my head was just pounding, so much so that I skipped eating because just the thought of food made me feel nauseous. However, since all the staff and crew were planning later that evening to gather to work on a skit we planned to do after the meal, I chose to lie down in the room where the skit work was going to be worked on to wait for them. It was not long into the meeting before Daniel, who was also a nurse, commented about how I looked flushed and asked me if I was okay. When he realized how awful I felt, I was given permission to go lie down and he got me something for my headache.

Every week at The Training Camp for CODCL there were new

groups of students coming and going and new expositors preaching on certain passages every night on the Gander Point side while on the Mockingbird's Cove side family camps usually met. Though occasionally both sides may have hosted groups of students or family camps. Many times, I and other crew would go to the expositions which was held in the meeting hall but after hearing the same passage preached upon several times, we eventually started to find other crew to hang out with and do things with. Then Saturday morning when that week's students had left, all the crew and staff would split up what section of the camp we all would clean. We would vacuum all the carpets, remove all old linens, towels and such and replace them with fresh ones and scour the bathrooms to get the rooms and cabins throughout both sides of the camp ready for the next group of students or family campers which would begin arriving that afternoon. Usually we worked from nine until noon to get the whole camp cleaned while the kitchen crew would meanwhile be reheating all leftovers which had not gone out to the dining area for our meals the past week. In addition to having a huge selection of food to choose from we also got to have ice cream. This was my favorite meal each week since I never minded leftovers. (It was not until when I was working October 2006 when they stopped cooking fresh meals each week and we had to eat leftovers daily for a couple weeks that I grew tired of leftovers.)

Also each week, in addition to our weekly Bible studies with a camp staff family, the crew would have a Sunday worship time where Kurt and Emma B who were in charge of the crew would lead a time of singing worship songs. Kurt would play his guitar and Emma the piano. They were a middle-aged couple with two teenage children of which the oldest occasionally helped the recreation staff and crew. Kurt and Emma both were tall, skinny, with dark blond hair, and blue eyes. After leading worship Kurt or Emma would share a devotional time before the crew was dismissed to interact before camp lights-out time, which was 10:00 p.m. every night. At lights-out time, the staff would occasionally go around to the various buildings and encourage campers and crew to head to bed so they would be refreshed for a day of studies or work the next day.

On my days off, I would usually look for others who had the day off and hang out with them. That is usually when I would discover more of the camp as I wasn't very adventuresome to go out and check out various sites on my own. It was my opportunity to explore Trillium City, too. My entire time at The Training Camp for CODCL, I didn't get very close to any of the other campers as I still wasn't very comfortable with developing close relationships. I mostly just tended to overhear when some of the other crew was planning on doing something and would get the okay to join them. That is how I ended up getting to go with a few crew members to Cherry Blossom City, checking out the Trillium City Library and the local thrift store which a person could name a price for an item they were interested in. Also the crew would try to occasionally do something as a whole group. Some of these activities included going out on three motor boats and checking out some islands, having an Euchre tournament until there was only one unbeaten team, and going out for movies. The one time we went out for a movie I remember how Archie Y, one of the most popular guys of all the girls, had been making the announcements which were made at dinner and supper meals how a group was going to the movies Sunday night which was open to all crew. He mentioned several of the movies which were playing but I remember him specifically mentioning Talladega Nights which casted the comedian Will Farrell. That night I joined them, as someone offered to pay for me to go, and since I thought Archie had been planning to go to Talladega Nights I bought a ticket to go see it. He ended up not going to it but I remember being with a handful of crew, who before a half hour was up were nervously laughing about how they felt that by watching the movie we were not being true to being the Christians we claimed we were. After several more minutes of this laughter and talk, I decided I was going to honor my Christian faith and walked out. So, for the rest of the evening until everybody finished watching their movies I hung out in the theater's main lobby.

As I said earlier, Archie was a favorite of the girls and I have a few other memories of a bunch of girls hanging out with him. One included how some of the girls had belching contests, another of when one of the few black girls at camp asked if she could cornrow his hair which she then braided very tightly, and another as some girls and he were swapping jokes. The one joke that I remember went like this: Two nuns walked into a bar and one ducked. It took me a while but I eventually got that one.

One of my best interactive experiences that summer with the crew was when because I knew that The Training Camp for CODCL paid travel fees I thought I would surprise Abby by coming to visit her for her birthday. In actuality, though I ended up footing the whole thing, it was something I was glad to do. To see if it was possible to surprise Abby, I had called her husband, Nathan, to make sure it would work. After I received confirmation that it would work for him, I worked with Leah K, who worked in The Training Camp for CODCL' office, to order an Interstate Bus System round trip ticket. Then Ed K, a crew member of Pilipino ancestry, who loved to drive, drove me with a few other staff members including my roommate, Ivanna, maintenance coworkers Radulf and Adrian, and a couple other crew women, Natezia and Rhea. These people made my journey to the bus station memorable and was made more memorable by Rhea who framed a picture of all of us and then wrote a letter on its back.

So, while that day made me feel quite special, a few weeks later when it was the Fourth of July I had tried to let my fellow crew members know that if any of them went to watch fireworks, I also wanted to go. Nobody apparently caught it though as I ended up getting left behind. When I realized that the fireworks were starting to be set off, I thought I'd try to walk to Trillium City to watch the fireworks which was something The Training Camp for CODCL actually discouraged due to the potential for danger. I hadn't even gotten halfway to Trillium City before Yvonne S stopped to ask if she could help me and then as she recognized me Yvonne gave me a ride back to The Training Camp for CODCL. I seriously wondered afterwards if I would be sent home since I had broken the camp rules but I am glad they hadn't made me leave.

It was at The Training Camp for CODCL that I had first realized that I was emotionally scarred from my childhood, first by reading some descriptions of diagnosing emotional abuse on paper work which all crew were required to read and sign off and then when Ed, on crew gave me the book Hiding From Love by John Townsend to read. Ed was the crew member I grew closest to and had developed a bit of a crush on. I had learned from one of the first Bible studies I had attended at Daniel and Yvonne's how he too had been emotionally scarred and he had said that the book had helped him. So, while I never got close to any of the fellow crew, I felt like working at The Training Camp for CODCL was a very good experience which was emphasized in a copy of a letter that I found that I wrote in September 2004 to a friend after working at The Training Camp for CODCL. I am including it as it shares just how I felt about my experience at The Training Camp for CODCL. It reads:

> Sorry I am so late getting back to you. I had a great summer helping The Training Camp for CODCL as part of their maintenance crew. I met a guy who has a background which was a bit like mine, and who has helped me to see how my background caused me to develop protective mechanisms which make it hard for me to respond as well as I should with people. I have talked to Ruth, our new staff worker at Catalpa City, about finding a counselor that hopefully will help me get over the protective mechanisms that I have which are harmful to relationships, including with my family. That is what I am really struggling with now. Often throughout the summer I felt resentment about how I felt like people at The Training Camp for CODCL were so much better at encouraging and with appreciation as well as a desire to keep things nice at all times. These thoughts then made me feel guilty for not loving them (my family) as I should. Then when I went home for a few days I felt so overwhelmed with things I wanted to do but felt wouldn't really last and with all the things that could be done. So I pretty much felt miserable while I was home and have been feeling guilty for not enjoying my short time home with my family more. So all of these feelings are why I am thinking about getting a counselor. The things that I am nervous about is that I don't have money coming in

right now to pay for counseling and that I would be going in for a wrong reason or something. Also, I am wondering if I should tell my family. I'm not sure they would think that I should get counseling but think that they and God are all that I should need to take my problems to. But I don't want them to think that I don't think that they care for me or whatever if I do tell them at some point. So right now this is what is heavy on my mind and what with classes starting, is causing me to feel a bit stressed out.

ABBY'S FIRST CANCER SCARE & MY FIRST MOVE TO ROSE CITY

In November 2005, during my final semester at CCC, Abby was diagnosed with melanoma skin cancer. Apparently she had had a little lump on her scalp for several years but thought it was from bumping her head after falling on some ice. By the time the doctors found it was cancer, the lump was about as big as my fist, so she had to have about a fourth of her scalp removed. The doctors took a portion of skin from her thigh as a skin replacement as they made sure to remove all edges of cancer from around the lump. So I went and visited her where she was staying with her mother-in-law, Raziela, in Daisy City for a few days over fall break as she recovered from the surgery before I returned back to college.

When I arrived at Raziela apartment, Abby had just had the surgery and was in a great amount of pain. With both her scalp and thigh recovering from having skin the size of a slice of white bread having been removed. The scalp looked like a cross between a fine mesh grate and waffle iron with grid lines throughout it. For years that grid appearance continued to be displayed on the hairless graft on her scalp which she did her best to keep covered when working or in public. Her leg also always contained a bit of a red scarring around it where the skin graft was removed.

While I stayed with Abby at Raziela's I barely strayed from her side except a couple times when I helped walk her and Nathan's white chihuahua which had just a few spots of golden brown and once to join Raziela at the Spanish preaching church she went to. Raziela barely spoke any English but mostly only spoke Spanish as she had only come to America from an US island to live sometime around when Nathan had been born. Her hair was dyed a pale, golden brown color and she herself was battling cancer prompting her to have her arm almost always in a compression sleeve and in a sling. After Abby's surgery, Raziela insisted that Abby join her in sleeping in the big king sized bed of hers. Raziela lived in an upstairs apartment of what looked like a house divided into four apartments. When one entered they entered the living room which the back half had been curtained off to make Raziela's bedroom, off to the left past the beaded curtain was the kitchen with a table rarely eaten at while I was there and behind it was a small bathroom and then a bedroom which Raziela let her older gay son have with his boyfriend. Coming from my background, I felt uncomfortable around each of Raziela's family, especially the gay son. Additionally to my spending the week with them during my break, Nathan's two older sisters visited several times as did many of their sons. I remember how one of the older sons was doing his math homework and was struggling with understanding what he was learning. When he got to solving the math problems, I remembered how he copied the math problems and then just copied the answer from the back of the book rather than working the answer out himself. I was aghast at his indifference to trying to get the answer for himself and that the teacher would accept that for an answer instead of requiring the students show their work. Meanwhile as I stayed with Abby when she felt up to it and wasn't in extreme pain Abby worked on making a quilt for Raziela using a square loom which usually came with nylon loops which a person could weave to create a potholder. And in my spare time I remember working hard on studying for Biochemistry as it was the one class I felt I was coming close to failing as I never got close to a B on any of my exams. As the instructor graded on a curve, I ended up getting lucky with a C. About a month later I finished my final semester of college graduating from Catalpa City with a degree in Diary Science Pre-Vet with a 3.4 GPA.

During my final two months of college due to Abby's cancer surgery and her being unable to work, Abby needed help paying her apartment rent, where she was living a half hour from where we grew up in Rose City. Abby and Nathan had only moved to Rose City between six months to a year earlier in 2005. So I helped Abby and Nathan that November and December by paying their rent out of my savings. After graduating in mid-December from CCC, I had my things taken to Rose City as Abby gave me permission to move into the apartment with them since I was helping with paying the rent, I had yet to find a job and did not want to live on the farm. I had considered it, though, as I offered to help with the farm if they would let the cows out to graze but they refused. Also, I had offered to do Dora's chores so she could go to college at Rose City for genealogy, as she loved reading papers and plat books of the surrounding towns where both Ma and her family grew up and where Ma raised us. From reading these things Dora would collect genealogical materials and then carry on conversations as if she knew the people and where they lived as well as Ma, Uncle Larry, and Grandma Nancy did, even though the majority of people she would have met before and not have spent time with after age ten. Dora turned my college offer down, though, as she insisted she was not smart enough for college. I then told her most colleges offer free tutoring to make sure their students can pass their classes at which point Dora insisted that the family needed her help on the farm.

So that December once I moved in with Abby and Nathan, I began looking and applying for jobs in Rose City. I also asked CCC CODCL alum and friend Curt X about which church he recommended as he had lived in Rose City since he had graduated a semester or two earlier. He recommended Rose City Alliance Church and when asked he gave me a ride there several times. I hoped to invite Abby and Nathan to join me at whatever church Curt recommended. Once Abby and Nathan returned to Rose City after Abby's cancer surgery I extended the invitation but Nathan referred to how a past church had failed to follow through on a youth activity when he was a kid due in his opinion because he and the other kids who signed up weren't caucasian as a reason why he would not go with me. Abby's reason was that she did not want to go to church if Nathan wouldn't. She did not want to have people ask her where her husband was or to put pressure on him.

Meanwhile, as I applied for jobs I kept my eye open for the job my friend Robin M, whom I had lived with before going to CCC, had told me was going to become available at the veterinary laboratory at Rose City Clinic in Rose City where she worked. When it was posted, I quickly applied and after getting interviewed I ended up getting the job at the veterinary laboratory as a seasonal veterinary lab assistant from February until June between the hours of 3-7or 9 AM. As I didn't have a car I was grateful that Abby lived only about 6 blocks from the laboratory as for the first several days to weeks I walked to work. Once Abby returned to Rose City after healing from her surgery she offered to let me use her car which a friend from Training Center for Troubled Young Adults had given her. Meanwhile Abby was also working at Subway which was just a few blocks from their apartment which once I brought the car back, she would then drive to work or I would drop the car off there if she had to work before I got back from work, give her the key and then I would walk home from Subway.

Then Nathan applied for a job at Rose City Trucking Co.'s CDL training class and when he got accepted he insisted that I start walking again to work as I would not be home by the time he needed to go to Rose City Trucking Co. and he did not want to walk to the laboratory to get the car to drive to work even though the sun would have been up by that time. Instead Abby suggested that I ask if a coworker would be willing to pick me up and take me to work. So, I had and Autumn Y offered to do so but she was scheduled to start earlier than I was. I still needed to wait to start working though at my scheduled time and so while I waited I worked on making squares using yarn and a loom to make a quilt which is what I would do with most of time every day at my sister's apartment when it was just me or Nathan and me home. When Abby was home I would leave the guest bedroom and join her in cooking or whatever she chose to do after work. Occasionally I would pop out of the guest bedroom and check on what Nathan was watching but usually it wasn't PG enough in its language, violence and terror so I would go back to the bedroom and work on squares to make a quilt. If it was just me though I would occasionally turn on the TV and watch whatever was on the Hallmark Channel. It was in the weeks leading up to Abby and Nathan's return to Rose City after her surgery that I got hooked on MASH and Hallmark movies so I liked watching them but Nathan hated MASH which I found out once when he came home unexpectedly with a friend and finding the TV on, he quite vehemently swore about how much he hated MASH for several minutes. He used the swear word which I always associated with sexual abuse about a dozen times or so in his tirade against MASH. This incident prompted me to confront Nathan about watching his language which he said he has tried to and wasn't successful at before. This prompted me to look for somewhere else to live as I was growing tired of Nathans' vulgar language and love of bloody, terror movies, adult swim channel and violent video games.

Meanwhile as I lived with Nathan and Abby, paying half their rent I working at the Rose City Clinic's veterinary laboratory. My job required me to clock in via the phone system. Once I was clocked in I would then start pipetting serum from off the tubes of blood which had been centrifuged and were in racks which number of rows and columns of tubes were equivalent to how many rows and columns of ELISA wells there were in the heartworm test tray with a spot for both a positive and a negative serum also. Then I would put a drop of an enzyme in each well. After several minutes I would then gently wash out the tray and then add another enzyme into each of the wells and after so many minutes as long as the positive well turned blue while the negative well remained clear any other well that turned blue would be indicative that the animal had heartworm. I was then to take my wells to my supervisor to observe and she would circle the ones she saw that were blue and she would have me pull the corresponding tube and at the end of the shift some of my co-workers would call the veterinary clinic which had sent that tube to let them know that that dog or cat had tested positive for heartworm. Once I was finished testing a rack I would recap and scan the tubes into the computer so that when the tube was stored if the veterinarian decided they wanted another test run on the animal's blood the tube could be found easily, pulled and the test run. After all the racks I was assigned to run the heartworm tests were tested, scanned, entered into the computer and stored, they would send me over to the chemistry side of the lab and ask me to cap and scan the tubes which were finished with having tests run on the blood in them so that they could be stored and easily found if the veterinarian decided further testing needed to be done.

While I worked at the laboratory I waited to hear again from the vet schools I had applied to. During the application process, they required three references, and I could choose whether I wanted to see or not see the reference's letters of recommendation. Later I was told an applicant is always supposed to choose to not see a letter of recommendation because it indicates that you trust your reference. Anyway, Dr. Reuben was the only one I knew very well whom I asked to write a letter of reference for me. I was not smart enough to ask my college advisor or Dr. Reuben about who else I should ask. So that final year I learned I had made a bad choice for a reference after reading Eric N, CCC's dairy science club advisor, letter of recommendation. I had chosen him based more on his position at CCC being THE dairy science instructor than how well we knew each other. As I had always chosen to see my references letter of recommendations I saw how he ended up not recommending me as he wrote something along the lines of how I was "too quiet to be a veterinarian but would be better suited working in research." I had considered becoming a part of the Dairy Science and Pre-Vet Club at CCC but with my studies I did not feel I had a lot of spare time for clubs and so CODCL was the only one I regularly participated in as my faith was the most important thing to me and those people I trusted most to have similar viewpoints on morals.

Anyway, this was the third year I had applied to College at Magnolia City, and this year I had also applied to veterinary schools at the veterinary colleges in the states surrounding the state I grew up in. I would have applied to the state I was born in also, but Ma adamantly discouraged my applying there, so as I did not think it worth angering Ma, I didn't apply to their veterinary school. In trying to get accepted into a veterinary school, I spent about a thousand dollars. The thousand dollars' expense came from my taking the GRE three times, submitting

---

the Universal Veterinary application form three times, submitting an application to College at Magnolia City's veterinary program three times, and submitting an application to both the colleges in the states surrounding the state I grew up in. For me that was a lot of money that I did not feel I could afford to keep spending by continuing to reapply if I got turned down again. Also, I was tired after four and a half years of intense schooling where I was torn between studying to try to keep my GPA up and trying to grow socially and spiritually. Also I was tired of taking the GRE, especially the essays by that point, and I did not want to continue to feel in limbo from year to year as I wondered if I would get accepted this time after reapplying. The feeling of being in limbo made me choose not to reapply for a desk assistant position my final year and a half at college and from letting myself be an option for CODCL's leadership which they choose new every year. The feeling of being in limbo was due as generally, the application process started in August as I retook the GRE hoping for better scores, with a due date for the Universal application by October and the individual school applications by December, and then the applicant had to wait until anytime between March and May to find out if they were one of the ten percent who applied that got accepted. So as I wanted to settle somewhere more permanently to feel like I was a part of a community instead of only a part until something else came my way, I asked a group of friends to join with me as I prayed God would either get me in to veterinary school if it was his will or that he would show me where he wanted me to be and what he wanted me to do.

Meanwhile as I worked at the veterinary lab, I also looked into getting involved in the CODCL chapter on the Rose City's Birch County campus and Bible studies at Rose City Alliance Church. Thankfully, I found people at both places who were willing to give me a ride to the events. The leader of the church Bible study that I attended, Nicoletta K, was the one who provided rides for me to and from the Bible study which was held Wednesday mornings at 10 AM and to a few other activities the women in the group hosted or went to. Then as one of the CODCL advisors on the Birch County campus also went to Rose City Alliance Church, she connected me with a student who took time to swing by and pick me up on the days they had their CODCL meetings as he was in the area picking up the pizza they would serve during their meetings.

As the job at the veterinary laboratory was only part-time, I continued to look for an additional job. I was never sure what job I exactly wanted to do but knew I wanted one with a purpose and had to be within walking distance which made my heart not be in it when I had gotten interviews a couple time with fast food places. While I looked for a job with a purpose, I put in applications at every business that I thought didn't require special training which I didn't have that were within walking distance of the apartment where I still lived with Abby and Nathan. I really hoped to find a job so that I could get an apartment of my own near Abby, where I would not have to live with Nathan.

Nathan and I were about as different as could be. I was a country girl. He was a city boy. I disliked swearing and horror movies. He swore and watched movies that contained swearing and horror a lot. I preferred doing crafts in my spare time. He preferred playing video games. I was quiet and insecure and he was loud and seemingly quite secure. Despite our differences and the above-mentioned things which drove me crazy, Nathan did also have qualities which did not drive me crazy. He encouraged getting outdoors and giving people hugs, and he was more like Ma in that he never struggled with making conversation even with people he did not know. Plus once when he, Abby and I were at a video store looking at videos to rent, I had seen the movie Jerry Maguire which I thought I remembered having enjoyed once but Nathan told me he was sure I didn't actually want to watch it. When we watched it I realized that Nathan was right and that I must have only liked the one scene and how that one scene made me remember having liked the movie.

By June, however, I ended up deciding enough was enough, especially with the swearing and horror movies. So, when Yvonne V, a friend from Rose City Alliance Church whom I met through the ladies Bible study, offered to let me stay with her and her husband, Ray, I accepted her offer. Also, about the same time I shared my desire to be able to reach out to my mom and sisters whom I felt were trapped yet on the farm, but that I couldn't really reach out to them as I did not have a vehicle to travel the half hour home to the farm. The lack of a vehicle also limited me in where I could look for a job. I had shared this desire as a prayer in the Rose City Alliance Church's bulletin as they had a place where the congregation could share prayer requests. This prompted Scott and Unity R who were church members there to offer to sell me quite cheaply a 1982 Chrysler Fifth Avenue vehicle they rarely used. I gladly accepted their offer.

During the six months, I attended Rose City Alliance Church, I had met Annie I, Yvonne V, Nicoletta K, and several other women during the Bible Studies which Nicoletta led on Wednesday mornings. I remember Annie inviting the church to hear Dr. John Patrick speak at the Rose City Clinic. So I had joined Annie and her family to hear him... I remember how Dr. John Patrick had emphasized the importance of getting to know family members. One example of how he encouraged his audience to do this was by sharing how he and his family would keep books where they would write favorite quotes and Bible verses down, and then they would share these quotes during meals and also why they did or did not like a book or movie they just read or watched. That lecture was what inspired me to start my own little book where I keep favorite quotes and Bible verses. In my quote book I have recorded a few other quotes he shared. One was: *"Believing in God is tacit knowledge. Just like you know those you love with just a brief glimpse of them even in a crowd. This is tacit knowledge – knowledge which is hard to explain with words.* The other was: *"When faced with the intolerance issue, one should ask who thinks a child should be abused. Then (when hopefully they all think a child shouldn't be abused) point out how some intolerance is a good thing."* Finally, I also recorded this in my quote book from his speech: *"When debating creationism versus evolution, draw the discussion back to the beginning."* In the years since I heard Dr. John Patrick speak, I have collected many more quotes from favorite movies, books, Our Daily Bread booklets, and many other sources.

BACK TO THE TRAINING CAMP FOR CODCL

I ended up not getting into any of the veterinary schools, and the veterinary lab job, being seasonal, ended in June 2006. While I worked at the veterinary lab job, Robin M asked me if I had ever considered becoming a laboratory technician if I did not get into a veterinary school. I told her I had never considered that type of work but once I learned I didn't get into any of the veterinary schools, I decided to look into it online. What I discovered from my online search was that I could take classes to get the degree at Jasmine City, Snapdragon City, Easter Lily City, and a college in the state on our west border. I do not think I really had considered Jasmine City, as none of my family ever did anything near there. Snapdragon City I considered, though, as Ma would work out at a gym there usually at least once a week, but I was also torn between there and the Easter Lily City and the college on our west border because they were close to CCC thus my friends whom had yet to graduate or continued to live in that area. At that point I still didn't have a car or much money so whatever choice I would have made would have required someone else taking me there. As I really struggled with making decisions, I never was able to decide which if any of those schools I wanted to go to. At that point in my life I still rarely thought about seeking others for advice so I never sought Robin's advice in the decision which probably would have saved me money in the long run or asked any of my friends to join with me this time in praying over if my taking lab tech classes was what God wanted and if so where he would want me to go. Earlier though I do remember having asked many of my friends to pray that if God wanted me to get into veterinary medicine that he would otherwise if I didn't I wanted my friends to join me in praying that God would lead me to where he wanted me to work. Overall I just had a burning desire to help others and being a veterinarian was an area which I had seen there was a need and was something I enjoyed doing when I volunteered and when I had successfully brought an animal back to health. So I had asked for help praying for God's guidance in this matter as I was growing tired of school and as I had asked the instructor who in my eyes I considered to be THE dairy instructor since he was in charge of the Dairy Club to write me a letter of recommendation as I thought a letter of recommendation from him would prove to the veterinary colleges how much I wanted to be a dairy veterinarian, the veterinary area with the biggest need as most veterinarians preferred small animals as that was the field where most of the money was. As I had wanted to see what all my references wrote for recommendations that is the box I had marked on my application which is how I discovered this professor had instead of recommending me had shared how he thought I would be better suited for working in research as he felt I was too shy to make it as a veterinarian.

Meanwhile, after about six months in Rose City and not even being able to get a job at a fast food restaurant, even though I got interviews and had put in applications at quite a few places, I debated about going to work back at The Training Camp for CODCL or a camp in several states further south, founded by an author which my friend, Nora V, whom I met through my CCC CODCL friend Curt X, who was friends with her son and daughters, really approved of and which the library at Rose City Alliance Church possessed several of the author's books. This camp was designed to assist children who had suffered from abuse similar to what my family had always shared my sisters had. The camp I had stumbled upon as I did job searches on a Christian job search engine. The Christian job search engine I had heard of while listening to my favorite Christian radio station, 88.5FM. The job at the camp required that I would have to find my own way for traveling to it to get interviewed for the job though. Since I did not have extra spending money to travel there just to get an interview and I knew how The Training Camp for CODCL would reimburse my travel fees, The Training Camp for CODCL seemed more appealing. Additionally, when I talked with a friend from Buttercup City Bible Church she mentioned how she loved the state several states further south as it was warm and humid there. As I really struggle with humidity since it increases my tendency to get headaches that comment was another strike in my mind against that camp job though I really wanted to help the kids who had suffered from abuse. Then as I got encouragement from Curt X, that if I wanted to go back to The Training Camp for CODCL he had some friends who were willing to provide me financial support so I could continue to pay off school loans while at The Training Camp for CODCL if that was where I chose to go.

When I first called The Training Camp for CODCL that summer of 2006 to find out if I could return to work for them, Leah K, who does most of the upfront office work, asked if I wanted to work as part of the summer crew or as an intern. The thought of possibly doing an internship made me think my going back to The Training Camp for CODCL would allow Trillium City, to become the place I could be at for a long time and one where I could become part of a community and develop friendships which I saw so many others had but I did not feel I ever really had due to my only living places so shortly and due to my unassertive, quiet personality. So I expressed my interest in an internship position but they were not available yet. I decided anyway to leave the state I grew up in and go work at The Training Camp for CODCL as part of their summer crew while I waited for them to create the internship positions. This time when I went to The Training Camp for CODCL, thanks to Scott and Unity R, I now had a car. This car was a silver 1984 Chrysler Fifth Avenue, which has had my favorite seats of all the vehicles I have owned as they were plush, thus very soft and luxurious feeling as well as blue, my favorite color though the back window wasn't one I really enjoyed seeing as it was so small.

My having a car made my being eight to nine hours away from

family easier since I no longer felt like I would be dependent entirely on Interstate Bus System and others' schedules to visit family. As I was raised very frugally though spending that type of money on gas wasn't something I would be likely to do any more than I had to. Another thing that The Training Camp for CODCL had going for it was that the staff at The Training Camp for CODCL I now considered to be my friends.

While at The Training Camp for CODCL that summer I often used my car to help fellow crew members taxi from one side of camp to the other as there was a bay between the two sites, Gander Point and Mockingbirds Cove. This summer I was assigned to live in a cabin on the Mockingbirds Cove site which is on the north side of the bay. The cabin I was assigned to stay in was one of the oldest cabins which the campus reserved for the crew. As to which department I was willing to work in, I told the staff I would be willing to do whatever they needed me to do. That resulted in my doing a wide range of things which focused more directly on assisting campers.

A typical day that summer would include my waking up about an hour before breakfast was served so I could get ready for the day by reading the daily devotional in my Our Daily Bread booklet, a Bible passage which corresponded with the devotional and the chapters Our Daily Bread listed that would allow me to read my Bible in a year which I had done ever since Tina P, the wife of Pastor Ulysses of Buttercup City Evangelical Free Church had recommended it back in 2001. Once I completed my readings for the day, I would head over to the kitchen and get some breakfast. Then I would head to the office at Gander Point and touch base with Emma B, the crew leader and office personnel, or Raymond Y, the maintenance supervisor, to see what they wanted me to do. One of them would give me an assignment or they would direct me to Daniel S, the kitchen supervisor, Leah K, an office staff worker, Robin YQ, the housekeeping supervisor, or another camp staff who might want extra help that day. About noon I would take about a half hour lunch joining other crew, staff and campers, and then return to whatever assignment I had been given or would get reassigned to a new assignment. Around five I could then call it a day and relax about a half hour before I would join the crew, staff and campers again for supper. After supper I would typically join the crew in an upper room of Mockingbird's Cove recreation hall, Osprey Nest, for games, music or whatever they choose to do.

While helping wherever I was needed that summer, I got to help an artistic guy set up his art supplies in the Wren room as he wanted it so that his fellow family campers could create a variety of different craft projects. The rest of the day I was encouraged to remain available in case he needed more help. I absolutely loved that job as I myself am a lover of artistic things. Other days, while helping Robin YQ, I was asked to help restock linens for guest's rooms, and do laundry especially when the camp prepared to close for the season as they washed everything so that they would be clean and ready for the next season of campers. Also at one point that summer I was asked to help knock down spider webs which were clinging to some of the buildings. Then as more crew continued to leave as the college year resumed for them, I increasingly was asked to help in the kitchen so that they would not be shorthanded cooking for the 50-250 people they still got the final weeks they hosted groups. Additionally towards the beginning of the time I was there that summer Kurt and Emma B who oversaw the music asked if I would help them get all the music they had on projector transparencies put into power point format as everything was going more towards power point instead of projectors. So I had and it was a project that I really enjoyed doing. Also that summer I had helped with many additional things like mopping, vacuuming and waxing floors, etc. but the ones I listed are a few things that really stick out in my memory as special or rare projects I was asked to assist doing.

After working at The Training Camp for CODCL that whole summer into early fall I was informed how the internship positions were still in the works and the staff were not sure when the positions would become available. The internship positions ended up not becoming available until the fall of 2007. Since I was only working as part of their summer crew in the summer of 2006 and The Training Camp for CODCL only had work during the summer to early fall months for crew, they released all their summer crew in the fall of

2006. Consequently, as fall drew near I knew I had to start looking for someplace new to work to pay my bills like my school loans, for my cell phone and to pay for a new place to live. Seeing that Trillium City is a very small town with very few businesses which stay open year-round, I had to look farther away. So I choose to look at Cherry Blossom City as it had quite a few more options of employment than Trillium City. Also, Cherry Blossom City was the closest big town to Trillium City which I was familiar with as the crew hung out there periodically on their days off during the two summers I worked at The Training Camp for CODCL. Cherry Blossom City also was where a former staff worker at The Training Camp for CODCL, Ramsey, worked as an CODCL staff worker at Mallard University. He still remained quite popular among all the crew and staff whenever he would come to help out for whatever period of time he had available to do so. While I looked for a job, Leah K and Emma B, friends I made working at The Training Camp for CODCL, made sure I always had a place to stay while I tried to determine what God had next for my life. In return I would help them with meals, taking care of their cats and I would help entertain Leah's young daughter, Rayna when Leah had a project she needed to get accomplished. One of Rayna's favorite form of entertainment came by getting to use a flashlight and when I'd get the flashlight I would make her some shadow puppets.

MOVING TO CHERRY BLOSSOM CITY

As I looked into options of moving to Cherry Blossom City, I asked Emma B if she knew of any church in Cherry Blossom City that she would recommend for me. Emma B recommended the Apostolic Church, which I went to for a few weeks to months. The church's style was a lot different than what I was used to with flag waving, dancing in the aisles, speaking in tongues, congregation participation and such which I never felt comfortable with seeing as I had always attended more reserved churches. As I began looking for a place in Cherry Blossom City to live, I had asked the pastor if he knew of any place for me to rent, because most of the places I saw advertised online were listed at $550 or more per month which was more than I could afford. The pastor referred me to his brother-in-law who had a place which he rented for $400.

In the middle of January 2007, I started renting from him the upstairs apartment which was located in an older house on Martin Street. The apartment was several blocks south of Egrets Avenue and about a mile east of Mallard University with a huge hill between the apartment and Mallard University. While it was listed as a two bedroom, the only way to access the second bedroom was through the first bedroom which could have equally passed for an office as the one wall was lined with cabinets. When a person entered the apartment upon climbing the stairs, one opened the door and immediately saw the bathroom which was at the head of the stairs. To the right was where the bedrooms were located and to the left was the kitchen and dining room and through a doorway you could see the living room. Each room had a window which I really enjoyed especially the dining rooms window which had a skyline view of the northern side of the city and the southern side of Apple Blossom City which included their industrial smoke stacks.

The first few nights in my new apartment I had relatively few essentials which were the things I had brought with me to The Training Camp for CODCL including my laptop. These few essentials were all that I owned as up to my moving to Cherry Blossom City I always lived in furnished places whether it was at college, family or a friend's place. When Leah K heard I found an apartment she offered to help me buy some additional essentials as she loved to shop. As I felt awkward about having people spend money on me in part probably due to inheriting Grandma Nancy's tendency for thriftiness. Since I knew I really needed somethings but couldn't afford them, I had agreed to let Leah K but I set a price limit on how much she could spend. The two stores we ended up shopping at were $1/item store and the inexpensive department store as I tried to be as cheap as possible. Some of the essentials she ended up buying me included: silverware, a dish set, glasses, a soap dispenser, dish soap, storage containers, dish rack, dish towels, shower curtain, dust pan and broom.

The apartment came with a kitchen table and a dresser. As I did not have a bed I spread several blanket that I did have on the floor of the office like bedroom and slept on the blankets further wrapped in a sleeping bag which Abby had given me for Christmas the year we first got jobs off the farm. About a week later, Matt Y had seen that people in his church had several items which they were giving away so he gathered the items he felt I could use and brought them over to my apartment. Some of the items he brought included a recliner, a plush chair, a folding chair, an end table on wheels, some pots and pans, a mattress and box spring which made it possible for me to have a bit of distance between me and the floor when sleeping making it easier to sleep during the night without feeling the cold as much which was the only time my apartment was ever cold. The people downstairs had access to the thermostat for the whole house which during the day they must have always had the heat cranked as my apartment was always quite toasty but at night my apartment started to feel a bit chilly.

Then as my birthday came a couple days before college started, which I share more about in a later chapter, I asked Emma B if it would be okay if I brought my laundry to her place on my birthday as I did not want to be alone on my birthday. She said it would be okay but that it would have to be about 7PM that I could come. So I went to her place at 7PM on my birthday and found her driveway filled with other cars. Upon entering Emma B's house, I saw that a lot of my friends from Trillium City had come to wish me happy birthday. They had fixed my favorite meal of lasagna, plus had fried chicken, vegetables and cake which they sent the leftovers home with me. Additionally, they each had a gift for me. Some of the gifts included a couple Penzey's spices, a bowl for popcorn plus a box of popcorn, one of my favorite snacks, an office starter kit: pens and pencils, paper clips, stapler, staples, staple remover, etc., and homemade slipper socks. That was the first party anyone had thrown for me and it made the day very special! The surprise birthday party also made the transition from Trillium City to Cherry Blossom City and starting college a lot easier.

COLLEGE AT CHERRY BLOSSOM CITY

As fall approached and no internship positions opened at The Training Camp for CODCL, I knew my time in Trillium City was drawing to an end as the town of Trillium City was so small, consisting of a population of around 276, that there wouldn't be job openings especially in the winter, non-tourist months. So, I knew I would need to look further out. The nearest big town was Cherry Blossom City with a population of about 14,000 was about forty-five minutes north. I knew Cherry Blossom City had a university so I went online to check if Mallard University had a laboratory program as I remembered Robin M my friend from Buttercup City Bible Church and supervisor at Rose City Clinic's veterinary laboratory questioning me about if I had ever considered working in a laboratory. Up to my having worked in the laboratory indirectly with Robin, I actually never had as I was overall oblivious to laboratory work other than knowing how the veterinarians I had ridden with would occasionally have samples which they put out for the Rose City Clinic's laboratory to pick up. Then as the work the vet lab had made me do was extremely simple and I remembered having enjoyed the work I decided it would be worth at least looking into. Mallard University, I discovered when I searched its website on my laptop, did have a Clinical Laboratory Science (CLS) degree. After I called Mallard University, I arranged a time to meet with Dr. Betsy Y, the advisor. When I met with Dr. Betsy, I found her to be a very business-like lady who walked quickly with a bit of a stoop as she appeared to be studying the ground as she walked. She was probably about my height and she had tight brown curls which were starting to turn gray. When I left from our meeting I had learned that I could transfer all my credits from CCC to Mallard University and all I would need to take would be seven more classes and an internship to get the CLS degree. As Mallard University was less than an hour from The Training Camp for CODCL and I knew the CODCL staff at Mallard University, Ramsey L, as he was at The Training Camp for CODCL frequently throughout the summer, Mallard University seemed promising and made me feel that I would not have to entirely start all over developing friends and getting established in a community.

Therefore, I chose to apply to Mallard University as that was the only college in the area I looked at which I discovered offered a laboratory degree, so I did not have to decide between schools. By getting the Clinical Laboratory Science degree, I reasoned that I would qualify to work in a laboratory for more than just seasonal help the next time I applied. What I did not know until about a year later was that most if not all hospitals which offer internships only offer them to students from certain colleges with whom they have contracts meaning I was unable to do my internship in Rose City; Cherry Blossom City or other cities I had worked, lived and developed a sense of community in. As I made these plans to enroll at Mallard University I also failed to think about what it would cost me which was a costly mistake as it wasn't until I lived in Cherry Blossom City for several months before I could prove I had become a resident in this state west of where I grew up so the first semester or two I ended up paying non-resident tuition. Then I also hadn't given thought about where I would have to do my thirty-credit internship or how much the internship would cost me.

So, part of my decision to apply for the program at Mallard University was because of Robin's question to me six months earlier about working in a lab, and partly because I was struggling to repay my loans, especially since the work at The Training Camp for CODCL was mostly voluntary except the $30 a week and room and board they provided. Even with the little bit extra I earned from what Curt's friends were willing to give me for support. I knew though if I returned to college that I could postpone repaying my loans which was another reason I decided to consider going back to college to gain a laboratory degree. As I waited to find out if I would be accepted at Mallard University, I made occasional trips to Cherry Blossom City to apply to jobs online using a computer at Mallard University's library. In their library, I would pull up the local paper online and look at all the job openings and then go to the various businesses, pick up an application and fill it out. At some businesses, I would stop by and just ask for an application even if I didn't see an opening listed and fill it out. So, I had filled out an application at Mallard University and at several of the local fast food places. After I had spent an entire afternoon filling out applications and job searching I would then attend Mallard University's CODCL group called Mallard University's CODCL.

One day I was showing another gal, Sara, from Trillium City the way to Mallard University as her boyfriend, Oleg, played drums for Mallard University's CODCL's worship time. Apparently that day my car's electrical system not liking that it was a rainy day, both its interior and exterior lights started dimming more and more as I drove. Several times I thought I saw oncoming cars flash their lights at me but as I knew I had turned on my light I brushed it off. At the time neither these other drivers or I did not understand that my lights were on but that the electronics with my car was draining the further I drove. Thankfully, Sara had thought she might not want to stay at Mallard University as long as I would so she was following me in her own car, because just two miles before we got to the Business Spur, Cherry Blossom City's main street, and about five miles from Mallard University, my car died. Sara ended up taking me to Mallard University that night and then back to Trillium City. The next day, one of The Training Camp for CODCL staff took me back down to where my car was parked on the side of the highway and tried to jump it. Afterwards they guided me to a shop in Cherry Blossom City to have it repaired. That time I replaced the regulator but the electrical system continued to give me trouble in the following months.

In the following months, I ended up replacing the alternator and the starter, but still my battery would drain. When the mechanics would check the battery, though, it was always good, so eventually they figured it must be a short somewhere in the electrical system. As the car had electronics for its windows and locking system one of those may have started to go or something else altogether. As trying to locate where the short was increasingly took any money I did have saved and then when the gas tank developed a hole so I could only fill it half full, about 5 gallons of gas I decided to sell my car after I made sure Scott was okay with my selling it but I hadn't parted with it until around April of 2007. So, for most of that first semester as I had gotten accepted into the Clinical Laboratory Science's (CLS) program I usually chose to walk the mile or two everywhere: work, classes and to church even during the winter, bundling up as needed in my winter jacket, winter boots and the insulated coveralls which Dr. Kurt from Ash Pine Veterinary Clinic had gotten for me around 2001. Once I had walked even after it must have snowed about two feet during the night as the snow was up to my knees except at the intersections which was closer to hip high where they had already plowed. Ultimately, I had decided to go for the CLS degree after meeting with the CLS advisor, Dr. Betsy Y, as she shared how my credits from CCC would transfer over and I would only need an additional seven classes and an internship which didn't seem anywhere near as daunting as four more years in veterinary school.

My advisor, Dr. Betsy Y, taught Immunology, Parasitology, and a couple semesters of Clinical Microbiology, which I needed to get my CLS degree. Dr. Rosemarie Q, taught two semesters of Clinical Chemistry which were additional classes I needed for my CLS degree. The final class I needed to take for my CLS degree was Advanced Calculus which I had ended up taking during the summer of 2008. I often got stumped and would go in for help and sometimes I would feel stressed heading in to work at Carry Out Pizza Shop as I was stumped but after working my shift would be feeling lot less stressed and usually was able to solve the problem which had left me stumped hours earlier.

Once I started taking classes with Dr. Betsy Y, one of my classmates, whom I often would partner with to study for our exams together, shared how Dr. Betsy Y was bi-polar which caused her to be adamant about the students being at her class **before** it started and make it to all the classes. Once I learned the hard way the necessity of arriving early as I didn't leave home early enough and had entered the classroom after she had so she made sure everyone realized I was late and gave me a such a hard time I determined I would never be late again. So even on the day when it snowed about two feet, I left home over an hour earlier than normal as I was unsure how long it would take me to get to Mallard University and trekked through the two feet of snow the entire way to college as I had previously heard how Mallard University never cancelled classes. Then as I waited for classes to start, I chose to read my Bible reading at the Mallard University library. Around the time class was supposed to start, I got the news that they had actually cancelled the classes. Since I didn't want to have to trudge through all that snow I hung around at Mallard University for a while before I walked back to my apartment. By the time I decided to walk back, the city had gotten the sidewalks cleared also which made it easier going home than it had been walking to Mallard University.

As I drew near to completing all my classes Dr. Betsy Y had encouraged me to start applying for internships so I had started inquiring at several hospitals to see if it would be possible to do my internship at their hospital. It was in early 2008 when I learned how the hospital in Cherry Blossom City would not be able to accept me for an internship because of contracts they had with other schools. By this time, Abby had just had a baby girl, Susannah after having miscarried her first pregnancy a little over a year earlier. Due to Abby's having lost her first baby and Ma having lost a baby within a year of its birth, Ma refused to acknowledge Abby's entire pregnancy with Susannah and had encouraged us to do the same. As I had disagreed and thought every moment of Abby's pregnancy was a gift even if she were to miscarry again, I celebrated with Abby taking pictures when I was visiting her and wanting updates whenever she had any. As I looked into internships and seeing as how I would love to see Abby and Susannah on a more regular basis and knew that I could do so by moving back to the state where I grew up I checked in at some of the hospitals over in that area. But when I went to check out the possibility of doing the internship at Rose City, I learned they also had contracts with certain schools. The laboratory manager there said to me, "Even if you applied we probably would look no further than to see that you weren't from a contracted school. But even if we did look further we still would not be able to offer you an internship."

This was also the case with hospitals in the towns I had lived in during college while working various summer jobs. So to get the degree I had to apply for an internship at hospitals in that state west of the state I grew up in the cities of Golden Rod City, Golden Rocket City, Mustard City, and Geranium City. As I applied to those four hospitals, I sent out an email to my Catalpa City, Rose City, Buttercup City, and The Training Camp for CODCL friends for them to pray that God would have me get accepted at the hospital he wanted me to go. I ended up getting accepted in August 2008 in Geranium City, so I decided I would contact the CODCL staff in Geranium City about my looking for a roommate and a cheaper place to live. They connected me with Ian who at one time owned a duplex which he rented out. As Ian started his own family though he had sold the duplex to Doug R so Ian gave me Doug's information. In turn Doug R connected me with Wendy N as he allowed her to be in charge of the female half of the duplex. After I went for a visit to check out the place and to meet my roommates, I ended up moving there in August 2008 in what was to be almost – if not THE – most eventful year of my life. Before I left Cherry Blossom City, though, Ruby C my roommate at Cherry Blossom City had told me I should write my story. Additionally, Ruby had thrown me a going-away paper party where the guests were invited to give me paper products I might need down in Geranium City. Some of the gifts included a couple reams of copier paper, napkins, paper towels, tin foil, Saran wrap, and sandwich bags.

FINDING WORK AT CHERRY BLOSSOM CITY

A few weeks after my car died the first time in November of 2006, and before I had heard that I got accepted into Mallard University, I ended up getting called for an interview at Golden Arches Fast Food Shop. After the interview, Rob, the head manager, said he would hire me. When he told me that, I mentioned how I already had bought an Interstate Bus System ticket back to the state I grew up in to visit family for a week around Christmas. Rob said he usually would not give a new hire some hours to work and then a week off, but since he knew I really wanted to start right away, he said he would. Rob also said he would schedule me to work morning shifts as he knew how deserted the highway between Trillium City and Cherry Blossom City usually was at night and he did not want to take the chance of my car breaking down and my being stuck on the highway all night.

So, for the first several weeks working at Golden Arches Fast Food Shop during the month of December I would drive from Trillium City to Cherry Blossom City to work. For the most part the drive was uneventful except for two times that month. Once when I had driven home from work I had felt a kind of wobble for most of the drive home in my front left tire. So, when I reached The Training Camp for CODCL I drove back by the maintenance shop at Gander Point and put some air in the tire. The next day as I drove to work the tire felt fine until about halfway to work when I felt a bit of a jerk so I pulled over to look at it. When I looked at it I saw it was flat so I called in that I was going to be late. As I prepared to change it, wondering if I really could seeing as I never had before, a kind passerby saw my dilemma so he stopped and said he would help me change my tire. The other time I had to call in was when there had been several inches of snow that had fallen during the night and the highways had yet to be cleared so I had maybe gotten about a mile or two north on Highway between Trillium City and Cherry Blossom City when my car lost control on the highway skid around for several long seconds before finally coming to rest in the ditch. A passerby headed towards Trillium City stopped and offered to give me a ride back to Trillium City which I accepted and asked her to drop me off at Leah's home. Then after I talked to Leah, she recommended I call our friend Noah N to help me get the car unstuck which he said he would be willing to do though he wanted to wait till there was more light in the sky as I had been scheduled to work at 6 so it was about 5AM when I had called him about my car being stuck. The supervisor working that day told me that it would be okay to come in whenever I could so I arrived several hours later. This supervisor and a few other employees I really enjoyed working with as they were very encouraging and friendly. I never saw them upset or cross at another employee and always seemed to have a smile for employees and customers which most of the other coworkers and supervisors did not have.

After having worked at Golden Arches Fast Food Shop about a month I learned that I was accepted into Mallard University and I got offered a job working at Mallard University's food court weeknights other than Wednesday from 6-10PM. When I told Rob, he worked my schedule at Golden Arches Fast Food Shop around my Mallard University schedule. Rob's willingness to: keep me safe while driving, as he worked around my job at Mallard University, and pre-planned vacation trips were some of the reasons I managed to stick it out at Golden Arches Fast Food Shop from December 2006 to June 2007. Otherwise for most of that time while I worked at Golden Arches Fast Food Shop I really struggled to feel like I could do the job. This feeling stemmed from how several of the managers had no patience with my making mistakes. The more they would chew me out, the more self-conscious I became and the more mistakes I tended to make.

While I found Rob to be friendly and thoughtful, he seemed the least tolerant of people making any kind of mistake as often he would watch all of his employees that he oversaw with a very intense gaze which I found intimidating. Additionally, Rob and a couple other managers had no problem chewing out employees even in front of customers. I learned this first-hand, as many days when I worked there I would get flustered, which would result in my making mistakes on customer orders or mishandling the cash given to me. This would make Rob and other managers angry at me and they would come up behind me and stand there and watch me for a few minutes. I could just feel their disapproval as they stood there which would be confirmed if I gave them a quick tentative look as I could see them watching me with a rather upset look. They often would follow the look up with some comment expressing how frustrated they were with my inability to remember who ordered what, with my having pressed the wrong key (thus an incorrect charge for a product), with my giving incorrect change, etc. even if I still had a customer in my line. Then as I sensed their anger and frustration, I tended to get more upset myself, increasing my tendency to make mistakes.

My tendency for making mistakes was not helped by the fact that between college and the job at Mallard University's food court I only worked on weekends at Golden Arches Fast Food Shop, so I continually had to remember from a week earlier how Golden Arches Fast Food Shop register worked and other requirements that I was to know. I never regretted taking on the Mallard University job which only required working during the fall and spring semesters while classes were being held. Some of the benefits of the job was that it paid better, had benefits including a retirement plan and gave me a chance to get to meet some of my fellow college students including several Criminal Justice and Fire Science students whom often come to the store wearing apparel marked as being Criminal Justice or Fire Science. The downside of the job was that there was so little training and I was so nonconfrontational, I sometimes wondered if some of the students stole some items but never had enough proof to bring it to anybody's attention. Also, due to my working at Mallard University, it meant I only worked a maximum of probably 15 hours a week, and only a day or two at Golden Arches Fast Food Shop which didn't help my ability to remember all Rob and the others really wanted me to remember. Once college let out though at the beginning of May, I started to improve as I started to work at Golden Arches Fast Food Shop for closer to 30 to 40 hours each week.

Finally in May, I feel the Lord inspired me to remind myself that I should look at the situation with my cross managers as if the managers were just having a bad day but that did not mean that I necessarily had to have a bad day. When I started reminding myself that every time I thought one of managers looked irritated, I finally stopped getting flustered whenever those managers came in my general area of work on the register. It had probably been about March though that I had started walking to and from Golden Arches Fast Food Shop whenever I had to work and as I would walk I took to stopping at pretty much every business between Golden Arches Fast Food Shop and home putting in applications as those managers at Golden Arches Fast Food Shop had been making me feel so miserable. This is how in came about in May 2007, that I got a call from Cathy Y about coming in for an interview at Carry Out Pizza Shop's. When I went in for the interview, Cathy took me from the front of the store and walked me to the back into a little room which I later discovered was the break room and sat down with me at the only table there and interviewed me. Throughout the interview Cathy always had a friendly smile and would often giggle in a quite laid back manner. She had made me feel very comfortable and I truly hoped it was an indicator that I would be offered a job.

Even though the job at Golden Arches Fast Food Shop had ended up not being as ideal as I initially thought it would be from my interview with Rob, I had been nervous though about the prospect of quitting Golden Arches Fast Food Shop in order to work full time at Carry Out Pizza Shop in case that was how I would feel at Carry Out Pizza Shop too, so I had called Abby. When I asked Abby for her advice, she reminded me how considerate Rob had been that first month about giving me time to visit family and not making me drive lonely roads at night. So, she recommended that I only work part-time at both jobs until I could determine if Carry Out Pizza Shop 's was a better job or not. When Cathy called the end of May and offered me the job, I told her I would accept it and tried to explain I wanted to be able to work there and at Golden Arches Fast Food Shop for a while, but when she sounded confused, I got flustered and said sure, I would take the job but that I needed to give Golden Arches Fast Food Shop two weeks' notice. I also told her that I was planning to go to the state I grew up in for my sister Abby's upcoming birthday. Cathy was fine with that and just said I had to attend the training session on Friday or Saturday morning about an hour before Carry Out Pizza Shop officially opened for the day. I chose Friday morning.

When I got there for training, Kurt L, the husband of Liz who owned that franchise, welcomed me and a couple teenagers who also had come for training. He then showed us how to remove a ball of dough off a flat sheet which we grabbed from the walk-in refrigerator. Then he showed us how we needed to roll the ball in flour and then flatten out the balls of dough a bit by pulling part of the soft, non-crusted part from the bottom of the ball to make the crust's edge and then knead the ball around till it was flat. The crusted part he explained was the part that wouldn't rise as much and where we would put the toppings. Then Kurt showed us how we would run the hand flattened ball through a machine which would stretch it to pan sized. Once it was pan sized we would stick it in a pan and set it aside until the people who were topping it were ready for it. After each of us new hires had made a few crusts Kurt then had us all grab a pan containing a crust and he showed us how to top the pizza. First he showed us how we would first put a ring in the pan which was to help keep the sauce and topping off of about an inch from the edge which made up the crust area, then to take a ladle of sauce which we were to even spread over the entire space inside the ring. Next we were to take a silver cup of cheese and sprinkle it over the sauce focusing on the edges as "everything tends to go towards the middle once it goes in the oven." Then he let us all select one topping to sprinkle a red cup of it on the pizza again focusing on the edges and then showed us how to stick it on the wire coils which slowly took the pizza through the oven. The coils were calculated to the amount of time needed to completely cook the pizza before the coils would have slowly carried the pan back out of the oven. Then Kurt showed us how to transfer the hot pizza out of the pan and into the box which we then cut into eight slices and boxed up. Kurt then allowed each of us to take one home with us. Kurt was that way. Usually whenever he came in he tended to provide a free pizza or two to the employees who were working that day, much to Liz's dismay. I think Liz was usually relieved when Kurt's construction job kept him too busy to swing by the store to help so she would not have to worry about losing money on his treating the employees to free food. After the training, I left immediately for the state I grew up in, spent the week with Abby and her husband, Nathan, for her birthday, and upon returning found that my roommate, Ruby C, had finalized getting Eli to agree to her renting his house on Chipping Sparrow Street and so she had moved all our things to the new place. Before going to the state I grew up in, I knew Ruby was considering moving to the new place, but I thought it was going to be after I got back that we were going to move. Ruby had also bought me a frame for my bed at that time. It was a pleasant surprise not to have to move anything.

I never did regret working at Carry Out Pizza Shop instead of Golden Arches Fast Food Shop. Everyone was quite friendly at Carry Out Pizza Shop. The breaks at Carry Out Pizza Shop weren't scheduled so people would just take breaks whenever things got slow. Cathy often would take breaks with Trinity I, whom I later learned was related to my Cherry Blossom Wesleyan Church friend, Carol I. Trinity quickly became one of my closest friends there as she would offer me a slice of pizza when she and Cathy would go on break together. After I started inviting Trinity to game nights that I would host but she never had been able to attend as she had to work those days, Trinity started inviting me to family gatherings where we would eat and then play games. Trinity was a lady about my height who with dark brown eyes and equally dark brown hair who seemed to usually have a smile and would usually be trying to draw me out. Another friend I made at Carry Out Pizza Shop who took me up on invites to my craft nights was, Lila, who was the daytime manager while Cathy was the evening manager. Lila had the same attributes as Trinity except her hair was a tad bit longer and more reddish, and might have been an inch or so shorter in height.

RUBY

It was January 2007 that I moved into Cherry Blossom City, to be 30 miles closer to work and school. The first night I hadn't been thinking and instead of parking my car in the garage behind the house off the alley, I left it parked on the street and received a ticket. Then to save myself some money as my living expenses rose with renting, I took to walking especially as my car started to give me more trouble starting and developed a hole in the gas tank.

The first time I walked to college a couple small white wooden churches caught my eye. The one was the Cherry Blossom Wesleyan Church and it had two services listed on its sign out front. The other church I had never noticed what time their services were held. When I saw the posted times that the Cherry Blossom Wesleyan Church was held I determined that the next Sunday I would have to check it out. So the next Sunday, I walked over for its first service.

Upon entering the building, there were stairs leading up and stairs leading down. I took the stairs up where I entered the church sanctuary. At the top of the stairs was a coat rack and along the back wall of the sanctuary was the sound booth with several chairs alongside it. In the following weeks, I learned how the sound booth was usually run by Ralph I. His wife, Carol, and their children usually sat beside the sound booth unless she was teaching the children which she frequently did. On the other side of the sound booth were several bookshelves full of books. The sanctuary itself had around a dozen or two rows of chairs before the platform where Pastor Andy preached and the worship team led the congregation in singing. That Sunday I had enjoyed the first service and thought I'd stay for the second Afterwards I had lingered a bit. I probably met some of the people that Sunday but can't remember other than Neal X who greeted and handed out the church bulletins whom also introduced me to his wife Rosemary.

What I do remember is several weeks later as I must have decided to leave early as I remember being on the stairs when a white-haired lady several inches shorter than me with a friendly smile and twinkling bright blue eyes behind glasses stopped me who frequently was wearing scrubs stopped me and introduced herself as Ruby C. Over the next several weeks whenever she would see me she would stop to at least say hi but often would engage me for conversation for at least a few minutes before second service began. That's how I learned how Ruby worked as a housekeeper at the local hospital and how I learned she was exactly six months younger than Ma. After a few weeks Ruby started to urge me to join her for the Sunday School class held during the first service in the basement of the church. The following weeks I did then join her and about a dozen others from the congregation for Sunday School which met around tables arranged in a square shape. Noah Q was the leader. He was a graying haired man about 6 feet and probably at least in his fifties as he had a son about my age—late twenties to early thirties. Noah's son and wife, Betsy also both attended.

A few weeks later Ruby also invited me to the Bible Study she attended on Wednesdays at Randolf and Yulia C's house. As the Bible Study met on Wednesdays which were my days off from working 6-10 at Mallard University's convenience store, I decided I would.

Ruby shared how Rolfe and Yolanda lived about three blocks from where I lived, so I chose to walk to their place. Rolfe and Yolanda lived in a sprawling one story white house with a wrought iron fence surrounding their front yard. The members of the Bible study usually would enter their house using the front door. That entrance brought a person in to their kitchen which also had an entrance from their garage which Rolfe or Yolanda usually entered sometimes after their Bible study guests had arrived. From the kitchen often the group would linger in the dining half of the room until the group was ready to start the Bible study.

Once the Bible study was ready to start the group would move to the living room. The living room required a person to take a step down to enter it. Usually the room was softly lit and not as bright as the other rooms were. In the living room some of the group members would sit on some of the couches or other chairs the room contained while others would recline on the floor. As the youngest member I'd take a spot on the floor. The living room also contained a wall of bookshelves and a piano, both items of interest to me as I loved reading and had always want to learn how to play more than the little bit I had self-taught while growing up on the farm.

The group consisted most regularly of Neal & Rosemary X, Ruby C, me and Rolfe &Yolanda W. Occasionally a few others would also join us. For our Bible Studies, we would either study a book in the Bible or watch a study video, like Ray VanderLaan or Rob Bell, and do a study based on the video. That is where I was first introduced to Ray VanderLaan.

When Ruby learned that I walked, she would then volunteer to drive me home afterwards. It was on these car rides when I started to open up to her and I told Ruby how I wanted to find a roommate to make me feel less stressed financially. Ruby then would share some of her own marriage troubles which were making her want a place of her own to live. When Ruby heard I was looking for a roommate she suggested we live together, but upon looking at the apartment where I was living she declared it a hole. When I got a brief visit out to Ruby's husband and her place some weeks later, the little I saw was elegant, a far cry from the place I lived in and I could then understand why she thought it was hole. Until I saw her place though I had not considered my apartment a hole probably because the place I grew up had become really run down and compared to my childhood home this apartment was in good condition.

When I said I would be interested in becoming Ruby's roommate, she then started looking for another place for us to rent. She found a house to rent on Herons Street which was about three blocks closer to

Mallard University. The house was a cute looking, white two story place with a few steps leading to a front porch which had been enclosed prior to our moving in. Going the few feet through the porch one entered the actual house. Upon entering the house one could see the French doors in the back overlooking the deck and what must have been close to an acre of back yard containing a playground set and rhubarb plants. When I saw the playground I immediately thought of Leah and her daughter, Rayna, whom I could imagine loving to play on the playground set. Leah and Rayna only made it the one time though but they didn't have enough time for Rayna to play on the playground. In between the front door and the back lay a room to the right which Ruby made into her study, library, and craft room. Right outside this room lay the stairs leading to a large brightly lit full bathroom which contained a laundry room too. Off of it was the room which Ruby let me claim for a bedroom, and off it was a spare bedroom and then Ruby's bedroom. Downstairs the kitchen and dining room lay at the end of a narrow hallway and contained the French doors. This kitchen, dining room area probably was my favorite part of the house and the area I spent most of my time when I was home other than my bedroom which I crammed my things in that I had gotten for my last apartment. While living at Herons Street house I mostly felt like a stranger living in Ruby's place and would look but not touch her things and only once entered her bedroom, when she had asked me to look for something she had left in her room.

As the landlord of the house said he was okay with cats, Ruby brought one of her cats to live with us. The cat was sweet, gray middle aged cat who tended to be an alarm-clock cat, as every morning before my alarm would go off, I would hear him walking around in my room stepping on paper making them make a crinkling sound or on my keys making them rattle which would wake me up. As there must have been another cat who lived there at some point, the cat took to peeing outside it's litter box mostly if not entirely in Ruby's study room. We lived in this house from around April until June, I think as there was still snow when we moved in and I was still going to the college. I know we moved out in June as I shared earlier about how one weekend after I went to visit

Abby for her birthday, I discovered all my things had been moved to the next house Ruby decided to rent. While we lived there, I continued to walk to school and Ruby would walk to the hospital where she worked.

On one hot summer day at that house, I remember waking up to a loud, profanity-filled argument taking place in the back alley of the house. I tried to ignore it but it went on for a long time. Finally, I fell back to sleep, only to be re-awakened by the arguing again. This time I peered out the window to see who was arguing and listened to it for about fifteen to thirty minutes, all the while hoping it would stop. When it didn't, I decided to call the police feeling like I was being a rude neighbor as I did so as reporting to authorities seemed like such a scary, fear inducing thing by my family's standards. But what prompted me to finally call was because I thought that if I was being kept awake by it, then maybe others were too and I really did want to sleep. When I called it in I reported how there was an argument with loud profanity happening in the back alley of the house at Herons Street but the actual house address where the activity was occurring I did not know. After calling it in, I continued to hear the argument for quite some time until I heard one of the people call to the others "There's a cop car, we better head inside." I don't remember exactly when it was but I remember calling the police department again just to tell them thank you for having responded to the call.

After living in that house for about a month or two, I remember Ruby deciding she wanted a new house to live in. Now that Ruby lived in town she also had taken to walking places and on one of her walks, she had seen a sign in front of where the youth pastor at Cherry Blossom Wesleyan church, Eli, lived indicating that the place was for sale by owner. She convinced the owner, a different Eli who had formerly gone to Cherry Blossom Wesleyan Church, to allow her to rent it. Eventually Ruby decided to buy the house after finding that every house she looked at and liked had an offer accepted on it before she ever really got a chance to offer anything for it herself.

GETTING ESTABLISHED IN CHERRY BLOSSOM CITY

As I thought and hoped this was my final move, I tried to get established in Cherry Blossom City by hosting game nights the first Thursday of each month and craft nights the third Thursday of each month. I had made up invitations which I started to carry on me so I could hand them out to those whom I considered friends who were mostly women.

So I took those invitations to church the next Sunday and I handed them out to several of the women whom I had gotten to know at Cherry Blossom Wesleyan Church. I had tried handing them out to the ladies at Noah Q's Bible study, but none of those came or they told me out front how they were too busy already so they would not come to either of my events. I also handed one to Carol I whose family was always sitting by the sound box where her husband would run sound. It was because of Carol's very friendly, smiling, sisterly demeanor which broke down my reserves and whom I got to know as I decided I wanted to start helping with the youth at Cherry Blossom Wesleyan Church which she oversaw. When I invited Carol, she asked if it would be okay if she brought some of her children. I told her that I would love for her to bring her children so often she brought her oldest, preteen daughter, India and her infant daughter, Isla.

Then one week Ruby C saw a new couple whom had just started to attend Cherry Blossom Wesleyan Church and she urged me to give the lady an invite. I hesitantly had as I was intimidated by the lady's husband as he was a rather large guy, and because I just was nervous around strangers, usually waiting for them to first approach me so that I'd get to know them rather than my approaching them. (I'd become more lax and complacent on breaking down my comfort zone since leaving CCC.) I'm glad Ruby C convinced me to give this lady an invite as she, Yvette N, became one of my closest friends in Cherry Blossom City. Our friendship probably grew to a fair extent as both of us were new to Cherry Blossom City, so that we were looking for friends. So as I would invite Yvette and her family (husband Tony and pre-school aged daughter Tonya) over to my place for games, she would invite me over to her place where we would talk, watch Tonya and occasionally the three of us would go for a walk or visit the beach which she lived a few blocks from.

By the time I started the game and craft nights Ruby C and I were living at the Chipping Sparrow Street address and I was working at Carry Out Pizza Shop. So I took my invites with me to Carry Out Pizza Shop and handed my invites out to the co-workers that I had felt most comfortable with. I had invited Trinity I, Cathy Y and Lila M. As Trinity and Cathy worked nights both of them told me that they would not be able to come to my events. Trinity remembered my inviting her to my game night though, which prompted her to invite over on the Sunday nights when her family was hosting game nights. Lila though said since she had some craft projects she was working on that she was glad to take me up on coming to those nights. Games weren't so much her thing so she only came to my craft nights.

Our closest neighbor's house and ours at Chipping Sparrow Street were separated just by both of our driveways and a grass section about as wide as our driveway which contained several bushes. This neighbor was an elderly, curly white-haired lady, Isla N who was a few inches shorter than me whom was frequently seen trimming her bushes, dead heading her flowers or washing her car or house. Ruby C quickly become good friends with her and soon I was too. Usually whenever we would go over Isla gladly welcomed us in and we would sit down and she would resume whatever craft project she was working on at the time. Eventually I took to bringing over the craft project I was working on at the time too. So when I started my craft nights I made sure that I also invited Isla. She ended up teaching me how to weave into monk's cloth patterns which were called Swedish weave. She taught me the pattern she used to make baby blankets, which was a pattern that included hearts, but after making a few of these I chose to experiment with making up my own patterns to weave into the blankets including a rocking horse and teddy bears playing baseball.

Another friend I made whom came to my game nights was Rodney S whom I met through a lunch that Ruby was taking me out to as she decided to also join him. Rodney was a friend she had made but hadn't seen in a bit so she had wanted to catch up with him and since the lunch turned out pretty fun as Rodney was a bit of a comedian whom had a rather infectious laugh. He was a therapist, which had proved helpful as the night right before I was to go to my first parasitology lab I had had a dream which ended in my hurting my middle finger on my right hand which he looked at but said just needed time to heal as it wasn't broken. In my dream, I had been wiping out the crumbs out of the Carry Out Pizza Shop pizza pans when I noticed that the stack in the far corner contained large black worms or small black snakes. As long as the snakes remained in the pan I had been okay but as soon as I dreamed that one of the snakes started to crawl out of the pan, I jumped to get away from it which resulted in my jumping out of my bed. As I had been asleep I landed on the floor and in the process sprained my finger, effectively waking me up. Ruby had been coming up from the basement which is where her bedroom was to use the bathroom which was located next to my bedroom and when she saw me sitting on the floor cradling my right hand, Ruby asked me if I was okay which I said I was as I was barely awake and as I worked on crawling back into bed. Later when I shared with Ruby about my dream she had a good laugh. The next day though taking notes, and using the microscope was quite painful but I think I managed to do both without bringing attention to my injured finger.

Then the other friends I had made whom would attend my game nights were Virgil and Ulyssa R, and their daughter Kori and son Nels, both pre-teens. Nels was a quite rambunctious boy who seemed to love tormenting his sister Kori while Kori in comparison seemed quite subdued and mostly eager to please. Ulyssa spent a good amount of time trying to encourage Nels to calm down as did Virgil though Virgil himself was more reserved. I remember how Nels favorite game was Battleship and he was always trying to get someone to join him playing it.

Each of these friends other than Lila and Rodney had in turn over the following year invited me over to their places to hang out with them and their families, which enabled me to know them better and become better friends with them.

My birthday in 2008 was also a memorable one. I had invited my friends over for craft night the Thursday before, like normal, and then invited them over again a few days later for my birthday. After that particular craft night, I learned that in the weeks preceding it, Ruby had handed out cards to the friends I had made in church saying she wanted to throw me a surprise birthday party on the same night I was inviting people over for crafts. She had baked me a cake just before this, and as my shift at Carry Out Pizza Shop 's was coming too near to her being able to finish the cake, she had called Carry Out Pizza Shop 's to ask them to stall me. Trinity I had complied by begging me to help the delivery guy get caught up on the dishes that had piled up in the washroom which I had thought nothing of as the washroom was piled with dirty dishes all over and it was drawing near to closing time so I just thought they were trying to prevent being stuck at work till two or later which sometimes happened when there were so many dirty dishes to wash. Additionally Ruby had a friend who professionally decorates cakes, whom she had asked to come over to our place to decorate the cake. Ruby then sprayed the house so that the house would not smell as if she had baked a cake. On the day of the craft night, Ruby sent me over to fetch our neighbor Isla N. As I had gone over a bit early, I thought I would take up Isla's offer to sit and chat for a while, but as the time for craft night came, I started to get antsy to get back so I could greet my guests. Isla seemed not to notice this and I did not want to appear rude by interrupting our time together so, it wasn't until after she got a phone call that we finally headed back to my place. Since I was in such a hurry to get home, I did not notice anything out of the ordinary as we crossed Isla's driveway and then Ruby and my driveway before entering Ruby and my place. It was only after I entered and all my friends who had come yelled, "Surprise!" that I realized what Ruby had done and then all her strange behaviors over the past weeks fell into place.

After I finished taking the seven classes I needed to take for my CLS degree, I had learned that I would not be able to complete my internship at Cherry Blossom City but instead would have to do so either in Golden Rod City, Geranium City or in one of a couple suburbs of Geranium City. Overall I had been pretty disappointed that once more I was having to uproot myself from my efforts to become a part of a community. A part of me was excited though as I wondered whom I would all meet down there especially if there might be the possibility of meeting someone special whom I might marry someday as I wasn't finding anyone at Cherry Blossom City.

GERANIUM CITY

At first when I moved down to Geranium City in August 2008 I was mostly awed by the big city life and enjoyed getting to see and explore a new city. It had seemed strange though seeing attendants at gas stores behind a bulletproof enclosure and that their bathrooms weren't accessible to motorists or pedestrians whom just dropped in to use the facilities. At Geranium City, I had moved into a duplex owned by Doug R who lived in the other half of the duplex. He was average height, slightly stocky man who usually was very friendly, especially with women, and was finishing up a residency at Geranium City Medical Center to become a surgeon. On my half of the duplex I lived with a couple ladies about my age. Wendy, Doug's friend, ran my half of the duplex. She was a tall, big boned blond who was very outgoing who when I first met with her she had shared how she also enjoyed hosting game nights and gathering with friends. She worked as an administrative assistant at a local company. She seemed very open to my hosting game night and having people over too if I'd live there which is why I ultimately chose to move there though I hadn't really found any other options which would make it possible to live off just the $400 stipend that I was going to receive each month from my internship at Geranium City Medical Center. Normally Wendy requested more than $100 for rent each month but as I was new to the area and doing my internship 40 hours a week so I was unable to find another job she told me that she would only require $100 for my rent. We had another roommate, Autumn, who was average in height, and a skinny lady of

Asian descent who was very friendly, as seen frequently by her ready smile, who loved to cook. She with her boyfriend, Stan who lived in the other half of the duplex, would usually be found after work cooking something up together and then sharing the food with whomever was home. Autumn was finishing up on becoming a speech pathologist at Geranium City Medical Center while Stan was doing residency to become a pediatrician.

The duplex I moved into was located on Gnatcatchers Street a few blocks off Waxwings about four miles from Geranium City Vultures Stadium. The duplex was a big brick house with a few large stone steps leading up to the big front porch. With a low wall dividing the two entrances. Here Doug and Wendy would occasionally play their guitars and jam out with some of their friends. These were some of my favorite memories I have with my roommates there other than the meals that Stan and Autumn would make most nights. As one entered the duplex one would go through the metal gate which none of my roommates felt needed to be secured and then the front door which was always locked when closed. Unless a group of my roommates and their friends were either on the porch or in the dining room the front door was always closed. Right in front of the door was the stairs leading upstairs where Autumn and Wendy's bedrooms were. There was another room upstairs but it was being used by another friend of theirs when I first moved in so I had a room in the basement which was accessed by stairs off the hallway parallel to the stairs leading upstairs. When I first moved in, the basement had things piled all over. So the first several weeks I took to putting similar things together into more organized piles on the tables and shelves that were down there and cleaning up the dirt and debris. Everyone in the duplex was in awe of the transformation when I had completed my organizing the basement. At the far end of the basement was a room equipped only with a toilet so I rigged up a 2.5 gallon juice dispenser up on a table to be my sink with a chair holding a 5 quart pail to catch the dirty water. On the table I would also have a bottle of soap and on a hanger in the general area, I had hung a hand towel. Beside the room with the toilet was a door leading to a room containing stairs leading outside which the other half of the duplex also shared.

So this door leading outdoors we kept locked but the doors separating the duplexes we kept unlocked which is the way which we used almost daily to go between the duplexes.

Being as how the duplex was located so close to downtown almost daily one would hear gunshots and multiple times a day a person had to deal with awful traffic jams which would make a ten minute drive take a half hour or longer. By October I had grown sick of the traffic jams and started looking for alternative routes so I could avoid the main streets. Some of the alternative roads though were filled with potholes as big as footballs which was probably the cause of my getting a bent rim around February 2009 leading to a flat tire that I found after getting off my internship at 5:30pm. By November after a few months of these extensive delays, I got very tired of Geranium City and began missing my friends in the cities I had lived previously.

Since my internship was to last ten months, the very first Sunday I lived in Geranium City I had decided to check out a couple churches there. I told my friends in Cherry Blossom City that since I really did not want to move again, if God wanted me at Geranium City, then I was going to do my best to find a church to become a part of to determine if that was God's confirmation that this was where he wanted me to stay. If God made it so I enjoyed Geranium City like I did Cherry Blossom City, then I would not come back to Cherry Blossom City. As I was moving to my new residence in Geranium City, I noticed several churches which were within walking distance, and since my roommates shared how they walked almost everywhere, I decided I would too. The first church I went to seemed very political and was mostly made up of blacks. Since I had only gone to churches made up mostly of Caucasians, I felt out of place there and what with their being so vocal on their political opinions and their worship style being so different from what I was used to, I chose not to go back. That church's service ended before my new roommates' second church service began, so I decided to check out their church. Their church had both blacks and whites there and a mix of black and white styles of worship, so I chose to continue going to their church. Plus, I liked the sermons. After a few months, the church got a new music minister and the worship style became very black. Also, in the beginning of 2009, the pastor began to talk almost every week about how he felt God was going to make their church membership expand to over five hundred new members. After each service he would invite the church members to consider accepting Jesus as their personal Lord and Savior. Then he would also invite church attenders to join the church and have them come forward so he and the other church leaders could give them membership things, get their information, and take their picture to put on the membership board. As the year progressed, the pastor would excitedly share how the membership was expanding and the progress they were making toward the five-hundred-new-members mark. Sometimes it seemed like they would get people excited about becoming members on a Sunday but not excited enough to actually keep attending the church. The pastor would still count them as members though. Meanwhile after he invited people to consider Jesus as their personal Lord and Savior I never heard anything more happen with these people which I felt was backward as these should have been the folks we should have been really excited about and tried to get more information from so we could keep in touch with them and help them to grow in their new faith.

Needless to say, this church's desire for members kept me from wanting to become a member and started making me think of wanting to find a different church. As the end of my internship was supposed to be only a few months out though I thought it really wasn't worth trying to find a new church and making new friends as by then I knew that I absolutely had no intentions of living in Geranium City past completion of my internship. Then to top off my frustration with the church after I had been going to the church for about six months the pastor preached about the woman caught in adultery in John 8. The pastor shared with the parishioners how, regardless of their sins, God loved them and that he would not cast a stone at the parishioners regardless of what sin they had committed or how long the parishioners had sinned. This was all fine and dandy except that I hope it was by accident that the pastor forgot to mention that when Jesus said to the woman caught in adultery, "Did no one condemn you ... neither do I condemn you," he also said, "Go and from now on sin no more." This last phrase is very important as Jesus wants us to be aware of our sins and his willingness to forgive them, but he also wants us to know he does not want us to continue on in our sins either after we accept his forgiveness.

In addition to getting involved in a church as I tried to get connected in Geranium City less than a month into having lived in Geranium City, I had asked Stan if there was a Bible study that I could get involved in. He shared with me about one he went to and offered to take me the next time it met. It ended up being at Eric and Martie I's place, who lived right across the back alley from us.

Eric was a tall skinny white guy who was passionate about the Lord and loved to fix up places. He owned his own construction company and worked long hours. Martie was a bubbly black woman who had an infectious smile and loved to pick on people, especially quiet ones like me, to try to get us to join in the Bible study discussion. I didn't mind as it helped me feel like if I had something to share she really wanted to hear what I had to say.

As Martie enjoyed company and had a son a month older than my niece, Susannah, I frequently went over there to visit. Then one Sunday night in November 2008, I remember going to Eric and Martie's for their Bible study where we talked about meaning what we sing. I remember thinking about how meaningful the song "Blessed Be Your Name," written by Matt Redman and sung by the group Tree63, was to me. It prompted me to think back to 2006 when I first heard the song sung in a church in Trillium City. At that time I had just been told a few days earlier that one of my favorite cows (which would have been a dear friend during my years without other types of friends) was going to have to be sold. (My family started to tell me when they were considering selling any of the cows from "my line of cows" – a favorite cow and her descendants. That was because several years earlier while I was at college studying my family thought Josh and Zeke, my steers, were getting too big and scary for my sisters so they sold them without telling me. When I discovered them gone, I thought surely they had to be someplace nearby and asked Ma about them. She told me: "They were starting to scare your older sisters so as we did not want to distract you as you studied for your tests we just sold them. We were sure you would understand and allow us to." Boy, was I mad, and I let them know that now I would be more distracted from tests than ever since I knew they would sell my favorite animals and things of mine without telling me first. Anyway, God used the song "Blessed be Your Name" to ease my sorrows whenever I learned that I was losing my favorite animal friends.

The day after that Bible study discussion, Monday, during a break where I was hanging out in a room about 5'X 6' equipped with a miniature refrigerator, a table and lined with bookshelves full of books with most of the other seven interns at my internship at Geranium City Medical Center trying to study, I got a call from Stan from the other half of the duplex asking me if I had a laptop computer. When I said I did, he informed me, "Not anymore" as it had been stolen along with four other laptops and a few coin collections which had been in the duplex. This really shook me up, as my laptop had all my favorite music and pictures on it, plus a lot of other things on it that I had not backed up, so it all was gone. Just like that, my most valuable material possession was gone through human unkindness. When the other interns learned what had happened they encouraged me to go home to be there when the police arrived which I did. While I waited for the police, I chose to give the loss of my laptop to God. As I mourned my loss, through my tears I sang in my head lines from "Blessed Be Your Name" about how I would still bless the Lord despite his taking things away. When the Geranium City police finally arrived out at the duplex they wrote down laptop owners' names, phone numbers, the types of laptops, the approximate worth, and any identifying marks for each laptop. The police asked if there was any sign of forced entry. They stood on the front porch the entire time they asked these questions never once looking at any of the doors, windows, or even inside either side of the duplex. When Stan said that there had been no sign of forced entry, the police told us how we should probably suspect one of the tenants of the duplex as being the thief and then before leaving they shared how laptops are rarely recovered so that we should not expect to get them back.

Of course, since we had just kicked out a drug-addicted family member of one of the tenants, my thoughts immediately went to him.

This led me to want to put new locks on the duplex to secure the place better, but nobody else who lived in the duplex that I hung out with afterwards seemed to care about the loss of security. They were all a bit put out about the loss of the laptops, but both Stan and Autumn ultimately decided that new laptops had been in order anyway because of how old their laptops had been. Maybe one of Stan and Doug's roommates, Vern had been more affected like I was seeing as he was a small town guy originally from the state where Ma grew up but since his wife was still back in the state where Ma grew up and he was busy with his internship, I rarely if ever had seen him so I never got his impression of having his laptop stolen but it probably was about a month later when he moved out of the duplex. Meanwhile, I feared that the duplex no longer was secure, but as I seemed to be in the minority, I kept quiet. As I feared the loss of security, I began to fear that my car, the next most valuable possession I owned and the only other thing besides my cell phone which was worth much money, would be stolen.

The following Saturday, less than five days after my computer was stolen and while I was living with all this fear, God had me read 1 Peter 5:7 " *Cast all your anxiety on him because he cares for you,*" and Psalm 70:4 "*Let all those who seek You rejoice and be glad in You; And let those who love Your salvation say continually, 'Let God be magnified!'*" (*New King James Version,* this verse I have since found is also in Psalm 40:16) during my morning devotion as I prepared to go to the Organization Releasing Children from Poverty in Jesus' Name event. The local area coordinator, Tori B, planned to pick me up and take me to the event. I had asked her if I could carpool with her as I was paying for thirty credit hours for the eight-month internship and making only a $400-per-month stipend, before federal and state taxes, so I did not feel like I had any money for gas to get to the Organization Releasing Children from Poverty in Jesus' Name event. So after doing my morning devotions I went upstairs to wait for Tori. When I looked out the window she was not there, but neither was my car where I usually parked it. Nor was my car anywhere in sight!

My heart sank, and near tears, I ended up calling the police and Tori to report my car was stolen. Tori then offered to also take me to

HALLELUJAH

the police station to file a report as the police required the report to be filed there rather than for an officer to come to my place of residence. Tori also said that if I did not want to go to the Organization Releasing Children from Poverty in Jesus' Name event she would take me back home. I told her I did NOT want to stay in Geranium City but wanted to go to the meeting. I am glad I did, as it allowed me to get my mind off the sorrows of the past week and focus on others less fortunate than me. Plus it let me meet a lot of nice people.

At the Organization Releasing Children from Poverty in Jesus' Name event, they had a student who had gone through their sponsorship program share about what the Organization Releasing Children from Poverty in Jesus' Name had meant to him and his family. He shared how he was one of many children within his family but the only one sponsored. Because of the Organization Releasing Children from Poverty in Jesus' Name he never got into drugs, alcohol or gangs like most young kids his age in his country did. Then as he learned about Jesus' gift of salvation, he shared the good news with his family and after nine years of praying that they would accept Jesus as their savior, each of his siblings and parents did. He also shared how his father who was an alcoholic has also given up alcohol.

Then each of us at the Organization Releasing Children from Poverty in Jesus' Name meeting was told to pick a packet and try to persuade another attendee to sponsor the child. I had chosen Moses J from a Central America third world island country who had seven siblings (the same number of siblings as I had family members growing up). Then at the end of the event the Organization Releasing Children from Poverty in Jesus' Name staff told us to take home some of the packets which were at the event and try finding sponsors for them. So I brought home the packet for Moses and a few other packets, determined that if I did not find a sponsor for Moses I would somehow find the money to sponsor him myself. After all each child was only listed in one place so each of those children that I took home with me would not be found at another event or online so until the packets reached their expiration date, which the Organization Releasing Children from Poverty in Jesus' Name put on each packet to make sure a child did not

193

go for months without the potential for a sponsor. The Organization Releasing Children from Poverty in Jesus' Name always wants to give the event or person trying to find a sponsor the chance to connect the child with a sponsor which each child only gets one sponsor. I did find a coworker, Nadine H, who was willing to sponsor one of girls for whom I had a packet, but not for Moses. So I sponsored him. Prior to sponsoring him, back in 2002 I had decided to sponsor my first child through the Organization Releasing Children from Poverty in Jesus' Name, an organization that uses the local church to determine which children are the poorest of the poor in their towns and then would seek to find sponsors for these children. These children are then guaranteed a meal every day, an education, medical care, and having Jesus' gift of salvation shared with them. Through their program the Organization Releasing Children from Poverty in Jesus' Name helped South Korea go from a country needing sponsorship to one which sponsored children in other countries. I have since heard of how children who had been sponsored growing up have since graduating and finding a good job have themselves started sponsoring other children.

When I first heard of the Organization Releasing Children from Poverty in Jesus' Name around 2000, I realized how fortunate I had been growing up as I always had food even if for most of my life my family rationed it; I always had an education; and I always had the knowledge of Jesus loving me even if while growing up the focus was on being good versus a personal relationship with our loving savior and heavenly father. For these reasons, I chose back then to sponsor a little girl from a Central America third world island country, Mandy G, who, with her seven siblings, was being raised by her grandmother (much like Grandma Nancy raised my sisters and me and how there was seven in my family too). Unfortunately, Mandy ended up moving away from the program less than two years later so I was given the option of stopping my sponsorship altogether or sponsoring another child. I chose to sponsor another girl from the Central America third world island country, Nita M. It was less than two years later that the pastor at Nita's program was caught embezzling the Organization Releasing Children from Poverty in Jesus' Name's funds for the children within the program, so they had to close the whole program down. The Organization Releasing Children from Poverty in Jesus' Name is very strict about maintaining financial integrity. So, I was again offered the chance to sponsor another child and as I was living in Cherry Blossom City at that time and Cherry Blossom Wesleyan Church had a ministry in a South American country, so I chose to sponsor a child with the greatest need in this third world South American country, and this was Rafe Z. I had been sponsoring him less than a year when I decided I also wanted to sponsor Moses J. To this day I still sponsor Moses, who has now started taking college classes as he seeks to become an agronomist.

When I got home from the Organization Releasing Children from Poverty in Jesus' Name event, though, I insisted on new locks to the duplex and a lock on my bedroom door. I told my roommates and the guys next door that I was willing to pay for the new locks, which I wanted for my own peace of mind that I had not had for the past week. Stan Z chose to pay for them though. After the duplex and my bedroom got new locks, I moved all my remaining possessions into my bedroom. The only exception was my library of books, which I had collected with encouragement from fellow book lover and former roommate, Ruby C who herself had filled an entire room with bookshelves containing no doubt over a hundred books which she would encourage me to read anytime I wanted.

In mid-December I had gotten a letter from the Geranium City police saying my car was found. When I called the police station, though, I was told, "According to our computers, your car still has not been found." As I had the letter right in front of me saying my car had been found, I persisted in trying to find out where my car was being held as I told them I had a letter saying my car had been found which they surely would not have sent me if my car had not been found. Finally, they actually listened to what I was saying and said they would check one more place. After they checked the other place they came back and told me, "You were right; your car has been found. The paperwork had just not been entered into the computer yet." Then they told me the impounds name where my car was being held.

Then for the rest of the day I looked in my unimposing manner for someone to give me a ride over to the impound. Finally, my friend Rhea N offered to drive me there. After we looked at my car and saw the thief had removed the ignition, Rhea offered to call her roadside assistance company for a tow to a garage in town which she recommended. The thief had also destroyed my brakes and muffler, both of which I had just had installed after I bought the car which was on its way to the scrap yard as the former owner didn't want it anymore as it needed a few repairs and wasn't very convenient for their growing family in the spring of 2008 in Cherry Blossom City. The person who had stolen my car had also removed the CD player from my car. Additionally, my passenger side mirror was gone and of course, the rear passenger window which had been broken to steal my car was still broken. The car stunk of cigarettes and my CD and tool collection was gone, including my jumper cables and spare tire. The thief only left a roll of toilet paper (not mine) in the car when it was recovered.

It took several more months to straighten out things so that the man caught with my car in his possession could start paying me back. This involved a lot of phone calls. Often during breaks in my internship I would try to call, only to find that the answering machine was full or that I would be told, "You actually need to call …" (a different number instead). After several weeks I finally started keeping track of who I called so that when I was told, "You actually need to call …," for a duplicate time, I could tell the business who was trying to have me call another business again that, "I called them on [whatever date] and they said to call you" or "I called them on [whatever date] and only got their answering machine which was full." Often they would then give me a new number to try, although occasionally they would take a note and pass it on to the "right" party. Finally, after all that work and a lot of waiting on my part for others to get back to me, I was able to start getting my car repair bills repaid by the man caught with my car. During this time, though, apparently somehow my address information got messed up, too, and I ended up having to go to several departments to finally get that straightened out.

In late November of 2008 I decided to join the Inner-City Take Back Program, a group that goes into large cities and teaches interested citizens how to take back their city from crime, drugs, gangs, and prostitution. The Inner-City Take Back Program met at the church I was going to. When I first heard about the Inner-City Take Back Program I was not interested, because Wendy N, my roommate at that time, who attended the meetings during the initial weeks, would share about "How it was fascinating as I learned how to be able to break a person's arm, leg, or knee by doing …" However, when I heard from Ariel, whom I worked with in the church's children's ministry, how she felt much safer learning the safety techniques the Inner-City Take Back Program taught, that I decided maybe I would like to check it out too. As I joined the Inner-City Take Back Program, I learned a lot of good self-defense moves and I would join them at least weekly to practice the moves or as we would walk some city streets to show that we were not willing to watch people break laws like dealing drugs, prostitution, fighting, etc. with occasional times that we would stake out at a house known to be a drug house.

Also around that time I joined the Central Geranium City Christians (CGCC) teen program which Rob B led. This CGCC teen program would offer to go around town and pick up teens in an old red and white standard sized bus where after we had picked everyone up, the group would listen to Rob or another leader share some on the Bible and then would be a time of fellowship with some snacks. Afterwards Rob would drive the bus back around, dropping off the students at their homes and would watch the student get inside their building before he would drive to his next stop. Through this CGCC program is how I met and really got to know my friend Nicole X. In addition to getting to know Nicole I also got to know Rob's wife, Ida better. In addition to her hosting some CGCC events at her place, I also worked with her at my church's children's ministry. As I still struggled with being outgoing, I am afraid I was not the best role model for the teen program though. Even so, these organizations were a couple of good things I got involved with while living in Geranium City, which helped me to work on stretching my comfort zone, though not as deliberately as when I was at CCC.

Then in the spring of 2009 I had a stocky, black guy about my height with a little scar on a cheek beneath one of his eyes approach me on my way home from walking downtown to use a gift card a friend had given me for my birthday a few months earlier. He asked me, "Do you have money for a fellow Christian brother who is starving to get some food?" Since I had forgotten how just hours earlier when I had walked downtown I had seen a truck providing a free meal for the hungry, and how I thought I would be smart and not give him cash, I offered to go to a store with him to buy him some food with the little cash that I had. In the meantime I just kept walking, so he started asking me, "How much money is a little money?' I stupidly told him five dollars. Then he kept begging me just to give him the five dollars, which I refused to do. So then he said he had a *piece* (a gun), no doubt in order to try to scare me into just giving him the five dollars. I decided I would do nothing until he actually brought the gun out, which I hoped was unlikely, as we were walking down a street past people, some lounging in front of their apartment complexes and others who were working on their cars all of whom seemed to be ignoring me even though I was talking much louder and more than I usually do as I tried to make sure they could hear me and would be able to tell I was being harassed. Minutes later as we continued to walk I felt something bump my thigh and feared he had finally brought out his gun. When I looked down, I saw that instead, he was just digging in my coat pocket hoping to find my money, and that it was not a gun. So I got angry and twisted away from him. Initially I was hoping to just get home to get away from the guy, but then when I realized that would let him know where I lived, I decided I would go to CGCC's main office, which was about the same distance from where I was walking to where I lived. As I twisted around, his hand came out of my pocket and I ran to the other side of the street about a block from CGCC. He of course followed me and came upon me on the other side. I did not think much of it until I felt him digging in my coat pocket on that side too. Oh, did that make me angry and I spun away again, but he flaunted the fact that he now had my keys and my ID that showed I worked at the hospital. I was so angry that I turned back on him and fought him for my keys, as I did not want to feel like I would again need to change locks in order to feel secure. As I fought him for my keys, I also stomped on his foot. Fortunately, I got my keys back but was okay not having my ID back, since I knew it would not give him access to anything. After all, he was a black male and I was a white female. All the while, he kept taunting me about having my ID still, but I didn't care. The ID had my picture on it, not his, and it did not have the address of where I lived so what did I care if he had it. The keys, though, were the ones protecting remaining material possessions the Lord had blessed me with, so I was willing to fight for them.

After getting the keys back, I arrived at CGCC's door and rang their buzzer. When the thief saw me ring the buzzer, he took off running, throwing away my ID which I then grabbed up. Needless to say, I was quite shaken about the event and it took me about half an hour to stop shaking after that, but at least I was not hurt physically and my things were not in danger of being stolen. Also thankfully there was a friend of a roommate there who offered to drive me home after she finished using the computers CGCC had available for use.

However, another event happened soon after that which left me shaken again. This time it was a skinny, young black woman who knocked on the door looking for my roommate. She begged to be able to at least come in and sit down as she said she was shaken up about having just been jumped by a guy. Once she got inside, she continued her story and expanded it with how she could really use some cash, as she needed to get something to eat. As she expressed her feelings of being victimized, my feelings of victimization over the past months and now by her actions accelerated, so I asked her to leave. As she started to make me feel like I was being cruel to her during her supposed time of being victimized, I gave her a few dollars on the condition that she would leave. She did, but she made me feel like I could not even trust the friends of my roommate. These events in Geranium City destroyed any desire at that time to truly trust or help people throughout Geranium City other than to continue helping the Inner-City Take Back Program and Rob's teen program.

ABBY'S SECOND CANCER SCARE & MY ACCIDENT, CAUSING MORE LIFE CHANGES

Sometime between the end of February and the beginning of April, we interns at Geranium City Medical Center learned that from April 18-22 there was a laboratory science conference, which the intern supervisor, Yolanda Y, said was mandatory for us to attend. Yolanda was an older white haired woman who used a cane to get around and I remember as wearing skirts and a sweater every day. She looked a bit intimidating as she didn't smile much but once I got to know her I found her quite friendly. As Yolanda stressed multiple times the importance of going to the conference, I fully intended to go, even though I was a bit stressed over the thought of how much it might cost. Not all the other interns intended on going to the mandatory conference though.

Not long after I learned about the mandatory conference, however, Abby called to tell me how the doctors had diagnosed a lump she found as being breast cancer. When I learned this, I went online and researched breast cancer a bit and then emailed my Buttercup City, Catalpa City, Rose City, Trillium City, and Cherry Blossom City friends to ask for prayers for Abby. On a follow-up appointment, the doctor at Rose City Clinic informed Abby that it was inflammatory breast cancer. When I researched inflammatory breast cancer I found that the odds of a 95 percent survival rate for those diagnosed with breast cancer went down to a 33 percent survival rate for those diagnosed with inflammatory breast cancer. Needless to say, this really got me scared, as I feared I was losing my best friend and I sent out another email informing my friends of the latest news on Abby. Then as I would swing by Yolonda's office often just to talk with her, I shared with her about Abby. Yolanda recommended I go visit Abby instead of going to the conference. Yolanda shared how she had lost a nephew to pancreatic cancer, a cancer so bad that most people who contract it die in less than a year of the diagnosis so she stressed the importance of being with a loved one as much as possible who has been diagnosed with cancer.

So on April 17, 2009, for just the second time during my internship, I did not stay in the laboratory area for the entire shift of 8:00 to 5:00 p.m. like the interns were told they were supposed to. Instead, I left as soon as the laboratory instructor told me she was done instructing me for the day so I could leave the instruction area. So I went home and grabbed all my things that I had packed and planned to take with me as I left Geranium City to go see Abby. As I was leaving Geranium City, Abby was going in for a second opinion at Inspired Medical in Snapdragon City.

As back in December, I had helped CGCC with an outreach project to help families be able to have a special Christmas as the parents were allowed to choose between clothes, shoes, games, etc. to select three items per child. After the event there were still close to a hundred shoes left over so I asked if I could go through the shoes and select ones that I knew the Cherry Blossom Wesleyan Church could use for an outreach they had. The Cherry Blossom Wesleyan Church's outreach was to a church in a South American country where they brought practical walking shoes without heels so that the South American country people could have their first pair of shoes which would not be likely to cause injury which heeled shoes probably would have in the rough terrain found in the South American country. I received permission to take some leftover shoes from the CGCC program, so as I set out to visit Abby I decided I would go by taking the route through Cherry Blossom City where I hoped to see friends and I planned to spend the night there. I had arranged it with my friend Rosemary X to stay overnight with her and her husband, Neal, and asked her to spread the word I was coming so that I could perhaps see my friends while I was in Cherry Blossom City for the visit.

As I finished packing and was about to set out, Asher C, who was staying on the other side of the duplex, asked me for a ride to his friend's place so he could pick up his bike which was his mode of transportation. Asher was a black, outgoing, carefree guy who struggled to keep a job but would usually have a big grin on his face and could be heard singing or found using the computer on my half of the duplex. He thought he sang pretty well but it always sounded off-key to me though I've been told how the guitar I received from my family has been off-key but I never was able to detect that. Since Asher's friend lived on my way to the highway going through Cherry Blossom City down to Geranium City, which I was going to take to Cherry Blossom City, I said that would be fine. I remember feeling a bit weird having another person – especially a guy – in my car as I rarely drove with anyone. So as I remembered how my drivers instructor had always encouraged Abby and me to use traffic lights rather than driving straight across or making a left hand turn onto a busy road, plus I hated how one could sit for many minutes for an opportunity to turn left onto Waxwings, a seven-lane road, I drove a block north to the intersection which had a traffic light. As I drove up to the traffic light it was red and a pedestrian was crossing the street all the while watching me as if to make sure I was going to stop for him. I stopped, and then I believe I watched him finish crossing and then watched the traffic as it came and went in front of me. I think it was only after the traffic had stopped crossing the intersection that prompted me to I look back at the light and saw that it was green, so I started across the intersection.

About halfway across, I do not know if it was a blaring horn or something else that caused me to turn my head toward the left in time to catch a flash of white out of the corner of my eye. I believe I internally started to pray, or at least I am sure my spirit did, as I knew I would not make it through the intersection. Then there were the awful sounds of grinding metal, shattering glass, and squealing tires as my car spun upon impact. These noises plus blaring horns are prone to make me cringe still to this day. Up until that time I had been very afraid that I was losing my sister, but when I realized I was going to be in an accident God helped me to realize how I had to be grateful that with cancer a person at least usually had some time to prepare for the death of a loved one, but that an accident could mean instant death. Between the start of the noise until suddenly I was aware of someone screaming like someone was dead or dying, I am not sure what all happened. Later I learned that the other car had run the red light in the left turn lane on a seven-lane road because they had a baby who was having a seizure. By the time the police arrived, the baby and an adult passenger from the car that hit me had found another car to take them to the hospital. Meanwhile, a passerby came over to let me know that he had called the police, so I began calling Abby, Ma, and Rosemary and told them or left a message telling them, "I won't be able to make it today. I just had a car accident. I'm fine, just have bruised my ribs and lower back. I'll have to take the Interstate Bus System bus now, as I'm sure my car is totaled."

My car, I figured, had to be totaled, as just the internal damages that I could see when I decided to assess the damage from the inside looked bad. The damages were, of course, broken windows on the entire left side, a dashboard reduced to about half its normal size, and a driver's seat that now was angled toward the steering wheel, from which I was not able to remove my keys from the ignition. Just those damages alone I was sure would cost more than I could afford, especially since I had not been smart enough to get comprehensive insurance on the car, which would have covered the majority of expenses due to a collision.

Then as I saw everyone else was outside the cars, I slid myself to the passenger seat to get out the passenger side and tried to stand, but the pain that shot up my back was so severe that I immediately had to sit back down again. So then I started picking up a few things that I saw had flown out my car upon impact during the accident and were on the road within my reach where I was sitting in my car which included pictures and my Bible. It still hurt to try to reach those things, but nowhere near like it hurt when I tried to stand and as I really did not want to lose the items, I picked them up despite the pain. Meanwhile, I continued calling people. Abby then called me back and told me how the doctor said her cancer was in stage III. As I had only been able to leave a message for both her and Ma, I told her how I was waiting for the police to arrive as I had just been in an accident. I told her that I was okay other than bruised ribs and lower back. I also told her I still was going to try to get to Rose City but that I was sure I would have to take the Interstate Bus System now since my car was totaled. It was while I was talking to Abby that I finally saw a police officer walk past my car's driver side on his way to the other car, so I told Abby that I needed to go so that I would be able to talk with the officer when he would come to my car. So we told each other to take care and how much we loved each other before we hung up. Then as I waited for the police to come over to talk to me the adrenaline started to wear off so that "my bruises" started to ache much worse.

When the police officer finally came over several minutes later to where I sat after talking with the people in the other car to get my perspective on the accident he asked me if I had been the driver of my car. I said I was so he asked me for my license and insurance papers. As I tried to comply with his request, I realized just how awful my ribs hurt if I moved my left arm even a little bit. Consequently, I chose to dig my license out of my coat's left pocket with my right hand, and my back hurt like crazy when I reached for the glove box to get my insurance papers. The policeman at that point radioed for an ambulance. Then while we waited for the ambulance, he asked me to tell him how the accident happened.

When the EMTs arrived, they told me not to move as they put a collar on me. Then very carefully they transferred me out of my car onto a stretcher and then into the ambulance. They asked me if I had a preference between Geranium City Medical Center or Medical Facility of Renown City Member and I said Geranium City Medical Center. Then they asked if my passenger felt the need to go to the hospital and Asher said yes, so that ambulance ended up taking me and Asher to the hospital. (I learned the next day when Autumn C visited me that Asher had whiplash from the accident and had been kept overnight for observation.) The paramedic who I thought looked rather fatherly apologized repeatedly on the drive to the hospital for how the ambulance bumped along the bumpy road as each bump caused pain to shoot through my body stemming from my back and ribs. On the drive to the hospital he also asked me to share with him the details of the accident.

Recently I listened to an author share about how while cutting down a tree, which had another tree resting quite heavily upon it, had the uncut tree unexpectedly fall. As it fell, the tree swung so that it severed off his leg. The author shared how from his accident he learned that a technique of emergency personnel after an accident is to continually ask the patient what happened at the time of the accident if the emergency personnel fear the patient is headed into shock as they use the patient's retelling of the trauma to keep the patient conscious and out of shock.

In the emergency room, the doctors again asked me to share with them the details of the accident as they prodded up and down my spine asking me to tell them where it hurt. It was as they cut off my shirt to be able to do a thorough exam that I started to shake uncontrollably. They also checked for internal bleeding via the rectum. Every time the doctors sensed I was experiencing discomfort they would apologize. Finally, they sent me off to get X-rays and a CT scan, after asking if there was any chance I was pregnant. I assured them there was not. From these tests, the doctors determined I had a couple fractured ribs and that my pelvis was fractured in a couple spots. The one spot being where nerves from the back entered the pelvis. While the doctors determined that my pelvis was fractured they shared how the fractures where stable meaning I would not have to undergo surgery but would only need to learn how to use a walker to get around. Ultimately, my having a fractured pelvis meant that I could not walk upright or without assistance, and that both of my feet had to do the same thing at the same time to prevent pain from shooting up my back. Also my left arm was almost useless unless I wanted to aggravate my ribs in moving it. So I had only one good limb, or two if you count my neck. Later when a boss I had in 2010 ended up breaking a cervical spinal bone when his bike got clipped by a disk, a piece of farm equipment, I realized how thankful I was that at the time of my accident I still had full range of motion with my neck.

At one point that first night when the doctor came by to check on me, I asked about the possibility of leaving, as I wanted to go to Rose City to visit my sister who had cancer. He said if I could prove that I could walk to the bathroom and back without assistance, I could leave. Of course, with my injuries I had not been able to walk without someone walking beside me that I could lean heavily upon. Once they got me back to the gurney, I lay as quietly as I could so as not to wake the sleeping giants of pain in my lower back and ribs. When the doctor asked me to rate my pain on a scale of one to ten with ten being unbearable, I had rated it as a seven, since I figured with a ten I would probably still be in severe pain despite lying still, but when I laid still my pain was at least bearable. Then sometime later that evening the emergency crew brought another woman in on a gurney, parked her beside me and asked her to rate her pain from one to ten. She said twenty and after the doctors left, she told me how she had fallen down some stairs a couple weeks ago and that the pain was still unbearable.

Later on when a nurse came by, I asked if I could make a phone call, as I wanted to let my friends in Geranium City know that I had not made it out of Geranium City. She wheeled the gurney over to a telephone where I punched in Martie my friend across the back alley's number, the only phone number of my Geranium City friends that I had memorized. When Martie answered the phone I told her how Asher and I had been in an accident and asked her to let my roommates know. Eventually that night the nursing crew transferred me from the emergency room gurney to a hospital room and an enormous bed. At least it felt enormous as its bed rails were at arm's length apart and I constantly seemed to sink too far down on the bed causing the nurses to always insist that I maneuver myself back up the bed. With the rails so far apart and having three limbs which exacerbated my pain tremendously with any movement, I always hated it when the nurses would tell me to scoot back up the bed.

That first night in the hospital, my roommate, Autumn came to see me. Once she learned that I had not eaten anything since before noon and it was close to nine at night, she went to get me something to eat. I think the nurses must have caught her after she bought it and told her that I was not allowed to eat anything that day and only liquids the next day as they were ruling out internal injuries. So the nurses offered to put the food Autumn brought me in a fridge. Autumn also came back the next day bringing me my Bible and a book to read upon my request the night before, as I preferred to read than watch the TV the hospital offered. That first night in the hospital it seems I remember waking up every hour on the hour and sleeping rather restlessly due to the fact that I usually start to wake as light increases and when I hear noises both of which I contended with that night as the hallway lights poured into my room keeping my room pretty well-lit and as I'd hear the nursing staff make their rounds on an hourly basis.

The day after my accident, when I again asked about getting out of the hospital, I was told that I could leave if I was able to use a walker to make it upstairs. I had told them that the duplex where I lived had at least three steps to get into the house. When they had me walk to the doorway and back that day with the walker, my friend Sheila Y, who had come to visit and was training to be a nurse, said it was awful watching me walk that short distance as it looked like it caused me such awful pain. As I was not able to do all they required of me that day, they had me spend another night in the hospital. During the second day, Doug R, the owner of the duplex who lived next door and was in his final year of residency for surgical medicine, surprised me with a visit between his rounds. That second night in the hospital I did not wake up as many times as the first night but still woke up quite a few times during the night.

On the second day after my accident, the doctor finally signed for my release after the therapist had me use my walker to walk about a dozen feet or two over to a stairwell and then go up and back down a few stairs with the walker. So I called Martie and let her know I was being released and she notified our friend Nessa I, who came to bring me home. Nessa was a tall skinny black lady who usually had a smile. As she drove me home, Nessa felt so awful and kept apologizing as I grimaced from the pain the entire ride home as I felt every single bump and once I got home as I ended up having to lean heavily on the wall on the side of the stairs leading into the duplex as I made my way up the stairs. Once I got into the duplex, I collapsed into the recliner and stayed there until that night other than the trips up the stairs to go to the bathroom.

Then that first night back at the duplex I tried to sleep in the bed in the spare bedroom upstairs, since my room was down in the basement with rail-less stairs going down to it, and the spare bedroom was upstairs with stairs that did have rails. Plus the spare bedroom was just down the hall from the bathroom. Autumn offered to help me during the night if I needed her. Since I knew she had to work the next night I determined that I would let her sleep through even though I constantly struggled that night to find a comfortable position to sleep in. I kept finding that either the pillows were too high, not high enough, or too far down my back instead of beneath my head, and then the bed did not have rails to help me reposition myself or help me to get up out of the bed either. Also it did not help that I had my blankets covering my feet like I always do when I sleep. That night though I realized how the weight of the blankets hindered the ability of my feet from moving together, a must for my pelvis.

So the next day I told Autumn how I thought I would try sleeping in the recliner, as the bed was so difficult to get comfortable in. So for the next month and a half I moved to sleeping in the recliner every night. For the first three weeks after my accident I had to use a walker anytime I wanted to get around. During that same period of time I had to sit while showering or to change clothes. Socks were impossible so I quit wearing them for a while. Plus I made it so that my shoes could just be slipped into real easily. Sheila offered to come over and help me that first week too. She helped me by bringing in an outdoor plastic lawn chair which I could use to sit on to shower and then encouraged me to make it up the stairs without the walker and then down the narrow hallway to the bathroom by leaning on the walls so that I would not have to have someone always bring my walker up for me.

Before sending me home the doctors had also provided me with prescriptions for Vicodin and an 800-mg Ibuprofen, which I took at the minimum time limits to try to control the pain and so that my ability to try to keep my sleep from going downhill. Then as both labels said that there were to be no refills and as I had not been able to schedule a visit with an orthopedic doctor for another three weeks, when I realized I would not make it the three weeks with what I had, I started to make myself go longer and longer without the painkillers and would alternate with which one I would take. As the painkillers did not completely make the pain go away and as I would take the medicine every 4 to 6 hours, I slept in spurts. Occasionally I was fortunate enough to sleep rather soundly, but always when morning came, I was still quite exhausted and could barely stay awake when I tried studying for my internship and the exam which would follow. While sleeping in the recliner, every morning I would hear the robins start singing and then hear Doug as he would wake up and start getting ready for work at 5:00 a.m. Then I would doze off again until Wendy and Autumn awoke at 7:00 a.m.

The day after I got home from the hospital, I had a list of things I needed to do. First I emailed Yolanda, the intern supervisor, to let her know I had been in an accident. She let me know that I should take whatever time I needed to get to feeling better. She did say I would have to quit my internship during that time though. So I quit my internship after I was reassured and had it in writing that I would be hired back when the doctor said I could go back to work. Next I asked my friend Sheila if she would go get my things from my car which was impounded. When she went to do so, she learned that either she needed a notarized letter giving her permission to get my things or I had to be with her when she got my things. As I was going down the stairs to get in Sheila's car, Dori P from church, who worked at CGCC, saw me with my walker so she stopped to ask me what happened. I told her about my accident and how I needed to go with Sheila to get my car as I did not know where I would get a notarized letter. Dori said that Sue P, who ran CGCC, was a lawyer who could notarize a letter for me. After Dori brought us the letter notarized by Sue, Sheila left and was able to get my things. She just left the items there which had been broken too badly during the accident. Sheila also took a picture with her phone of the outside of my car, paid the impound fee, and sold my car to the impound for me.

Even though this was the most physically painful experience of my life, I have to say I felt God's love from the people he surrounded me with: from the doctors to Kurt H, a friend who brought me a laptop his boss was going to have him sell on the Internet but agreed to let me have, to Natasha Y. She was one of my internship teachers who befriended me when my car had been stolen by giving me rides from home to the hospital and back home again. Then when Natasha heard about my accident, she held a fundraiser to buy me a roundtrip plane ticket to visit Abby. To raise the money, Natasha had shared in an email sent to all the laboratory personnel about my thefts, my accident, and about how if I was going to visit Abby who was sick with cancer I would have to fly, as traveling by car or bus were out of the question because the pain would be unbearable. So people throughout the lab sent her money for me. Some even sent money who did not know me but who wanted to help anyway. Natasha then had a coworker, Raina I, buy me the roundtrip plane ticket as Natasha wasn't comfortable buying things on the internet while Raina was. So Raina bought me the tickets which allowed me to fly to Snapdragon City where Ma picked me up from the airport and then drove me over to Abby's so I could spend a week with Abby.

When I came back from my week visiting Abby and the rest of the family, I resumed my internship and Natasha and Raina alternated on giving me rides to and from the laboratory. When Raina drove, she would share how she had recently live-trapped a mama cat and brought her and her kittens into the house. Raina had been afraid for the cat and kittens as she said she lived on a street that had enough traffic on it that she didn't want any of the kittens or their mom getting hit by a car. Then Raina would keep me entertained by sharing with me the kittens' antics. As my internship drew to a close, Raina offered me a kitten for a graduation present and I couldn't say no. That is how I got Isaac, my playful, all-white kitten who made more noise than I realized was possible for a cat. Raina gave me Isaac on my final day at the internship. Since Ma and Uncle Larry weren't coming till the following day and Doug was allergic to cats, I had asked my friend, Nicole X, my friend whom I'd made through CGCC's teen program if she would keep him overnight for me. She had gladly done so and she was the one who decided on the name of Isaac for me.

Isaac was quite a character as he loves to chew on hard plastic items like balls one find in ball pits, keytags, charge cords etc and paper, which was especially annoying when he did so before my alarm would ring in the morning. Additional things he likes to do which are cute but sometimes annoying is that he loves to lick faucets in order to get them to drip water, fish all the water out of his water bowls, and crawl up on books or paperwork that I am working on, and just plain laying on things that are on tables and such causing them to move and eventually fall off the table. As many told me that I should spray him when he was naughty, I would try to do so but Isaac loved licking the water back off himself so it seemed he started to purposely try to get me to spray him. When I realized that my attempts to spray Isaac seemed to be a regarded as a reward and was starting to create streaks on my walls where I had missed him and had gotten the wall instead, I discontinued trying to spray him. The things I have found most successful actually has been the peeling of an orange, opening up a lotion bottle, or just plain ignoring him are the best ways to discourage him from doing things.

So by the time my internship ended, all I wanted was to be out of Geranium City with its traffic, crime, and swamped law enforcement and city officials. I did not exactly want to leave the friends and co-workers I made there who had shown me such love, especially after my accident, but the distance from Abby – my sister and best friend – and her baby was so far, and there was no way I was going to be able to continue working in Geranium City without having to deal with the traffic on a daily basis. So I began searching for a job somewhere, anywhere in the state I grew up in so that I could be within two to four hours from Abby and her daughter Susannah, plus be closer to the rest of my family. While I searched, I also applied to the hospital at Cherry Blossom City, and I would have accepted a job there if offered it, as I knew I had friends there already and I enjoyed living there.in Cherry Blossom City.

Recently I found a letter which I had written and taken to the emergency room doctors and asked to have delivered to the EMTs who had helped me the day of my accident, along with a picture of my car. It reads:

Praise the Lord! Nobody was seriously hurt! Lord, be with the baby and its mom through this time, as I cannot imagine how rough the accident was on them, especially as the baby already was having problems. Things which have been helping me through trials (since November: two thefts, robbery attempt, sister with cancer, and accident): Psalm 70:4b which says, "And let those who love your salvation say continually, 'Let God be magnified!'" As I love my salvation, I pray that I will continually magnify God even to people who I do not know, as normally that is not my personality. I pray the Lord finds me faithful as Job but I truly hope it is God's will that this be the end of the re-mining of my faith for a long stretch of time. To my God and Savior, Jesus Christ, be all the glory, honor and praise, Renata Rivka (Bethel Believers Church—Corner Waxwings/Gnatcatchers).

THE MEDICAL FACILITY OF COMBINED PRACTICES

In August 2009, Uncle Larry and Ma came with a U-Haul and picked up my things and me from Geranium City and tried to tell me that was their graduation present for me which I protested to Abby about so they ended up giving me another graduation gift. After Ma and Uncle Larry had gotten everything moved into the U-Haul they had brought to haul my things, Martie came over to say goodbye, bringing her son, barely before I left. I ended up leaving Geranium City with quite a few more things than I had come with as Wendy was headed to do missions in Africa and Autumn was moving back to Canada where her family lived, so they had offered me several bookshelves, the recliner I'd slept in, some clear, floral dishes, some music, movies and a few other things they didn't want that I opted to take with me. Ma and Uncle Larry dropped me and a few of my things off at Abby's where I again lived while I looked for a job. The things they didn't leave off at Abby's they took and stored at the farm. The next two months I continued applying to almost all Medical Technologist (MT) positions I found available within the state I grew up in. While I waited to get accepted at a job, I studied really hard for the MT certification exam, played with Susannah and Isaac, and helped Abby. As Nathan and Abby were concerned that Isaac might suffocate Susannah, the only time I was allowed to let him out of the dog crate they had me enclose him in was when I was awake and was watching him. So while I looked for a job,

I asked my friends that I had made in Rose City, Catalpa City, Cherry Blossom City, Trillium City, and Geranium City to again join me in praying God would lead me to a job in the city he wanted me in, where I could have the best impact for him, and where I could grow the most. In October of 2009, I got hired for a job in a brand-new clinic facility in Rosemary City called the Medical Facility of Combined Practices.

When I learned that I got hired in Rosemary City I started looking online for an apartment within walking distance of the clinic and I found a couple. Ma then drove me over to Rosemary City to look at the two apartments and after looking at them both I ended up choosing the one that looked less like a hotel with halls of doors leading to the apartment which only source of outdoor lighting came when one was inside the apartment. The apartment I chose came with free cable but heat, water and utilities one had to pay for themselves. This apartment complex had three buildings with three stories and eleven apartments per building and was on Lark Sparrow Lane. Its parking lot was lined with garages. The apartment building I lived in had a front and back entrance both of which contained windows letting in natural lighting. My apartment was down a flight of stairs which had doors at both end of the hall enclosing where the three apartment and laundry room doors were located. I was grateful for this the one time when Isaac decided to escape my apartment as I chased him up and down the hallway a few times before I was able to get him to go back into my apartment. When you entered from the front of the building my apartment was the second door on the right. When you entered you were standing in the dining area and straight ahead was the kitchen, off to the left was a nice sized living room and behind it was the two bedrooms and the bathroom. On that visit, I signed the paperwork and paid the deposit for the apartment. Then ten days before I was to start my new job, when I was informed that I was approved for the apartment, Ma took me and my things that I had at Abby's over to my new apartment and left us off there. The rest of my things didn't come over till a week later when Uncle Larry brought them. So that first week I was again living minimally without furniture with just a television, Isaac, the computer Kurt H gave me and some changes of clothes and books. By the time

Uncle Larry, along with Ma and Abby, brought my things to my new apartment I realized I really needed some chairs as I hadn't taken into account how hard not having a chair to sit on would be for my back. As I only had one chair even after Uncle Larry brought over my furniture, I asked Uncle Larry if we could go shopping for chairs. So we looked up where to find second hand stores and then went to Second-hand store. After trying a number of them out for comfort, I settled on some yellow, padded chairs which allowed me to sit properly: feet flat on the ground, thigh parallel to ground and back flat against its back. The chairs continue to provide comfort better than couches, recliners and similar types of furniture for my back even if in every other way the other types of furniture seem more appealing. While I lived in Rosemary City though, I hadn't come to that realization yet, so I often chose to watch television in the recliner I brought from Geranium City or a swivel chair Ma found on a curb and brought over for me. Though as Isaac chose the swivel chair most of the time and it collected fur, it usually was filled with fur unless I took the time to clean it. Isaac also really loved my TV as he was quick to crawl on top of it and try batting at the screen where he saw things moving.

Three days after my family brought me my things and helped me shop for some chairs, I started working at the Medical Facility of Combined Practices four days a week for eight hours walking to and from work each day. Then several of my coworkers, who learned I was walking to and from work each day, started offering to pick me up and drive me home. I accepted the rides home as after eight hours of working and being on my feet or using the tall laboratory stools, my back and left knee would be hurting pretty badly. In the mornings I usually would choose to walk, as I did not want it to be anybody's fault if I was late to work. The rides with my coworkers gave me a chance to get to know some of them better.

As I was starting at the Medical Facility of Combined Practices, my co-worker Carol P was assigned to train me in the hematology and urinalysis part of the lab work which included a machine apiece and microscopic work She was pretty thorough and worked with me most of the week to make sure I was comfortable with what I was doing which I definitely was a lot more comfortable after that week than I was at the beginning. Meanwhile Ulyssa S was assigned to train me in the chemistry part with its two different machines, both of which the lab had two of. Ulyssa taught me the basics in two days and then left me on my own. Finally, Bertha H was assigned to train me on the coagulation and PSA machines. She also taught me the basics and then left me on my own. So overall I feel like Carol was quite thorough in her training but Ulyssa and Bertha not as thorough. Then after about two weeks into the job, Regan F, the laboratory's cell lead, told me, "If you need more training in any area let us know." As I was not very assertive, I never told anyone she told me that and I had not asked her how I would know there was an area I needed more training in until I was faced with something I didn't know.

So I said I would. However, the goal was constantly stressed that everybody was to get the specimens, which came to the laboratory tested in less than five minutes: from being sent through the tube system, accepted as having arrived in the laboratory, and then stuck in a machine for the test(s) to be run. Between that goal and the expectation that the laboratory staff was not to wander from their position other than during breaks, I have to admit there were a few times I had questions and yet I did not wander over to another area in the laboratory to get answers to my questions, which probably played a part in my not doing as well as I could have in the laboratory.

After a few months, I started to be told by Regan and then by Sheila, the newly hired laboratory supervisor that "People in the lab are concerned about the mistakes you are making. You need to be able to do your job without mistakes or start looking for a new job." One of the mistakes was of my failing to catch caller's names which I had improved as I immediately wrote down the callers names whenever I'd answer the phone, plus the question they were posing to me, which as I had just started working in the lab I rarely knew what was being asked so I would be handing off the phone to one of my coworkers, often Regan. Each of the mistakes I had made only a few times and had already corrected before either of them had talked with me about the mistakes. Each of the complaints made against me I could trace back to one person every time. Nevertheless, because Sheila told me "people in the lab were concerned," it made me concerned that others were also complaining about me without talking to me directly as I would overhear them complain about some of the other laboratory personnel whenever those people weren't in the laboratory. Therefore, I became paranoid and would usually try to figure out the answers to my questions without asking others, except for Carol P and Clint C who seemed to care that I feel comfortable asking them any question I had and would assure me that everyone makes mistakes especially at the beginning.

When I was told maybe I should look for another job, I started to apply for other jobs, but I ended up losing my job first after just six months. It was a learning experience for me. Losing the Rosemary City job was due to many additional contributing factors. I failed to be assertive and confident with my co-workers. I was in a city where I did not know anyone. I was learning a new job. I was the only medical technologist in that laboratory without prior experience. I had just recently moved there. I was still in considerable pain when standing, when sitting on the laboratory's bar-stool-like chairs, and when bending or twisting. Additionally, within the first week of working at the laboratory, Ma had called me to inform me that Uncle Larry had been struck by a semi-truck and that the jaws of life had to be used to pry his foot out of the wreckage. (He was not able to walk for six months after the accident as the doctors worked on rebuilding his foot, and they had to rebuild his nose too.) Then it was not until January 2010 that the doctors had finished treating Abby for the cancer. By January 2010, I was being told how I had to do better at work because "people were concerned" about my ability to work there. As I was struggling with this, God had me read in Romans how *"Not only so, but we also glory in our sufferings, because we know that suffering produces perseverance; perseverance, character; and character, hope."* (Romans 5:3-4)

After I ended up being forced to quit my job at the Medical Facility of Combined Practices, I determined that if I was ever made to feel like I was going to be micromanaged for making mistakes or felt like I couldn't trust my coworkers to be honest with me when they had problems with my work that I would immediately start to look for another job as that environment turned the job toxic way too quickly for me. Also, it made me determine that I would need to do a better job being assertive when unfair requests were made of me. Plus, I determined to remind people when I would hear them talk poorly about other people when the others weren't around how it makes me wonder if these people would tell me if they have a complaint about me and if that is how I feel then probably other coworkers probably also feel that way. Unfortunately, the last one I was never very assertive about following up on but when my latest job made me wonder if I was going to start getting written up whenever I would make a mistake, I did talk with my manager about how from past experience I would not stay in a job that made me feel that way. At that time my manager told me how he thought I was a good employee and how he did not want me or any of my coworkers to feel like he was trying to micromanage them so that I should let him know if any of us thought we were being micromanaged.

Before I was told that I was going to have to leave or be fired from the Medical Facility of Combined Practices, I decided I wanted to schedule an appointment with one of the doctors for my back pain. The Medical Facility of Combined Practices was a building which had merged multiple medical clinics (internal medicine, family practice, among others). The laboratory consisted of personnel from both internal medicine and family practice. The three people I knew from family practice I got along better with than the two I knew from internal medicine, so I chose to call the office of family practice to meet with one of their doctors. When I called them, the receptionist asked which doctor I wanted to see. I of course had no idea, so she shared some about what the different doctors specialized in. When she mentioned how Dr. Victor Y specialized in back injuries I chose him. During my appointment with him, and upon learning how my younger sister Abby was battling breast cancer, Dr. Victor recommended I get a mammogram. I do not remember if it was him, a nurse, or the receptionist who answered when I called to set up the mammogram who told me I should make sure I stated the reason for going for a mammogram was due to a younger sister being diagnosed with breast cancer. Otherwise, since I was still in my thirties and insurance programs do not cover mammograms for people under the age of forty, insurance companies would consider a mammogram as an unnecessary test and would not pay for the test. If the reason for the test did not get put down, the insurance would make me pay for the mammogram and the medical staff did not want me to get stuck paying for the mammogram. Dr. Victor then recommended I go see Dr. Neva HY after I had gotten my mammogram since she was a breast specialist. A few months later I had gone back to see Dr. Victor for my knee when my back felt like it was improving after going to a chiropractor several months, but my knee wasn't. Dr. Victor then scheduled me to see a physical therapist instead of telling me it was probably just stemming from my back injury like several doctors I had seen prior to him had told me.

By the time I saw Dr. Victor, I had been told one way or another, quit or be fired, it was my last day at the laboratory at the Medical Facility of Combined Practices. When I learned that my insurance was good through the end of the month, I mentioned it to the nurse. She then pulled strings so I could get the mammogram and visit in to Dr. Neva before the end of the month.

The first time I went to see Dr. Neva I was so nervous just because I was in the same building where I had just been released from my job. Dr. Neva and her assistant, Rebekkah, were able to put me at ease. I ended up going to see them multiple times in the following months, and they helped me know whom I could ask in the Fox Cities area for assistance to cover follow-up mammograms and how to do a self-breast exam. Then when a follow-up mammogram showed some change in some calcifications, they said Western Cities Medical had a program for the uninsured and low income by which they might be able to help cover the biopsies of the calcifications and other follow-up care which might be needed afterwards. I applied for this assistance and got it, but not before the date scheduled for the biopsy.

UNEMPLOYED ATTEMPT TO WRITE STORY

As Renata sat waiting for the doctor or her receptionist to return that Friday afternoon, she started to reflect on her life. Here she was at 31, still single, just lost her job which she had only had for six months and waiting to find out what the doctor wanted to do to make sure the calcifications found on her mammogram were not cancer.

The concern about cancer at such a young age stemmed from her younger sister, Abby having been diagnosed with inflammatory breast cancer a bit over a year ago. Thankfully with aggressive treatments the cancer which had been at stage three was now gone so that Abby was currently in remission. Renata knows that she is extremely grateful for this fact as Abby still is her best friend as Renata has in the past five years found herself living in five towns. This is why Renata is feeling so down about having lost her job. Here she had just six months earlier gotten a job in the field which she had just gotten her degree in and taken the test to become certified in. Yes she had managed to get all A's and B's with only one C, did a year's internship and had passed her certification exam with over 100 points to spare failing her first job as a Medical Technologist. Heartbroken Renata wonders again what went wrong and why.

As she thinks, Renata concedes to herself how for some reason she really struggles with communicating sometimes especially with certain people or over things which she does not feel overly passionate about.

Say for example there are times when she sees food on the other end of the table which looks wonderful but she does not know the people between her and the dish so she decides to content herself with what she can reach and is willing to wait for the other dish. After all, others probably will also want that dish and then she can also help herself to some of it, too.

What causes her to prefer waiting rather than asking for the dish Renata wonders? Upon reflecting upon the question Renata feels there may be several reasons. One she feels that to speak up would interrupt thoughts or conversations of others. Two, Renata knows that when she speaks without being called upon it causes people to refocus their attention on her and overall Renata is okay not being the center of attention (except maybe when she is trying to help a favorite non-profit like the Organization Releasing Children from Poverty in Jesus' Name). Though, Renata admits to herself she really is fine being the center of attention in really small groups where she knows the majority of the people or when it is one on one. In fact, Renata admits that in the situations she sometimes doesn't even try to get the attention off herself by asking questions of the other person or people.

But wait Renata chides herself, I am getting sidetracked. I want to figure out why I am struggling with speaking out. Upon further reflection, Renata realizes how as a child that was how most conversations occurred: individually or with maybe four people max. Her childhood really was different, Renata realizes. Her ma, Nora, had been divorced from her husband, Arthur, shortly after their 10th anniversary as she discovered he was sexually abusing Renata's older sisters, Dora and Sandy. Then Ma had ended up living again with her mother, Grandma Nancy, and older brother, Uncle Larry. At the time of her divorce and for quite a while afterward Ma needed Grandma Nancy and Uncle Larry's help as she had four daughters under the age of eight. The way Renata sees it though, Grandma Nancy and Uncle Larry then were able to keep Ma mostly under their power of persuasion. After all they gave Ma and her daughters free food and lodging for the next twenty some years. So what if Ma feels like they kept her from feeling like she could do anything right. That was just Ma's interpretation of their comments.

It was Ma's fault she went against Grandma Nancy and her husband, Robert's wishes and married Arthur whom they knew was not who he claimed to be. So what if all her life Ma never could please Grandma Nancy prompting Ma to want to find someone who loved her how she wanted her mom to love her and so when Arthur made her all these promises she chose to believe him as she saw it was a chance to escape Grandma Nancy's continual disapproval.

Many years after her divorce Ma had commented to Renata and Abby how she believed she had married Arthur as a way to get away from Grandma Nancy. (A fact which Renata and Abby had already discussed amongst themselves. In fact Renata also wonders if her uncle, Larry had not initially moved from his hometown in the state where Ma grew up to Lilac City—where he bought a farm from some brothers who he had worked with for several years—in an attempt to himself get away from Grandma Nancy.) It really was sad, Renata thinks, how this family which really struggled while growing up had after several years of separation had ended up being together again. Especially as things still seemed rather strained a large extent of the time.

Many times Renata remembers how Grandma Nancy would tell Uncle Larry how he always was "see me go" all the time. Grandma Nancy always was reminding Uncle Larry how finances were tight. Renata also remembers how many times growing up she would hear Grandma Nancy tell Uncle Larry not to playfully swat at her or her sisters as they would hate it if Arthur would take them to court and Renata or one of her sisters would have to tell the court how Uncle Larry hit them. Even if the swat was only in play as the court would be looking for a yes or no answer not an explanation. Also later, when Renata hit her late 20's, she remembers feeling sad when she learned how Grandma Nancy told Uncle Larry that having six women already in his life was probably enough. After all he saw the difficulty Ma experienced getting divorced, so why would he want to get married?

Of course, Renata admits to herself, that is partly why she is still single. She does not want to end up marrying a guy and feeling like she and any children she may have will need to go move in with Grandma Nancy or Ma or have Ma or Grandma Nancy move in with her for any length of time if something happened to her husband. A short period she would be okay with, as Renata knows she has told Ma how if she needs to get away from Grandma Nancy and Uncle Larry, Renata does have a spare bedroom that Ma can use to get on her feet as she gets herself a new life in Rosemary City where Renata now lives. Also Renata told Ma that Sandy and Dora would be welcome also as Renata would hate for Sandy and Dora to feel like Ma abandoned them. Of course Ma still has not taken Renata up on the offer as Ma told Grandma Nancy she would look after Grandma Nancy so Grandma Nancy would not have to go to a nursing home. Also Uncle Larry is just getting back on his feet after getting his foot crushed by a semi in an accident so Ma feels like she cannot leave him either. Even if Uncle Larry and Grandma Nancy tell Ma she never thinks of them but always only about herself most of the time including on her birthday.

"Wait a minute," Renata thinks to herself, "How did I end up here? I was trying to figure out why I would rather wait for a dish than ask for it. Well I already thought that I do not like to interrupt and I do not like to draw attention to myself. Though I guess I had not thought how when I draw attention to myself and start to speak I sometimes get so flustered though this is usually for things more complicated than asking for a dish. Partly I think as I am very subconscious of all the people listening to me and partly due to how my mind likes to think ahead so I start to talk and my brain comes up with additional thoughts. So after a period of time if I do not focus only on the one thing I am saying, I get lost in my own train of thoughts, confused on how best to describe them so usually I do not. Sometimes the confusion makes it so that I just up and quit speaking without finishing my sentence with "I don't know." Which of course is not the full story but would they really want to know the full story?

Then Renata hears a knock on the door and the doctor, Dr. Neva walks in and tells her how an MRI could be taken. The MRI is very good at showing if the calcifications are negative or not for cancer. Though the deposition of calcifications are often just part of the normal aging process, Dr. Neva assures Renata. After Dr. Neva asks if Renata has any questions, which Renata of course did not at the present, Dr.

Neva says her receptionist will be in shortly to let Renata know when she should come in for the MRI.

Shortly after Dr. Neva leaves, Renata hears another knock. This time it was the receptionist informing Renata how they had set up an appointment on the following Wednesday for the MRI and then on Thursday to follow up with Dr. Neva.

Finally Renata was headed home again where she packed the rest of her weekend trying to keep herself too busy to think, going out that night with a friend where they heard about the concerning number and facts of human trafficking, then helping serve breakfast at the local homeless shelter, watching movies on the Hallmark channel, hanging out with the churches young adult group playing Apples to Apples and attending a couple churches and partaking in their services. The first service was preached this time by an elder rather than the pastor and was about the need to mature and the second church was the conclusion to the series of "It all adds up" which was about the necessity of reaching out to people and loving them. Not loving others because of what they may do for you but loving others even when they do nothing for you.

As Sunday night rolled to a close, Renata thinks how she really does not mind not having to go in to work. Oh she would not mind if the job made her forget other problems but this job never had. No it just added problems of its own. There were those who complained to such an extent that Renata often wondered if someone had an issue with her would they really bring it to her or did their concerns bypass her and end up at her supervisors first? No Renata really did not miss that part of the job. She mostly misses the friends she felt she made there and regrets how the working environment at her job ended to make her more time and co-worker conscious rather than patient focused. Of course, Renata now sees how the work environment was a bit like her childhood. They both had one person who mostly seemed impossible to please and both would rather complain about others but not to the person who could possibly fix the problem. In other words, the people seemed to prefer venting over addressing the problem head on.

Though, Renata admitted to herself, sometimes taking a problem to the source did not always work. Take for example the time she tried to explain how she felt a coworker reminded her subconsciously of the most intimidating person in Renata's life. The co-worker told Renata she did not mean to be intimidating but continued to treat Renata in the same manner. Ultimately between that intimidation and the comments how issues were a concern of the others in the lab (as in all the other techs versus just the one) and Renata's frustration in communicating, Renata found herself without a job.

The following Tuesday Renata decided she wants to finally take advantage of the beautiful May weather. So she heads for the church which she knows has a women's Bible study. When she arrives, the women were already studying the names of God, focusing on El Shadi and Adoni. During the study, Renata learns the El Shadi meaning and how Adoni means Lord and Master. One of the women, Nina, whom Renata had not met before later commented about how we are to God is similar to how cats and dogs are to us. The way Nina saw it we are to be like dogs: excited when we get to spend time with God and always looking for how and when we will next do something with God. Often times though Nina commented she felt more like a cat: Not wanting to spend time with God when he wants to spend time with her but coming when she wants something from him Also Nina had mentioned how God had revealed to her a couple verses which were helpful. The first was from Luke35 about how even if the judge does not give what was asked of him at first will give it after continual asking, which Nina said gave her encouragement as she was struggling as a son she kept praying for showed no interest in believing Jesus to be his savior. The other verse which Nina said had helped her through a period her faith was being tested was when Jesus told Peter in Luke 2: 31-32, "*Simon, Simon, Satan has asked to sift all of you as wheat. But I have prayed for you, Simon, that your faith may not fail. And when you have turned back, strengthen your brothers.*"

Renata hearing Nina share verses which were helping her, decided to share a verse which was helping her through the loss of her job. The verse Renata recited was Romans 5:3-4 how "*Not only so, but we also glory in our sufferings, because we know that suffering produces perseverance;*

perseverance, character; and character, hope." Renata laughed as she said, "The tribulation from my job should really be producing a lot of hope."

After the study as Renata was planning on walking home, Nina asked Renata if she wanted to join Nina and her friend, Rhianna, for lunch. Renata debated as she really is not a person who tends to eat out but rather as she told Nina, "I usually do not eat out as I can get myself something to eat at home a lot cheaper."

As Nina said she would treat Renata, Renata gave in even though she struggles with the thought of people buying things for her, too. As Nina drove to go pick Rhianna who had a doctor's appointment which was why she had not been at the Bible Study, Nina discovered Rhianna was not going to be ready to be picked up until noon. So as they had about an hour to kill, Nina asked Renata what she wanted to do. Renata told Nina how she had planned to drop her resume off at a couple veterinary clinics as she walked home. So Nina said she would be glad to take Renata to the veterinary clinics. Two of the veterinary clinics, when Renata asked if they were hiring said that they were. The one clinic had been excited too when they saw she already had experience working at veterinary clinics. While Nina drove, Renata and Nina share personal stories.

Renata learned how Nina's husband had passed a few months earlier. He had always wanted a motorcycle which Nina viewed was more of an individual activity rather than family activity so he never had gotten one. After his death a couple of their friends had told Nina how having motorcycles had actually brought them closer, so Nina decided to get a motorcycle. Now though Nina said, "Well I managed to ride it a couple times but then it tipped over. Now I am afraid of it so people have talked me into putting it up for sale. My feeling is that if God does not want me to have it, someone will buy it otherwise it will not sell if God wants me to have it."

Also Nina had told Renata how, "Growing up I lived in a little country town where the nearest neighbor was about a mile away. Then as I had not been involved with extracurricular activities school had been my only source of social interactions."

"Yeah," Renata said, "I understand that frustration. After fourth grade my family decided to homeschool me and Abby, my youngest sister. Then as they disliked how the Catholic church was going (their praying to Mary and saints like they were God) my family pretty much stopped attending church. They only went once a year then to keep their Catholic obligations, except Uncle Larry who went weekly. As we lived on a dairy farm, we had things which kept us quite busy. Busy enough that for about ten years we were on the farm probably twenty-three hours, seven days a week. My grandmother had been hurt by so many people that even though we had neighbors right across the street and between six to twelve within a mile radius she chose to not let any of them come over. Part of this was due to how one of the neighbors who had several teen boys would ask to borrow machinery. The machinery either never came back or if it did, the machine was broken. Another neighbor though would not let my oldest sister, Dora, come over to play at their place but their daughter was always coming over to play at our place. This mother was heard to practice witchcraft so when pipes would break after my grandmother caught the smell of her perfume, my grandmother was certain it was due to witchcraft. Ultimately as my grandmother says this neighbor knows where all the pipes are in the house, my grandmother refuses to fix the pipes as she is sure the neighbor would have them break again."

After telling Nina this story, Renata sees they are at the destination to pick up Nina's friend, Rhianna. Nina asks Renata, "Would you mind scooting to the back seat, Rhianna has a bad back so she needs the front."

So Renata scooted to the back and they went for lunch at Taco Bell before Nina dropped Renata back at home to look for some more jobs.

Friday morning, Renata found herself unable to sleep until her alarm went off as she thought about how she needed to read her Bible, do her exercises to help her lower back and left knee (which had been injured in a car accident a little over a year ago) and get dressed. After all she was meeting one friend for breakfast and then hanging out with another friend in a town about thirty miles away who had two girls the ages of two years and two months.

From experience, Renata knows her days seem to always go smoother if she reads her Bible in the morning so she gets her Bible and her Bible in a year guide with a devotional out. Renata reads them and then works on her exercises which she neglected the night before as she looked for jobs until almost midnight. Finally she dresses and heads out to meet her friend, Rachel.

When Renata enters the restaurant at about 9:15 for what she thought was a 9:30 meeting, Rachel greeted her by saying, "I was starting to wonder if you forgot."

"I'm sorry," Renata apologizes, "I thought we were meeting at 9:30."

Rachel and Renata walked over to the greeter who hands them menus and points to an empty booth. Upon sitting Rachel asks, "So how is the job search coming?"

"Well on Tuesday, I dropped off a few resumes at veterinary clinics, a couple of which said they were hiring. Also as I look for jobs I see a lot of job openings for Certified Nursing Assistants in the area, so if I do not get a job soon I am thinking I will go for the education to become a CNA. In the meantime I have applied for a few jobs as a Medical Technologist, some for senior care and a few banking jobs."

Renata starts to help herself to her meal which had arrived and asks Rachel, "So did you grow up here in Rosemary City?"

"No," Rachel said, "I grew up in Poppy City. I never dreamed of or wanted to move from there as I was real close to my family and loved the town. I was content to go to a local college and then I met my husband. It was after we married that we moved several times and ended up here in Rosemary City."

"Well as I wanted to be a large animal veterinarian when I left for college," Renata said, "I had three options in the state I grew up in to choose from: Catalpa City, Phlox City, or Magnolia City. As I knew my veterinarian friend who convinced my family to let me go to college had gone to Catalpa City, that was the college I chose."

Renata fell silent as she started to reflect on all that happened to get her to college. It definitely had not been easy. Renata remembered how when she was 18 she had told her family that she wanted to go to college to be a veterinarian. They told her she should wait until there was a correspondence class. Renata had bristled at the thought as she wanted to get off the farm. Renata said nothing though as she knew that to protest would result in a fight and being told she was sinning. (One of the many ways to be told she was sinning.) Instead she continued to dream and took the Veterinary Assistant correspondence class. Her family had kept mentioning how the class was available so she should take it, so Renata had just so her family would drop the subject.

Then Abby had started listening to Packer games which was on a local country radio station, the only music the family allowed Renata and her sisters to listen to. The Packers had gone to win the Super Bowl. The kicker made the longest field goal and the kick returner (or was it the punt returner) ran for the longest run back in Super Bowl history. The next year, Grandma Nancy allowed them to start watching TV which got Renata totally hooked on football. She started reading everything she could about the Packers and watching every NFL game. As she began reading every book about the Packers, Renata read a book by a disc jockey on a Christian radio station who interviewed the Christian players. After reading how a player had recovered from a season ending injury, listening to Christian music Renata decided to look for the Christian radio station. She was sure her family would not protest as the lyrics had to be family friendly without bad hidden messages her family feared were in non-country music. Between the radio station urging listeners to "*not forsaking our own assembling together, as the custom of some is, but exhorting one another; and so much the more, as ye see the day drawing nigh*" according to Hebrews 10:25 (*American Standard Bible*) and the Billy Graham crusade, Renata had insisted she go to church or else she was not going to watch another game.

Now Renata recognizes that probably was not the way she should have gone about getting to church but it worked. At first Renata's family had insisted Abby go with her and until both of them turned twenty-one Grandma Nancy had wanted them to go to a Catholic church. Renata had for many weeks and met nobody. The closest she came was when they gave the handshake of peace. As Renata expressed her frustration to Abby, her sister encouraged Renata to look for Saturday night services at another church to go to. As they looked around they found a small church whose pastor and elder were gardening outside the church. They insisted it would be okay for her to go in and take a look inside.

It was their friendliness which prompted Renata to attend the church, Buttercup City Bible Church, when Abby was scheduled to train for a new job on a Sunday. Thankfully the Catholic church was having a festival which caused both churches to start at the same time that week. When Renata got home, Ma had asked her where she had been. So Renata had told Ma who got upset and told Renata, "You better talk to Grandma Nancy!"

When Renata told Grandma Nancy, her grandmother merely said, "You are twenty-one. It is your choice."

Thanks to Abby's selflessness (or had Abby never wanted to go to church) and encouragement Renata continued going to that church as that first week she had probably met at least half the congregation and talked for a long time with Pastor Martin S and heard how the church had activities planned every month for the rest of the year.

Pastor Martin had mentioned he knew a couple veterinarians, Dr. Michael G and Dr. Kurt Y. When Renata mentioned she wanted to move off the farm, Pastor Martin had suggested parishioner, Robin M, who had grown up on a dairy farm and as for Renata's steers he shared how Dr. Kurt had a place in the country where they maybe could stay.

Renata who had been volunteering at the veterinary clinic her family used, decided to see if she could volunteer at the clinic Dr. Michael and Dr. Kurt worked at. That is where she met Dr. Rueben a veterinarian 5 years her senior who always would ask her enthusiastically, "So you going to ride with me today?"

The first few times Renata said no as she had arranged to ride with Dr. Kurt. After that she started riding with Dr. Rueben. When Renata decided she was fed up working at the cheese factory, where she worked part-time, as all her friends that she made there were basically chased from working there, Renata started to ride daily with Dr. Rueben.

Meanwhile Renata had also moved in to live with Robin and her husband, Louis M. It had taken four angry months before Renata had gained her mother's approval. Yes it had been her mother not her grandmother which kept Renata from moving for several months, much to Renata's shock and dismay. But between her moving out and Dr. Rueben's odds and ends assistance on the farm in return to Renata's "assisting him," Renata's family had decided she could pursue her veterinary dreams.

Renata finished her reflection and talked with Rachel a bit more before they finished eating. Rachel gave Renata a hug and then they went their separate ways.

Renata then had gone to visit her friend, Nicole S, in Gladiolus City after she left Rachel. She had enjoyed her time with Nicole. Renata and Nicole had been entertained by Raya, Nicole's two-year-old daughter who got excited seeing a squirrel and pointing out trees which had bloomed. Renata also got to hold two-month-old baby Elizabeth while Nicole worked in the kitchen.

While at Nicole's, Renata had realized and mentioned to Nicole how, "This period of unemployment has been a lot less stressful than the final month or so at my job had been. I feel more confident that I can work again as a Medical Technologist or any field I get hired into. I now know I just need to make sure I know where they keep binders about the instruments and instrument policies. I plan to find out how the training process is done and about how committed they are to teamwork and assisting each other. Those things ultimately helped make my last job fail. I also have realized how the job had reminded me of how things had been growing up."

"As I grew up everything ended up going to the lead person. The rest of the people then complained about everything. How the lead person did or did not do this or that. How the leader's way of doing things ultimately was the way to do things. It was the lead person's job to know everything and manage everything creating tension between the leader and the others. Ultimately the tension and complaining at the job caused me to be frustrated with the negativity. Then when I was told the concerns of my coworkers were being brought to my supervisor, I ultimately wondered whom I could trust. Were the people who said they would tell if they had an issue with me or were concerned with my work or was it just the leader? If it was just the leader why did none of my coworkers stand up for me?"

"I really need to remember how Jesus said to 'Love your enemies, do good and lend, hoping for nothing in return, and your reward will be great.' To love my enemies, I need to remember to pray for them and do the best job I can for them. My problem is rather than confront them when they do something, I usually retreat into silence."

"There are times when I want to talk to the person who intimidates me but usually I foreplay the scene in my mind. The scene usually has them angry, disappointed, frustrated or a similar reaction so I choose not to say anything because I would rather be angry, disappointed, frustrated, and such toward me than them. This is especially true in the case where I may not be the only person whom feels the brunt of the anger, disappointment or frustration of the person I am intimidated by."

"Tricky," Nicole tells Renata, "but I think as long as you try that is all that matters. If you just give them a call and see how responsive they are or are not to you, you can just tell them you had been thinking about them so that you thought you would call. You also could tell them you are praying for them and that you want your relationship to grow."

After their conversation, Nicole asked Renata if she would be okay with going with her to drop off some food for a couple who had just had a baby. Renata said that would be fine. So they did a little bit of visiting and when they had returned Nicole's husband, Albert, was home from work. Therefore Nicole threw together supper, which they all enjoyed. Then before Renata headed home Nicole, Renata and Raya went for a walk. Nicole and Renata were quick to point out animals to Raya for her enjoyment and they admired the many flowers and remarked over the different style of houses they saw.

UNEMPLOYMENT PERIOD

As my laboratory job in Rosemary City was nearing its end the laboratory supervisor started bringing up how if I would quit it would need to be as I knew I would be getting fired if I was to get unemployment benefits. So in May 2010 when my job ended I was again reminded how I could get unemployment benefits since the only reason I quit was as the laboratory job told me I got to choose how I wanted to end the job by being fired or if I wanted to quit. So I quit and applied to get unemployment benefits.

A few weeks after I had started to collect unemployment benefits, I was required to get some training in order to keep getting unemployment benefits. The training was held in Pansy City at North Central Second-Hand Retail Store's Organization Helping Jobless Become Better Employee Candidates. One of the handouts the Organization Helping Jobless Become Better Employee Candidates gave me listed stressors which you were to mark if you had experienced them within the past year. According to the handout, which had three levels of stress, the number of stressors (accidents, moving, new job, cancer) I had experienced in the year leading up to my job termination had put me in the top level of stress. After my job ended, my back improved dramatically, with the help of a chiropractor which I had started to attend a few months earlier. Also I found I was much less stressed, although still a little bit stressed as I looked for another job.

I continued to try to get another laboratory job by applying to all that were remotely close to the Rosemary City area, but my confidence was shaken from the attitude I got at the last laboratory job so I really wasn't sure that I was fit to work in a laboratory. As I looked back on my mistakes, I realized as Raine had always stressed, how awful some of the results could have been if they had proven to be incorrect and the effect those results could have had on patients' lives. Plus, I disliked how I never actually got to know any of the patients and instead only worked with my lab coworkers who were pretty vocal about their frustrations except when the person that was committing the frustration was around. Another reason why I eventually decided laboratory work wasn't actually for me was because I had to depend almost entirely and strictly on my school learning to know why each test was being run, since we never met the people we were doing tests for and we, due to HIPPA, were discouraged from looking into a person's medical records.

I kept trying for laboratory jobs, though, because I had the training, but now I was only applying in the Rosemary City area (with an occasional glance to see if there was an opening in either Rose City or Cherry Blossom City's hospitals), as I really had grown tired of being uprooted every six to eighteen months since 2006 and starting over in a new city. Besides, my friends and I had prayed God would bring me to the town where he wanted me, so I bookmarked all the local hospitals and applied for every laboratory job I found, as well as other medical jobs which I felt I would qualify for. While applying for jobs, I also prayed and asked my friends to pray that God would lead me to the job he wanted me in and to the one he knew my back could withstand as my back was so miserable if I stood still too long, whenever I bent over or stooped, etc.

As time went by and I didn't get hired by any of the laboratories I applied to, I decided I really wanted to be employed rather than just collecting unemployment, so I started to apply for additional types of jobs. During my extra free time, I had considered and attempted writing a book about my life as my former Cherry Blossom City roommate, Ruby C had encouraged me to do. See last chapter which is what I wrote during that time. As the style I was writing in at that time required a lot of free time to get lost in thoughts so I could write my thoughts down while incorporating actual events happening at that time, the last chapter was as far as I had gotten.) Plus in my extra free time, I considered what it would take to create a place for people of any age to have a safe, social environment to get together to play games, do crafts, read, etc. without the pressure to buy anything, for those people like me who had spent the majority of their life broke. The closest examples of what it was I wanted in this regard was what I would hear on Whit's End in the *Adventures in Odyssey* series created by Focus on the Family, and my childhood playhouse, which was an old, vacant house with four intact rooms. There was an additional room, bathroom and an attic like space but they all had areas which were rotting so we were discouraged from entering those areas. The one time I learned why as I walked a bit too close to the hole I saw in the floor and ended up falling into the cellar. It hadn't been a far fall and I didn't get hurt. As I had never been down there before and as it was too dark to see where I was in relation to the exit, I was too scared to move from where I fell. Abby had been with me and saw me fall so she had run for my mom who lead me out of the cellar. I do not remember too much about it other than it was very dark, had a wall between where I had fallen and the opening, that it's floor was coated in ice and that I narrowly missed pipes when I fell. In that old house's four rooms, my sisters and I each had our own "apartment" and a "place of business" which we ran out of our apartment. Dora's business was a store, but I don't remember the others. Grandma Nancy also allowed us to take the junk mail she, Uncle Larry and Ma got for us girls to use as pretend mail at our apartments.

In my extra free time while unemployed, I had also attended a class or two for starting your own business, but due to my debts, lack of money, and reserved personality which rarely succeeded in Rosemary City to get anybody to attend game and craft nights I sought to start in Rosemary City (which, I struggled in feeling like my starting the business wasn't much of a real possibility or of knowing what would really be needed to get it going successfully. I still daydream about it at times, how I would like to have a place with a room to house a library, another for crafts and games, another for mini concerts and/or a theater, and still another to play movies. I also would turn the backyard of the place into a large community garden. These would be the free options of the place, while maybe I would also include a store for people to sell crafts, garden products, and other things. For anybody to be able to purchase these things, I would provide "job opportunities" like doing some weeding, running my movie theater for me, manning my craft and game rooms, etc.

During my three months of unemployment, I tried to make my looking for a new job a full-time job, like I heard a person should while unemployed, by devoting forty hours each week to looking online for jobs via a few job search engines and applying for all jobs which I thought would be possible to work. To keep my sanity though, I also would look for volunteer opportunities to complete my 40 hour a week as the thought of applying every week for 40 hours a week stressed me out. My looking for volunteer opportunities is how I came to work for a week apiece for Rosemary City Alliance, the Organization Releasing Children from Poverty in Jesus' Name, the Organization Providing Essentials for Those in Need and the Program Providing Lodging, Food, Transportation, Etc. to those Spreading the Gospel at Hibiscus City's Pilot Informative Event.

While volunteering with Rosemary City Alliance I helped in their Program Providing Bible Learning to Children which is where the church taught their congregation younger than 18. Mostly I worked with the kids around the pre-K to kindergarten age. As Rosemary City Alliance easily had 150-500 people at each of their five services, I usually was a helper for the 6-12 kids we would have during their 5PM church service. Mostly I would try to encourage the kids to sit quiet while the Bible story was being read to them and a couple songs were played and then to encourage the kids to sit nicely and color until their parents came to pick them up. When I expressed interest in volunteering some more, they asked me if I would be interested in helping with their field trip activities. Every year Rosemary City Alliance would host this event which they opened to local schools throughout a whole week, where a different school each day would bring their first and second graders. These first and second graders were split into four groups and then rotated through four areas. The one area they would play in the indoor sandbox which would have gold coins hidden in it, another area they would do some type of game, another area was singing, and the other was the snack area where they would get ice cream and one of the helpers there would offer a topping which they put on the ice cream for the child. A few weeks or months later after their field trips were done I also spent like a week helping them make a huge macramé gold statue for the Babylonian skit they did of Shadrach, Meshach and Abednego. Finally, I helped serve a meal during their teen program's 80's theme night, stuffed fundraising envelopes and I helped paint some hallways.

With the Organization Releasing Children from Poverty in Jesus' Name, I helped at several concerts by setting up a table with several packets of children from third world countries of the poorest of the poor in the area which the church in those third world countries agreed to partner with the Organization Releasing Children from Poverty in Jesus' Name with the understanding the church would be vulnerable in showing the Organization Releasing Children from Poverty in Jesus' Name just how the funds sent were being spent to benefit the child. The Organization Releasing Children from Poverty in Jesus' Name insisted on this vulnerability which allows them to show any sponsors who visited just how their finances helped the child. If a church used funds inappropriately the Organization Releasing Children from Poverty in Jesus' Name would hold the projects leaders accountable and if none of the leaders showed remorse over how the funds were used the Organization Releasing Children from Poverty in Jesus' Name would withdraw out of the project as they insisted on running the projects with integrity. Once the child packets were laid out we would answer any questions the crowd who came for the concert might have. Occasionally the artist would share how helping these poorest of the poor with the Organization Releasing Children from Poverty in Jesus' Name had ministered to them and then would ask their audience to raise their hand if they were interested in sponsoring a child. If they were, the other volunteers and I would do what we called a packet pass where we would walk up and down an aisle handing out the packets to whomever had their hand raised. The artist would usually share before their concert when they planned to have us do a packet pass. While the audience was all enjoying the concert some of the volunteers were given the chance to go in and enjoy the concert as long as we beat the audience back out to the table. After the concerts were usually when we would get the most people to come up to our table and sign up to sponsor a child. In addition to concerts, I also would help similarly at the North Central Christian Festival except during one's entire shift of volunteering a person was required to stay at the table as there was always someone walking by one of the two or three tables we had set up and we rarely got to enjoy any of the concerts unless we were at the table located right next to the stage. The North Central Christian Festival was a Christian festival that usually was held starting the second Thursday of July and would go to Sunday. Sunday there would be one artist performing worship and then a speaker, providing an outdoor sermon. Sundays were always free the. North Central Christian Festival has five stages a few of them were more rock than I really was interested in, the main stage would have the best-known artists and there is a stage hosted usually by the Christian Fiscal Organization which would have comedians, illusionists and some less known artists. The main stage and the Christian Fiscal Organization stages were the ones I spent most of my time at when I would have off from volunteering with the Organization Releasing Children from Poverty in Jesus' Name. The last two years I went, I had some friends, Ian and Ulyssa S, who were camping out there who would invite me over to their campsite and join them and a couple of their grandkids with meals so I ate better than prior years where I typically ate canned foods and crackers.

Another organization I started to volunteer with during that period I was unemployed was Program Providing Lodging, Food, Transportation, Etc. to those Spreading the Gospel. I was talking with a friend, Ida T, as I helped set up for a Vacation Bible School (VBS) at Rosemary City Evangelical Free Church, about trying to find things to do to break up my time applying for jobs and she suggested I call Betsy Y as they were starting the Program Providing Lodging, Food, Transportation, Etc. to those Spreading the Gospel and they were looking for more people to help them for a week. The Program Providing Lodging, Food, Transportation, Etc. to those Spreading the Gospel provides opportunities for missionary aviators to come to

Hibiscus City's Pilot Informative Event which was held the final week of July. To do this Elmer and Betsy Y, a retired couple, would contact local churches to see if they would allow a missionary to preach on Sunday and if they would be willing to provide one of the meals. Elmer and Betsy would also try to find homes for each of their missionaries to stay the week they were at the Pilot Informative Event plus an automobile for them to drive. That first year, I helped them set up the large tent and several dozen long tables where Program Providing Lodging, Food, Transportation, Etc. to those Spreading the Gospel provided meals. Next to that tent was a small tent which I and another volunteer or two, usually one or both Nettie Ns, would take the missionary's bags, assign them a number and store their bags back on a shelf while the missionary went to the dining tent to eat and then return for their bags once they finished eating and headed back to their organizations display at Pilot Informative Event. That week in addition to meeting Elmer and Betsy Y, the two Nettie Ns, and lots of missionaries, I also got to work with Uriah Y who was a chef, who also provided his services as a head chef for the Program Providing Fellowship and Food for the Lonely and Poor. This led me to apply to help volunteer at the Program Providing Fellowship and Food for the Lonely and Poor the following weeks while I continued to look for a job.

The Program Providing Fellowship and Food for the Lonely and Poor I learned when I contacted them about volunteering, provides the Rosemary City area with a free community meal, Monday, Wednesday and Fridays for those who are hungry or lonely. It was held in a church a block south of Crane Street which was Rosemary City's main street of businesses. The guests were welcome to go downstairs, sign in to the guest book and wait until time for the meal to be served. The guest book was used to know just how many people were being served so that the founder of the organization, Ruby H, could give the information to the lady who wrote grants for her which helped them get the money they needed to continue the service. Once the volunteers arrived they were asked to look at the volunteer list to see where Ruby H had them working and then to put on a cloth apron and gloves except the two people Ruby H had down to volunteer in the dishwashing area. These two people did not need gloves and would put on a rubber apron as the one would scrape the trays, then spray them before putting them in a rack which once filled would be slid in the dishwasher to clean, while the other person took the clean dishes out of the dishwasher when it was done and put away the clean dishes. Meanwhile a couple other volunteers would scout out the guests for parents with young kids or the handicapped and would offer to get their food for them. Of the remaining volunteers, there usually were three people in the serving area with each person serving up the portion size that Uriah or whomever was the head cook that night had recommended. Another two volunteers would serve the guests milk or water and a desert. The two remaining volunteers would help remind the guests to sign in before the meals or to take some bread or canned good as they left and the other person met people at the door to make sure the guests knew the food was downstairs which they could get to by using the stairs or elevator and then thank the guests for having come as the guests left. Each of the volunteers were encouraged to also partake of the meal and join the guests as they ate. Ruby H liked to give everybody a chance to do each of the positions so I got to do each of the positions several times as I volunteered with Program Providing Fellowship and Food for the Lonely and Poor. Even after I found a job at North Central Second-Hand Retail Store, I continued volunteering for them periodically and would also partake in their meals as I fell into the "lonely" category and as a coworker from North Central Second-Hand Retail Store often ate there too, I usually would join her and her friends. By volunteering occasionally still at the Program Providing Fellowship and Food for the Lonely and Poor I felt less guilty about partaking of the food which others may have been more qualified for.

Another place I volunteered at while looking for employment was the Organization Providing Essentials for Those in Need. It is an organization consisting of several trucks which would go town to town. When it came into a town once a year, it would provide the citizens a play area for the kids filled with lots of inflatables, a tent where local businesses could share about the services they provide, another tent where the citizens could get free medical and dental care, an area which offered free haircuts, and another area which offered free family portraits and then as the guests left they offered the guests several bags worth of free groceries. The area I worked in was the kids zone where I just made sure the kids remained safe as they played.

College Organization Developing Christian Leaders Job

At the end of July 2010, I called my friend Emma B, who had worked at The Training Camp for CODCL, to wish her a happy birthday. When Emma heard I was looking for a job, she gave me the phone number of Michael V, an CODCL staff worker who lived in Rosemary City, as she thought he might know of a job opening for me. When I called Michael and told him Emma B had given me his number as I was looking for a job, he told me how he had a ten-hour-per-week job opening which, if a person raised funds, could increase to even more hours. So I applied for the job and got it in August of 2010.

When Michael talked with me before hiring me, I told him about my veterinary background and my desire to provide a place for people to be able to hang out. So Michael told me that he realized this job was just a stepping stone for me between other jobs, so if I found another job which I found more suitable he would let me go my separate way, but until then he would gladly give me ten hours each week to work for as long as I wanted to work for him.

The job Michael had was an office job, which looked appealing for my back. It consisted of helping Michael, who oversaw CODCL staff throughout the state I grew up in and the upper half of the state east of it by answering phone calls, emails, printing off document, etc. We connected at just the right time as the Lord knew how Michael was going to be needing someone in town to help him, because a few weeks after Michael hired me, while he was out biking on a country road like he often did, a farmer in a pickup pulling a disc clipped his bike. Michael shared how he picked himself up from the dirt and tried to flag down the farmer but either the farmer didn't see him or chose not to see him. Either way the farmer did not stop but had driven away. A bit later a lady was driving by and stopped to help him. She realized his need for medical care and helped get him to the Western Cities Medical. She shared with Michael how she had almost not driven through at that time as she had thought to finish working several hours earlier that day but something came up and she hadn't which she now saw as God working because it meant she was able to help Michael. From his bike getting clipped this resulted in Michael fracturing his C2 spinal bone which meant God was looking after him when he jumped up to try flagging down the farmer as the C2 protects a major artery which with the fracture could have been deadly if the C2 would have moved and even nicked the artery. The fractured C2 was the most serious injury Michael had sustained but he also had a few other injuries which kept him from being able to come in to the office and working for several months.

Thankfully, God had made it so that I was there to help Michael, though because his being injured came at an inopportune time as CODCL chapters which we oversaw were starting to ramp up in preparation for a conference at the beginning of November. The conference usually had around eight hundred students from multiple colleges all over the state I grew up in who would get together in a southern city over a weekend to take miniature Bible study classes, called tracks. There were around a dozen different tracks the students could choose from. The tracks were designed to help them grow in their faith in God and to lead some students to accept Jesus Christ as their Savior for the first time. Each track had one main staff worker who lead the track with several additional co-leading staff or volunteers. The track leader was responsible for putting together the track material which was to be used that weekend and was supposed to get it to Michael at least a few weeks before the conference. That way we could in the week leading up to the conference print off enough of each material for every student who signed up for the track to get one of each material.

While Michael was not able to make it to the office, staff worker and area director Steven H and former administrative assistant Victor stepped up to train me so that I could do much of what Michael typically would have done. This had required me to go down to Magnolia City from 1-4PM one day to meet with them. When I went down there, they showed me the website I would be working with as I helped students sign up for tracks, switch tracks, make payments for the weekend or whatever else I was requested to do. Meanwhile Steven H and Victor also stepped in and helped do some of the other things Michael typically did so that the preparations for the weekend ran smoothly. So over the next two months, I was responsible for making all changes needed for every student who had an issue signing up on the website. Michael also had me pick up a gift basket which he ordered from a local cheese store to give to the printer, pick up the conference brochures from the printer, and then distribute to each staff worker the number of conference brochures they felt they would need. I in turn had to learn how to weigh the packets so that I could print off mailing labels to ship the brochures to each of the staff. I then had to record how much it cost to ship each of these packets and record how much ink was used on printing off all the material, and gather all the travel expenses for each of the staff so that Michael could keep track on just how much had been spent on the conference so the expenses could be reimbursed.

Since a short while before Michael had gotten injured I had also been hired to work part-time at the North Central Second-Hand Retail Store. Michael was gracious enough to allow me to come in for a few hours before or after working at the North Central Second-Hand Retail Store as long as he could have a general idea when I planned to come in so he could let me know what he needed me to do. Once I realized how much I really needed to work full time for so that I could get benefits, I had debated for many months which job I should, and I seriously started asking God to show me which job he wanted me to do full time. As I saw the CODCL job as directly making an impact for God, I tried first to get full time at CODCL.

So Michael helped me look into doing some fundraising. While fundraising, I enjoyed the excuse to call my friends as it gave me an opportunity to catch up with many of them but I was not very good at convincing many people to send some of their hard-earned money my way so I could work more hours for CODCL. After almost a year of fundraising, I decided there was little likelihood that I could raise enough money to get thirty hours of work, which was what I needed to get to in order to receive health insurance benefits. I needed the benefits because of my lingering back and knee injuries and due to the results of the mammograms I had done.

So, when the most I got after fundraising for a while only helped me get enough for a maximum of fifteen hours and I remembered a compliment by Erica R, a team leader at the North Central Second-Hand Retail Store, about my being gifted working with people with disabilities, I decided I would work full time at North Central Second-Hand Retail Store and just part time at CODCL. Another thing that the North Central Second-Hand Retail Store offered was that I daily got to work with people while CODCL it was hit or miss as Michael was often out connecting with staff workers around the state I grew up in or the upper half of the state to the east. Even after I decided to go full time at the North Central Second-Hand Retail Store, I continued to work for CODCL. After working for a while with CODCL, Michael was also assigned to oversee the staff at campuses in three states west of the state I grew up in. After Michael was given these extra campuses to oversee, he and some of the other staff wanted to reach out to the growing Asian American populations. So Michael asked me to call these colleges to try to determine how many Asian American were on each college to determine the need for Asian American CODCL conferences which I did for him. Another project I did for him was to collect and compile surveys determining how well the area directors were doing their job of assisting the campus staff workers.

North Central Second-Hand Retail Store Job

Even after I got the CODCL job, I had to keep looking for a job if I still wanted to earn unemployment which was helping me be able to pay all my bills. Unless I fundraised CODCL was only able to give me a maximum of 10 hours each week so I needed the extra income the unemployment checks provided as there was over a $5 and 22 hour a week difference between my CODCL and my former laboratory job. While applying to more jobs I had gotten interviews at several laboratories and for other medical-type jobs, but the companies always found someone more suitable for their needs. So I ended up applying for non-medical jobs too and got interviews for jobs at the Mentorship Club and at Petunia City's North Central Second-Hand Retail Store. Both of them looked appealing, as the former would allow me to impact children's lives directly, and the latter would allow me to work with people who had disabilities. It was the latter that offered me a position first, so I chose it as I wanted to get off unemployment and I had been praying God would bring me to the job he knew would be a good fit, especially with my back in the condition it was in. They hired me in September 2010.

The job I had applied for was as a seasonal donation assistant but area team leader, Amber N, and store team leader, Shannon N, also had a need for a seasonal cashier which they thought due to my size I would probably be better at. Due to the condition of my back, I agreed that working as a cashier sounded like it would be the position I would prefer over accepting donations. So when they hired me, it was to be a seasonal cashier.

There were three North Central Second-Hand Retail Store stores in Rosemary City. One located by the mall which was just east of Wild Rose City, another was just north of Pansy City and the one I worked at was just west of Petunia City. It was a pretty large store, with four checkout lanes which most evenings those first few months I worked they needed a cashier at each lane. It had two entrances into the huge backroom. The one closest to the front had a swinging door and was where the clock where a person had to swipe their name badge to punch in was located and most items were run out to the sales floor or returned to the production area while the door by the back were double doors and were used to run the furniture out to the sales floor or once the furniture was sold, it was brought back to the donation door.

The first few days as a cashier, the team leaders assigned Alexander N, a young man around his mid-twenties to train me. He was pretty thorough and knowledgeable with his training, showing me a bunch of tricks to keep things flowing more easily through the entire day. One was to always look when the cashier had a break in customers to make sure there were three packs of bags on the bag rack and if not, to restock the rack so three were kept on the rack so that even on busy days a person shouldn't run out of bags. After training me for a while Alexander then watched me cashier for a while until he thought I was comfortable cashiering. After a few days, I started to feel like I was getting a hang of it and would usually work alone. It took me several months before I truly felt comfortable using the paging system but I eventually got it down, too. In addition to ringing up the customer's purchases, the cashiers were responsible for working on the return rack, keeping the store picked up and things put away. Most of my fellow cashiers did not enjoy working on the return rack and keeping the clothes hanging properly on the racks versus being draped over the rack or lying on the floor. Me on the other hand, loved working on the return rack and straightening out the store as it gave me lots of opportunity to keep moving which I enjoyed as my back and leg hurt quite a bit less when I was moving around compared to when I was cashiering and only slightly moving and rotating above the hips. Also if I had been scheduled to help close the store, as a cashier, I was responsible to make sure everything that customers had decided against wanting to buy or keep had to be returned to the proper area of the store. The first several times I was confused every time I saw an item I hadn't had to return previously as to where it was to go. Eventually I realized how the tags were very informative on telling what department the item was supposed to be in (wares, domestics, glass, etc), the price was on it in a couple areas, and the color of ticket was listed on it. The only thing the tickets did not say was the specific item that it was like a doll, metal art, wooden shelf, etc. unless it was a new goods item which North Central Second-Hand Retail Store actually bought to sell.

Then around December as the season which the seasonal cashiers had been hired for was drawing to a close, the team leaders started to ask the seasonal cashiers about training them in other areas of the store. Amber N asked me if I would be interested in training in apparel's store pull to see if they thought I would be worth keeping on after the season ended. I had been nervous as apparel looked very intimidating but I said yes as I really wanted to keep the job at the North Central Second-Hand Retail Store as the team leaders and the team members that I worked with made the job a good experience. As I always say now, it's the management and co-workers which really can make or break the experience at a job. A few days later, when they finally started to train me in the apparel's store pull and explained what it actually entailed and I got to do it for a little while, I felt sure that I would have no problem doing it. Pulling apparel required me to look at the tags on every piece of apparel looking for the color which had been on the sales floor for around a month, which had not sold, even when it's tag color was the color of the week so that it was on sale for 50% off. I also would be responsible to pull off the items that were put on clearance the week before. When they started scheduling me to pull my time switched from working 5:00pm-10:00pm approximately half the time to being scheduled from 8:00 a.m. to 12:00 p.m. everyday four days a week. The team leaders requested that I get around 1000 pieces pulled each day before noon with the assistance of 4-12 program participants whom generally had a handicap of some type whether physically or cognitively. There were usually three job coaches, also, which oversaw these program participants, assisting them to do the job as it was requested. Depending on the severity of the handicap, the job coach might have to most of the work themselves while for others, the job coach could direct them, then leave them for a time period before coming back and verifying the program participant was successfully doing the job requested of them. Every day I would oversee the pull with the program participants and job coaches, and have the required number of apparel pieces pulled, clearance stickers applied and run out to the clearance racks, well before the 12:00 time period I was assigned to complete the pull. Then, the team leader in charge would request me to switch over to hanging, ticketing, and running apparel out to the floor and they would reassign the program participants into other jobs they could handle. I loved pulling apparel. At first I was a bit intimidated in telling the job coaches what they needed to have their program participant do (what areas to pull, what clearance price was to go on what, etc.). As time went by, however, it got easier and I started helping job coaches find additional jobs to assist the apparel area once the pulling got done for the day (such as applying foam stickers to hangers to decrease the likelihood of the apparel from falling off hangers, sizing and colorizing, taking hangers out of boxes and putting them on hanger racks, letting them do some hanging of apparel, etc).

One time my team leader, Erica R, came to me and told me she had just hired a young lady who was nonverbal and who had never had a job before. Erica said she was going to have me work with her since she believed I was gifted in working with people with disabilities. Erica also tried to have me oversee a young man with a very short attention span with apparel pull as she felt his job coach did not do a good job with him. Later that day when she asked me how it went, I shared my frustration as I felt I did not do a good job with him either as I could never get him to focus very long and he preferred to grab the colored tickets that needed to be pulled which were easily seen rather than looking at each item and finding the pull items whose tickets had been hidden from being easily seen.

This gift of working with people who had disabilities, God helped me grow in different ways. One way was by being a comfort to Ma when my uncle or grandmother would take out their frustrations on her, although Abby was by far a greater comforter. It also grew with Sandy, my older sister, who has a developmental disability which has kept her more like a child in many ways. Another way of developing this gift, I believe, was taking cantankerous or stray animals on our farm and helping them to see what kind of a friend I could be to them by taming them.

I had been working at the North Central Second-Hand Retail Store for about half a year or so when Dr. Neva told me that the crystals found in my latest mammogram had enlarged since the earlier mammogram and after several more tests, she said she wanted to remove them. After trying a few less invasive techniques to remove them, she discovered that the only way that worked for me due to size and density, was to surgically remove the crystals. Since I didn't have insurance, Dr. Neva's assistant, Rebekkah, helped me find a hospital program which would help cover the expenses. This hospital program required me to fill out quite a bit of paperwork, which I found daunting. Once I got it all done and turned in, I hadn't found out I got approved until the Friday before the date I thought the surgery was set. When I called Dr. Neva's assistant, Rebekkah, to tell her I was approved, she told me that they had only tentatively set the date for the following Monday, but since they had not heard from me, they had filled the time slot with someone else and that the next available date would be the following Thursday or Friday. So I ended up calling Erica in tears to tell her my appointment was being rescheduled, which meant I could work on the days she had scheduled me off but I could not work on the days she had me scheduled to work. Erica reassured me that it would be okay if I swapped days. I could come in on the days I was scheduled to have off and take alternative days off for my surgery which she had scheduled me to work. She also said if I needed to keep my mind off the stress that all of this was causing me, I was welcome to work that weekend, even though I was not scheduled. As I already had plans, I reassured Erica that I would not need to work the weekend but appreciated her being so understanding about my stress. Additionally, on the day of my surgery Erica swung by the hospital to make sure I knew I was not alone during the event bringing with her my first remembered vase of flowers. Ma had also come from Rose City to be with me for my surgery. The crystals were found to be benign as well as the lump Dr. Neva had found.

So it was the comment by Erica about my being gifted that got me wondering if I should go full-time at the North Central Second-Hand Retail Store. As I weighed the pros and cons of going full-time at CODCL or at the North Central Second-Hand Retail Store, the latter option seeing as every hour I worked I would have quite a few people I would work with, thus the job at the North Central Second-Hand Retail Store seemed it would give me more people I could directly impact as I tried to magnify the Lord through my life. So I started talking to Petunia City's North Central Second-Hand Retail Store's team leaders (by that time Erica was store team leader in Hibiscus City) about the possibility of getting more hours.

The team leaders kept me in mind when positions opened. Between December 2011 and April 2012, I went from just being part time with 10 to 19 hours a week to full-time at 30 hours per week to 40 hours per week. The downside of going full time was that I no longer could be in charge of the pull and the team leaders insisted I learn to sort apparel. The store team leaders made sure that the majority of their full-time team members who worked in apparel knew how to sort as that was the job that took the most work. So, the team leaders had Sara V teach me how to sort. Thankfully prior to my leaning to sort, I had been involved in a few apparel meetings where the team leaders would pull a few dozen tops from the sales floor which were going to get pulled and would have the team members determine potential reasons why the item didn't sell. Some of the reasons I heard at the meetings would include that the item was: stained, torn, snagged, pili, faded, outdated, sized wrong, over or underpriced, etc. Due to hearing these meetings, Sara was able to train me to her standards of quality pretty quick with it taking a bit longer in my getting down all the categories of apparel down so as to properly price them. The time of training with Sara was wonderful as she was very easy going and friendly which made her become one of my closest friends at work. She was tall, skinny, bronze-skinned, and had sun bleached hair that reached halfway down her back. When she heard about Abby's battle with breast cancer she got me a pink fleece Columbia sweatshirt with a pink ribbon on it and offered to go on a 5K fundraiser walk for breast cancer with me. Before she had gotten to go on the 5K with me though, she found out she was pregnant and a few months later got another job in the Gladiolus City area as that was the area she was living.

It was the beginning of 2011 when Abby started to experience a nagging cough which the doctors treated initially with antibiotics, as a cold. Then when the cough persisted, they gave her an inhaler for asthma and after the cough still persisted the doctors treated her for pneumonia before taking an x-ray. On the x-ray the doctors saw a slight thickening of the lung wall and since none of the prior treatments touched her cough and instead it seemed to be growing worse the doctors finally scheduled a biopsy of the slight thickened lung wall they found by X-ray. From the biopsy done on her birthday in June, they found out her cancer had returned. During this period, Abby struggled with the nagging cough, which according to Ma who had moved in with Abby and her family told me how winded Abby got by just climbing the stairs to her apartment and which was triggered by talking – making conversations with her over the phone impossible (further aggravated by my having a phone plan which had such poor reception that I HAD to be by my apartments patio door in order for it to not drop calls or make the call crackle). It was while she resumed treatments for cancer that Abby and Nathan were told they had to find a new apartment. Apparently, the landlord had made a clean sweep, requiring most of the tenants of the building to move. A few months earlier Ma had moved in with them. She had torn her rotator cuff and she wanted to be there for Abby and help her take care of the dog and Susannah. When the doctor told Abby that the cancer had returned, he also told her that the doctors would only be treating the symptoms and not the cancer, and that now it was just a matter of time. Abby then called me and told me the doctor's news. Needless to say, I was quite shaken and made plans to go see her on my first weekend off. I thought that with how bad her cough was and because the doctor said it would just be a matter of time, she probably would not live to see Christmas. So I brought Abby and Susannah's Christmas presents to them, which I had already bought as I wanted to make sure Abby got to enjoy the gifts and see Susannah enjoy hers. Abby got upset with me as she did not like the impression I gave her that I thought she would not live until Christmas.

When I told the team leaders at my job about how Abby's cancer had returned, they all kept reassuring me they would help me however they could. I toyed with the idea of moving to Rose City at that time, but since the chemotherapy made her cough go away which seemed like a good thing, I decided that as I really did not want to move again, I wouldn't. Abby also kept telling me not to move just for her because she knew how much I did not want to move again.

It was about that time when Matthew M, a guy from the North Central Second-Hand Retail Store who always seemed to have a smile and a friendly word for everyone, whom I had learned went to the Morning Dove Church, asked me if I would like to go to a play a friend of his was in. This was the first time some guy had asked me to join him in something which could be considered a date, so as I felt we had a common faith and possibly a few other things in common, I told him sure. So he told me where the play was held. I met him there and we watched the play together. I did not really like the sexuality that the play had and neither did Matthew. In fact, I loved the way Matthew openly shared his feelings about the play and wanted to know my feelings, so when he asked me if I wanted to have supper with him sometime I said yes. When I went to his place for supper a week or so later, I asked him what his thoughts were for us: friendship or something more. Matthew said it was just friendship at that time but would consider something more. Again I was impressed with Matthew. Since I was more attracted to another guy physically than Matthew, and because Matthew looked more like Ma's age than my own (even though he was only halfway between Ma's age and mine) since he was already graying and Ma was only beginning to gray, I was not willing to tell Matthew I would consider anything more than friends during the next few months that we hung out together. Also I tried to determine how I felt about a few additional facts he shared with me, plus as I knew how he lived off disability and only worked part time due to a back injury (while I persisted in working full time without disability despite my back injury). Overall I did not want to rush into a relationship like I felt Ma and Abby had. As I tried to determine how I felt, I know that I loved how he would call me several times every week and would make weekly plans to do something with me, but my doubts kept me from being more than friends. Matthew had also invited me to a niece's birthday party and to his family's white elephant gift Christmas party as he had nine siblings, lots of nieces and nephews and both parents. In January 2012, he told me that he did not feel anything more than friendship for me either, so he said if I wanted to spend time with another guy instead of him, I could do that without hurting him. I was relieved at hearing this, as it helped me as I struggled with my doubts.

Matthew, a few weeks into our spending time together, when he learned Abby was battling breast cancer was the one who told me about how Valley Automotive was having a Drive for a Cure event, which was a fundraiser for breast cancer. He took me to the event where he test drove most of the vehicles though he kept offering to let me drive. As I didn't feel the need to drive, I let him as he was excited about the prospect of getting to drive all those new, higher end vehicles and I was just happy to spend time with him supporting a good cause. As I told Matthew how I knew that the lady directing traffic for a festival along the route was my friend, Nelly V whom I knew from Rosemary City's Alliance Church, Matthew would honk and we would wave every time we passed her. I texted Nelly to let her know it was me driving by, and I told her more about the event, which prompted her interest in joining me in participating for at least a half hour in subsequent years. The Drive for a Cure event offers vehicles for people to drive who may never drive them otherwise (such as a Hyundai, Land Rover, Mercedes, Nissan, Porsche, Range Rover, Fiat, Mini Coopers, etc).

Valley Automotive supplied a mapped 10- to 11-mile route for us to drive the vehicles and Valley Automotive then contributes one dollar for each mile driven to a cancer research foundation. The driver needs to be at least eighteen years old, must sign a paper, get a wristband, and then stands in line to drive as many cars as they want to drive over the Friday and Saturday that the event is held on.

After Matthew took me to the play and I shared with him about Abby's battle with cancer, he shared with me how he had just been diagnosed with lymphoma. I felt a bond with him at that point, as I knew he knew what I was feeling with Abby's diagnosis. That was probably part of the reason why, at that point, I did consider dating him and while at the same time felt that I did not want to tell him I would not want to date him either, if that was the way I felt led. Thankfully, though, he helped me with that decision by telling me our relationship would stay as a friendship.

Meanwhile, Abby resumed chemotherapy and after a few rounds her cough went away. Since the doctors did not have an actual tumor to monitor the effects of the chemo on the cancer, but instead only found a slight thickening of a lung wall (which is how they detected the cancer), the doctors told my sister she needed to let them know about any cough she developed. Since they had put her on chemotherapy for several rounds and her cough had disappeared, the doctors then had given her the choice of switching to hormones to suppress estrogen production as that was what her cancer was feeding on for treatment, which was less stressful on her body compared to chemotherapy. So this was the route she chose. After six months of hormone treatments, however, her cough came back, and in April 2012, her doctor told her the cancer was back, so she started chemotherapy again. She again underwent several rounds of chemotherapy which made her cough go away. After those rounds of chemotherapy the doctor again decided to put her back on hormones.

THE ORGANIZATION RELEASING CHILDREN FROM POVERTY IN JESUS' NAME AT ROSEMARY CITY

It had been shortly after I moved to Rosemary City that the lower area coordinator of the state I grew up in for the Organization Releasing Children from Poverty in Jesus' Name told me her group was getting together in Clover City and told me she would love to meet me. I told her if she could make sure I had a ride to the event, I would gladly go. So, she lined up a ride for me and I got to go and that is where I first met Raymond and Dori S. When they heard how I did not have a car, they offered to give me a ride back to Rosemary City but wanted to take me to some second-hand stores first which I was glad to do. I had learned how car rides could be quite a bonding experience and they were such a fun-loving couple. While they were serious when discussing the Organization Releasing Children from Poverty in Jesus' Name's work, their infectious humor also would keep coming out. They both tended to smile a lot and while Dori was probably about my height with curly blond hair, her husband was probably at least a foot taller with graying dark hair. That day they took me down to Hibiscus City's Flycatcher Thrift Shoppe where they had a section where they sold everything in it for just $1 per item. They also took me to another store or two that day before calling it quits and taking me home.

Then a couple months later they were in the market of getting a

new car, so they offered me the choice of their red two door Ford or
their silver four door Honda Civic LX which they were planning on
replacing and just charged me at I price I would be able to afford. I chose
the Honda Civic as I hoped to use it to provide transportation to people
who may need it. I haven't done much of that type of transporting but
having four doors has been useful when I have my niece over, especially
the period when I delivered newspaper in the wee morning hours and
choose to let her sleep as I took her down to my car. Raymond and Dori
then brought the Honda over to Rosemary City when I told them I was
interested in buying it. When they had learned about the condition
the laptop Kurt H had given me was in, they gave me their old laptop
which was a newer laptop too. This couple is a hoot to be around. They
enjoy the fun side of life with giving and taking little jokes and puns.
They are also animal lovers, although because Dori is allergic to some
animals, they just provide for the wildlife that surrounds them outside
their home.

At the Organization Releasing Children from Poverty in Jesus'
Name meeting I also met Esther J. She is pretty straightforward, direct
person. She has such passion for the Organization Releasing Children
from Poverty in Jesus' Name and for those whom the Organization
Releasing Children from Poverty in Jesus' Name helps. Together with
some teens she meets with regularly at her church, Esther has taken to
making and selling jewelry and the funds go to sponsor children. They
have to sell enough to sponsor a child for a full year before Esther will
let them choose a child. Esther herself sponsors quite a few children
and she brings her binder where she keeps all her letters from her
sponsored children to all the Organization Releasing Children from
Poverty in Jesus' Name events she works. Often Esther is found at the
Organization Releasing Children from Poverty in Jesus' Name event
sharing some of these letters and photos she has of the children whom
she has gotten to visit. Over the years since I have been volunteering
with the Organization Releasing Children from Poverty in Jesus'
Name, Esther and I have ended up manning tables together for the
Organization Releasing Children from Poverty in Jesus' Name at several
concerts and at the North Central Christian Festival too.

Also at the Organization Releasing Children from Poverty in Jesus' Name meeting I met Raphael and Shannon S, an elderly couple whom always seemed to have a smile. Shannon's hands were quite crippled by rheumatoid arthritis when I first met them, and Raphael had to help her with many of her basic needs. When they learned how Abby was battling cancer, Shannon told me how Raphael had battled cancer and was currently in remission. Before my three-year stay in Rosemary City was over, however, I learned that Raphael's cancer had come back and he was not expected to live to see their fiftieth wedding anniversary. He did, though, and he outlived Shannon who passed away in September 2013. This couple God used to provide comfort for me as I sought peace about Abby's cancer. In the following months, I would use a picture I had of them, which I framed, to remind myself how God can keep cancer from claiming a person in the time frame a doctor predicts. I remember working with them during my first Peter Eide concert whom they were big fans. They also had taken me out once to eat.

While in Rosemary City, I also helped Straight and Narrow Church as they over several services had a few tables set out completely covered in children from India whom were from churches near where they already supported mission works. Also, Rosemary City Alliance had a pastor in Northwest third world African country which they supported so they took up keeping several packets of children from his church who needed sponsoring. This pastor from Northwest third world African country I got to hear speak one time, and a story he shared that day has stuck with me ever since. The following is how I remember what the Northwest third world African country pastor shared. He had shared how when he had gone to college he had befriended a Muslim man but due to discomfort in their differences in beliefs, the pastor had never actually shared about his Christian beliefs. Several months passed and as the pastor was returning to Northwest third world African country, he and the Muslim said their goodbyes. As he said, "Goodbye, my friend," to the Muslim, the Muslim disagreed as he told the pastor how, "If you truly consider me a friend, you would have tried to convince me to become a Christian as I know that your beliefs consider that I will be going to hell if I do not accept Jesus as my Savior. So you can't really think of me as a friend if you weren't willing to at least try to convert me to your beliefs to keep me from going to hell." I feel like this is a very good point but what with my perfectionist personality which is also a people pleaser, I don't feel like I'm a very good friend to a lot of people as I don't try to convert them as I cave to the assumption that they do not want me to force my religion on them.

ROSEMARY CITY EVANGELICAL FREE CHURCH

When Nora V from Rose City Alliance Church learned I got a job in Rosemary City in October 2009, she was excited for me and shared with me how she had a couple children living over in Rosemary City. She told me how she knew there was a great Alliance church in Rosemary City. In fact, Nora also shared how the church had a great young adult ministry in which both of her children who lived in Rosemary City had met their significant others. This prompted me to google the directions to Rosemary City Alliance from the apartment which I had found to live. It looked to be about five miles from my apartment. I remembered how, when I first moved off the farm, I had walked about that same distance back to the farm several times, so I was sure I could walk the same distance to this church now.

On the first Sunday in October 2010, I set out walking to Rosemary City Alliance Church. On my way, I passed a gas station, and it wasn't until a few blocks later that I realized I needed to use the restroom. So I debated about going back, but I could faintly see a traffic light about the same distance in front of me. I chose to keep going forward. As I continued to walk toward Rosemary City Alliance, I heard a train whistle and noticed tracks up ahead. Oh, I hoped and prayed that the train was not going to be crossing there, as my bladder would not let me forget that I still needed to go to the restroom and it reminded me how I probably should have stopped at the gas station. Thankfully, I made it past the tracks without having to wait for a train, but as I neared the stoplight I saw there wasn't any gas station, store, or similar business where I thought I could inconspicuously stop to use a restroom so I feared that my bladder was going to try to force me to use some bushes. Thankfully there was a building nearby, however, that had a few cars near it, and I saw some people entering and leaving the building. Due to its shape, my first impression was that it was a Jehovah's Witness which due to their differences from what I believed I really did not want to enter as I did not want them to try telling me my faith was wrong or tell me how we believe the same thing as I had some do in the past when I had talked with them. After all I believe that Jesus IS God, sent to die for us to take away our sins so that we could have ever lasting life with him. But I REALLY had to use the bathroom so I thought that I should at least see if I could get in and find a restroom. I successfully entered the building and saw written above an opposing door on the other side of what looked like a sanctuary were the words "Following Jesus, Engaging People." That put my mind somewhat at ease though not entirely, as I thought the building must be a church of some kind, but still Rosemary City Alliance was where I ultimately wanted to go. After using the restroom, on my way out, a woman asked if she could help me with anything. I told her I had just been out for a walk and needed to use the restroom, to which she replied that she was glad they were able to help me with that. So with the single purpose of making it to Rosemary City Alliance's 9:30 a.m. service, I left the building. But my curiosity made me wonder what organization this building belonged to. I saw by a small painted on sign on what was the building's front doors that it was the Rosemary City Evangelical Free Church. At that point, I remembered how Betsy S from the Buttercup City Evangelical Free Church had shared with me about how they had a sister church in Rosemary City which was a really good church. So I looked at the posted service hours, which were 9:00 a.m. and 10:30a.m. Then as I noticed it was around 9:10 a.m., but the parking lot and building were mostly empty my curiosity was stirred. So I went back inside and seeing the lady who had earlier wanted to help me, I said to her, "I see your church service is at 9:00; are you not having it today?"

The lady ended up being Liz S, the church secretary. Liz gave a little laugh and said, "Our church likes to reach out to the community a couple times a year, and this Sunday happens to be one of the Sundays when the church goes out into the community and provides services. You are welcome to stay, though, as the congregation will meet back here in about an hour to share what they did. We will also have pizza at that time, which you are welcome to stay and enjoy."

The thought of community outreach on Sunday intrigued me and the free pizza sounded downright good, so I stayed. This gave me a chance to talk some more with Liz and a few other people in the congregation who had stayed at the church to help set up for the pizza afterwards and who were watching the children. Liz S and Georgia V, one of the women watching the children, then both offered to give me a ride home after church. I took Georgia up on the offer. Georgia in turn introduced me to several more of the moms at the church and offered to give me a ride to church every Sunday, which I accepted, as I had already decided I really liked the Rosemary City Evangelical Free Church after just those few hours with them.

Over the following years, I continued to really enjoy the sermons at the Rosemary City Evangelical Free Church and all the friends I made there. They had a Sunday school class during the 9:00 service, which I would go to, and then I would go to the 10:30 worship service.

Several weeks later, in December, Rosemary City Evangelical Free Church had a ladies game night at the church which I went to after work. (By that time, Raymond and Dori S had helped me find a car so I was able to drive myself to the event.) That night I met my friend Rissa H for the first time, when she came over and gave me a bit of a pat. She had blond hair which fell just a bit past her shoulder which she had a tendency to flip back over her shoulder when it would fall forward. As I do not often get physical affection of any kind from people (unless they ask me if it would be okay for them to hug me), so that pat of hers really stuck out to me as I did not know Rissa prior to that night. As the night wore on, I could see she was one of the main people in charge of the games and that she just was that type of friendly, outgoing person. It prompted me to want to get to know her better, so when a few weeks later she asked me if I wanted to go eat out somewhere – her treat, I said sure. She asked me what my favorite type of food was and then took me to Fazoli's. While we were eating, we shared our stories and learned we had a lot in common, as we both struggled with our upbringings with a dominant woman. It was also at this meal that I learned Rissa worked at my favorite radio station 91.9FM, a sister station to 88.5FM which helped me find the courage to leave the farm. I learned she worked at 91.9FM as shortly after I had gotten my car, I had swung by the station just to see the station which meant so much to me, but at that time I hadn't known Rissa very well so I hadn't stopped to say hi. At the meal, Rissa had expressed her sadness that I hadn't stopped to say hi. Throughout my time in Rosemary City after that, Rissa was the one I often went to when I just needed someone to talk to or needed some advice, as she was about my mom's age as she was getting married the year I was born.

As I continued going to Rosemary City Evangelical Free Church I decided I wanted to get involved there, so I asked if I could help with the children's ministry. First, I was told I had to fill out paperwork so they could check out my background. Shortly afterwards, Pastor Horace N asked me if I would like to help with AWANA, which encourages children to memorize Bible verses. I said I would. Through AWANA I started to get to know Kimberly I, who was a stay at home mom for several rambunctious kids. We would usually take a few minutes every week just to catch up a bit with each other. From these visits, I learned we both had a dairy background and she just reminded me so much of my sister Abby that we really hit it off.

After I had been in Rosemary City for about a year I decided the apartment on Lark Sparrow Avenue was more expensive seeing it was almost $600/month without heat being included. While it was fun having free cable, I didn't need it so much as I wanted free heat. As I still had hopes that my family would come and stay with me occasionally, I still focused on finding a two-bedroom apartment. So, I went looking and found an apartment on Robin Drive which was on the second floor, a balcony, let in more light while including heat and being $100 less a month. It also had one garage stall and one parking space assigned to each apartment. The apartment had a secured entrance, requiring one to have a key to enter. Then straight in front of the door was the stairs leading up to the second floor. My apartment was the second door on the right. Inside the apartment one found themselves in the dining area with the living room to the left and the kitchen straight ahead. Then there was a bit of a hall with the bathroom and two bedrooms off of it. Downstairs on the other side of the wall where the stairs were, was where the mailboxes and at the end of the hall was the laundry room.

As I decided this was where I wanted to move to, I talked with Kurt I, the youth pastor at RCEFC, to see if he would be willing to help me move my things. He was and he found a few other people to help him and together they got all my things moved to my new address. As they were helping me move my things, Suzy M, a lady in her eighties in one of the downstairs apartments decided to treat the moving guys with a pizza as she, "knew how hungry guys get when working so hard."

Throughout the upcoming year while I lived in that apartment, I got to know Suzy pretty well as she made sure she got her exercise by walking the hallway on the first-floor numerous times every day. Suzy welcomed me to her apartment, which was the second apartment on the right on the first floor, several times a month and we took to occasionally playing Scrabble when we got together, too. The rest of the times we tended to work on craft projects, she with her knitting and me with my looms and afghan making.

Then another couple from RCEFC, Dick and Iola X, who were probably around 15-20 years my senior, offered me some loveseats which they were getting rid of. As I thought it would make my place more inviting to have people over, as up to then I only had the recliner I brought with me from Geranium City and a plush swivel chair my mom had found on the side of the road and gave me, I told them I would love them. The cool thing was that each of these items either were green or in the loveseat's case had just enough green that I thought they all matched pretty good. This couple also would occasionally invite me over to their place for supper and the chance to watch football together.

One day in the middle of the summer the year that I lived at Robin Drive, I had been visiting my friend Rissa at her job at 91.9FM when a strong storm rolled in. We watched the sky turn very black in the middle of the day and trees bending nearly double. When I drove to my apartment afterwards there was branches down all over as well as numerous trees and power lines. While I don't recall having to detour in order to get home, as I drove home I had seen several streets that were blocked off due to downed trees and power lines. When I arrived home, I saw there were a few shingles that had blown up on the roof over my apartment in the storm which the rain had then blown under. Inside my apartment, I saw that the rain had come into my apartment and had puddled on some papers which were sitting on top of my laptop that was on my dining room table. Thankfully I was able to save each of the papers which were the papers I had scanned to make computerized documents of them for CODCL. I had brought home earlier as I intended to work on them as during the scanning process sometimes the computer hadn't been able to accurately read the document so the scanned documents were not always an actual replica of the original documents. So I was working on making sure the scanned document matched the original, but if not I was correcting the scanned copy to make them match. The times it was the most difficult was when they used charts which the scanner struggled with comprehending the charts. Anyway these were the papers which the rain water was sitting on when I came home so I took them and spread them out on the floor in the guest bedroom. Thankfully my computer also was okay. Then since the rain water continued to drip into my apartment, I put down on my table a pan with a cookie sheet under it to catch all the water. My apartment's electricity ended up being out as it was in most if not all of Rosemary City and some of the neighboring neighborhoods which prompted my friend, Matthew M from the North Central Second-Hand Retail Store, to buy me a flashlight so I would not have to stumble around in the dark. What he didn't know though that I had for years worked on getting down how to get around without lights as much as I could ever since I remembered reading about how Helen Keller learned to make her way around while being blind and how cats use minimal light to see plus I used Uncle Larry's dislike of having us use electricity more than we had to. (Some of his frustration probably came from how we occasionally forgot to shut lights back off at night so that the lights were on all night and back into the next day.) Then that evening my friend, Wioletta, had invited me over to place for a spaghetti supper which I gladly accepted and afterwards we played a game of Scrabble with her boyfriend, Earl and she offered to let me bring over the food from my refrigerator and store it in her refrigerator until my electricity came back on since she had not lost her electricity.

At Rosemary City Evangelical Free Church I was also blessed by the ladies Christmas tea they held every December. At the Christmas tea a hostess would set her table with her own dishes and decorations so each table was unique. Then the men would serve the meal. Afterwards they would have a speaker share the gospel story and a few times they had a woman who would draw a picture and when done would darken the room and when turning on a black light there was another picture visible.

Then each spring Rosemary City Evangelical Free Church would also host a women's retreat. Thanks to some scholarships being available to me, I was able to go a few times. I enjoyed being able to go as these events allowed me to get to know some of the ladies better. The one-year Robin T, who led women's Bible study, was the one who led the Bible sessions on the difference between Mary and Martha. Another year it was my friend Rissa H who led the Bible sessions. There were a number of Bible sessions throughout the few days of retreat, followed by smaller groups who discussed what we heard and tried to find applications for our lives. Then there were meals provided and some free time in which the one year I went with a group of ladies about my own age, whom I remember as all being married with children, out to eat and then to do some shopping. Mostly I went just for the companionship.

It was while I was at one of the women's retreat events that I felt prompted to write a letter asking Grandma Nancy about what would become of my older sisters Dora and Sandy if she, Ma and Uncle Larry ended up passing away. As I was sure she did not hope they would outlive Dora and Sandy who still helped "run the farm". Though to my knowledge they never earned much more than room and board, or were entrusted with the more essential nuts and bolts of running the farm like the finances, doing repairs, calling someone other than family for help, etc. Also I had asked Grandma Nancy if she had forgiven people as in the Lord's prayer we ask the Lord to forgive us as we forgive others. I asked this as throughout the years she continually shared about what people have done against her which I shared earlier in the chapter Grandma Nancy. Grandma Nancy, whom has since passed away, wrote in reply to my letter. I am sharing parts of the letters so you my reader can possibly see why I and most if not all in my family was intimidated by her. To my concerns about Dora and Sandy, she replied, *"When I told Dora and Sandy about the way you alone view the lives they are living here on the farm and you think there should be something better in life by moving out and they both say—Dora says, "NO WAY" and Sandy says "NO" and they love to be where they are at. We give them all of their needs and whatever they tell us they want now. They will not be left destitute. Larry has a will in his inheritance and their welfare is well taken care of in their lifelong futures. Dora will know how to handle it according to the way they'll both like it. They think they aren't telling you anything about how or where you should live your life. Why should you try to interfere in their lives? Please don't do that to them! Another memorable thing about this is when Sandy was about six years old she cried and said, "I want to stay by Larry!" She felt safe and secure here on the farm with Larry. Women have been seeking jobs (at something they can handle and like to do) as milkmaids on farms. It is a respectable job.*

Then in reply to my concern about if she is forgiving according to the Lord's Prayer she shared how, *"God the Son long ago taught us to pray, "The Lord's Prayer", and that is the (capital S) Son, gathering us together Himself saying, our "Our Father." Therefore, through, with, and in Him we are (if we think of what we are saying) getting and giving forgiveness, by way of Our Father. As for as the word forgiveness (as you are using it) it has only the human interpretation (which has some value) but merits only as much as a polite mannerism; such as, excuse me or beg your pardon. For me, it must be the God based forgiveness. Why don't people listen to what the Son tells us about the word, as He uses it in the Father in the Blessed Trinity Lord's Prayer, keeping what the Son in the same Blessed Trinity, the ones that are both meant in the original Apostles' Creed, when He says*

"Our Father. He joins us together with Himself as He says "Forgive us our trespasses as we forgive those that trespass against us." This way, through the Son is the only true way through which the real, true forgiveness comes and must come to us from God the Father through the Son. Then God's true kind of forgiveness is that it is (in His way granted by Him—both to us for our sinful trespasses, and from us including all that are involved. When it comes to our end of life judgment, this the way we are told that the Son, that died to take away the sins of the world will be there to judge the living and the dead.

Thank you for your concern, but you must let go of your "know it all" attitude and do the First Commandment. Never "my way," but with the Son we must do as He says, "Lead us never into temptation, then we can reconsider that these are things the human self thinks are best. Also, according to Romans Chapter 8 to the end of the book of Wisdom" And we know that in all things the Father works "good" to those that love Him, and have been called according to His purpose. Can't you see His hand in this? Whereas, you seem to be substituting your wishes to supersede the will of the Father as He urges Dora and Sandy to have His way that is taking them eventually to His place that He has for them in Paradise. "Let go, let God." Do the First Commandment, God's way at all times."

These replies were very much the way Grandma Nancy came across whenever anyone disagreed with her up till the day she died. I always hope that I do not come across this way but in too many ways, I see my thoughts, words and actions are more of the characteristics of Grandma Nancy's which I honestly do not want to display.

Meanwhile as I hoped Rosemary City was my last move and I wanted to connect with people more. I tried to do what I had done in Cherry Blossom City and invite people over to my place for games. I never was very successful at this, however, other than on my birthdays, so there were only a few times where a few people had actually come over. I was seriously discouraged about it especially after Michaela C, who I thought was a friend, told me that I sounded desperate when I would send out emails to the friends I made in Rosemary City inviting them to come over. Michaela also discouraged me when she would tell me she would come to an event at my place after I sent out the invitation, but then on the day of the event she would tell me another friend of hers had invited her to do something else so she couldn't come after all. It started getting to the point that as soon as I saw her excited reply to my email that she would come, I would mentally not plan on seeing her show up. Eventually I stopped inviting her altogether, as I got the impression she did not actually consider me a friend she wanted to spend time with.

ROSEMARY CITY ALLIANCE

I did eventually make it to the Rosemary City Alliance Church but not until Raina S, the daughter of Nora V from Rose City Alliance, and I connected over the phone and she offered to drive me sometime in November 2010. Raina and her husband, Rhett, usually went to the 6:30 p.m. service but would volunteer with the children's church or go to a Bible study during the 5:30 p.m. service, so I would actually go to both evening services. I really enjoyed Pastor Rob's sermons as they were pretty applicable and he used a bit of humor to keep them lively. So I was quite saddened a year or so later when I learned he got offered a different position and was moving to the eastern US to preach. Raina had been about eight months pregnant at the time we first met, so she and I spent a good portion of the services sitting down since her feet bothered her and my back bothered me which wasn't helped by the fact that the floor sloped with seating in an auditorium fashion.

Rosemary City Alliance was about a half mile from Rosemary City Evangelical Free Church. Rosemary City Alliance was a huge building easily encompassing a whole block, maybe even two or three, and had a couple parking lots which probably also encompassed a block apiece. Rosemary City Alliance had entrances on the east side and the North side. The north side led straight to the huge fellowship area which was off the sanctuary while the east side was over by the classrooms with a narrow window lined hallway leading over to the fellowship area. As there could easily be 500 people per its five services, this hallway could bottleneck quickly if people stopped to talk so usually the people from the earlier service would be walking to pick up their children from the classrooms or headed to that parking lot while others coming to the next service would be coming in from the east parking lot. Once a person reached the fellowship hall area it was possible for people to stop and talk but I can't remember doing so much even though that would typically be what I've done at all other churches I attended prior to Rosemary City Alliance as well as since.

The first Sunday I was there Rhett and Raina introduced me to Samuel and Lisa M who were trying to encourage people to get involved in Bible studies that week. Samuel was a tall guy with a shaved head and glasses who would probably been intimidating if he wasn't so friendly and laughed a lot while Lisa was about my height and was more serious. Samuel and Lisa told me how they led a Bible study on Monday nights and they offered to give me a ride to it as they shared how they lived not too far from where I lived. At that point, I still had not gotten another car since my accident. They also offered to give me a ride to church if I wanted them to. I took them up on the offer to the Bible study but said I would continue riding to church with Rhett and Raina as I planned to continue to go to Rosemary City Evangelical Free Church in the mornings so would prefer going to Rosemary City Alliance in the evenings. Samuel and Lisa M usually went to the morning services. After introducing me to Samuel and Lisa M, Rhett and Raina S took me to the event for young adults, which were held after the 6:30 pm church services. There they introduced me to Trudy Q, a big, cheerful, outgoing honey blond haired lady, who loves to laugh. Trudy and I got to talking and learned how we both had been homeschooled. Later as Rhett and Raina needed to get going, they asked Trudy if she would mind taking me home and Trudy cheerfully said she would.

This became an almost weekly routine for me until I got a car: I would go to Rosemary City Evangelical Free Church in the morning, then to both evening services at Rosemary City Alliance Church, followed by their young adult program, after which Trudy would take me home. The young adult program was usually pretty laid back. There were a few game tables, some tables containing snacks and drinks and several games. Mostly people stood around chatting with their friends partaking of the snacks and beverages while a few people would play a game or at one of the game tables. Usually I would join the people who were just standing around chatting as that was what Trudy usually did as well as the friends she would introduce me to. Initially Program Uniting Singles was led by Rob and Ava R, a couple that was about my age though possibly a few years younger but they eventually headed to North West Africa at which point there wasn't anyone exactly in charge though most of the time afterwards I remember Ray, whom I remember sharing a bit about having been a partier while going to College at Jasmine City before he became a Christian. He briefly went to the Bible study I went to and a few times he held it at his house where I got to meet his big black Labrador Retriever.

These opportunities to ride home with Trudy after the young adult program, helped me get to know Trudy pretty well, which was also helped by her inviting me to her family's Thanksgiving celebration so I would not have to be alone for Thanksgiving. Trudy's family consisted of both her parents and a couple younger brothers and three sisters. Though I am not sure if the oldest sister who was already living in the state west of the state I grew up in had been home for Thanksgiving. Additionally her family had invited Pastor Rob and his family to join them for Thanksgiving. So there were quite a few people partaking in the meal. After the meal, Trudy and her mom transferred all the leftovers into smaller storage containers and put them out on the porch as it was snow covered so it worked for a refrigerator. Afterwards there was a bit of game playing and watching TV or a movie and throughout the rest of the day they would help themselves to the leftovers.

Then about a week or two later I got a call from Trudy to find out when it would work for her to come over to my apartment. So, we set up a day and time and she ended up bringing me my first Christmas tree, ornaments, candle warmer, tablecloth, a candy jar, candy (my favorites which are Reese's Peanut Butter cups) wrapped in red, green and silver wrappers and a tree skirt. I was so overwhelmed as I had been wondering what I was going to do for Christmas since I didn't feel like I really had any money to buy anything to make my place feel like Christmas. Trudy also had invited me over for Christmas if I didn't go home and to her family's place to see the New Year in. When I went to see the New Year in, there were many other family friends also gathered. All night there was lots of game playing, snacks to munch on and conversations. When the New Year arrived Trudy and several family and friends all went out their house banging on pans, calling out, "Happy New Year!"

Trudy and I continued to hang out periodically over the following years while I lived in Rosemary City and is one of the friends I call whenever I head over to the Rosemary City area especially if I hope to be able to spend a night in Rosemary City. Trudy was also the one who made sure everyone knew it was my birthday when I just sent an email inviting people over to my place on my birthday but hadn't mentioned in the email that it was my birthday the first year I was in Rosemary City. The following years I shared how it was my birthday when I would invite people over. Trudy also introduced me to a lot of her other friends whom have since become friends of mine like Nelly V (who invited me to join her group of friends when they would get together for games and who joined me a couple times when I have done the Drive For A Cure event). Trudy also introduced me to Nada Y who was also homeschooled. Nada was someone I would invite to come and spend time at my place; however, she was usually unable to come. Finally, she chose to tell me straight out how with her busy schedule (two part-time jobs) she struggled to find time to hang out with the friends she had had for years, so she doubted she would come to my place because she felt it was important to try to find time to maintain her current friends. Yes, I was disappointed, but I appreciated her honesty so that I wouldn't feel like my invitation to her would only be considered as long as something else better did not come along for her. The latter was something my friend Michaela C tended to do though she probably never meant to make me feel that way. Though she did tell me one time that I came across desperate as I tried on a weekly basis to invite people over to my place. Overall I just feel sincerity and keeping one's word is not something a person should take lightly which Michaela and I appear to view differently as I try not to commit to going to something because if I do, I do my best to go and instead turn down doing things which would come up later even if the latter appeared to be something I would prefer to do. This oversensitivity to others reactions, is something I am still having to work on too.

Rarely did I have anybody join me for any of my game nights though. I usually was most successful when I just invited one person over and they invited others. During my time in Rosemary City the person I most frequently remembered coming over for games was Esther X. I first met her at Program Uniting Singles at Rosemary City Alliance but then she later started to come to Samuel and Lisa M's Bible study too. Esther was a girl that was partly Native American and had the dark eyes and hair typical of those origins. She also had had Fetal Alcohol Syndrome which is what prompted her family to withdraw her from school, never taught her how to drive or use the bus system which was about three blocks from where they lived, or encouraged her to get a job. They would make sure she went to church though but the one they were attending, God's Army Bible Church or later at Rosemary City Alliance but both had several hundred other people attending so she really struggled to feel like she knew anyone. Esther desperately wanted to change her environment though which prompted Samuel and Lisa M to help provide her the chance to get her GED which I do not believe she successfully completed. I also had offered to help her learn how to use the bus system and apply for jobs. None of those things were what Esther really wanted though as she shared how she met a guy online, who offered to pay for her to move to a far western state to live with him. After everybody carefully asked her to reconsider as we feared she would get hurt by the guy, she shared about meeting another guy whom would help her get away from her family. I know I shared with her a number of times of my personal experience of how bad using a guy to get away from family was as I shared how Ma had but after having had five daughters, Ma had ended up living again with the same family members she had married to get away from. I expressed my concern that that could be what would happen with Esther too if she wasn't careful which is why I was trying so hard to help her gain social skills which could help her become independent.

Unfortunately, Esther's determination to find a guy ended up resulting in her moving in with a guy who if nothing else was verbally abusive. I learned this when she asked me if I wanted one of the kittens she had as her landlord said she could only have a maximum of two cats and she had four with the three kittens. I had agreed to take one of the kittens and as I went to pick him up, Esther asked if I would be interested in going for a walk. I was okay with that as that entire time I was over at Esther's her boyfriend kept verbally, and quite loudly sharing how stupid she was and that he had known she was going to get into trouble for having taken the cat in. If I remember correctly, her boyfriend continued to verbally berate her on our walk as he tagged along. I myself was pretty scared of him but also was plenty mad at him. Eventually Esther ended up leaving him but not before she tried to commit suicide which is when the hospital intervened and sent her to a home. The place they sent her, a person had to call and get the staff's permission to visit her or any of the other residents and then she had to sign out sharing where she was going and then back in when she got back. Overall, I think that place probably was what she needed as it started to teach her some independence skills.

Other than Esther coming to the game nights I tried to hold, I only remember a few other times when I successfully managed to have other people over for games. One was Ryan H, a guy whom I met at Rosemary City Evangelical Free Church as he ran their sound board and whom had asked me once if I would be interested in a Timber Rattler baseball game. While baseball I found slow and easy to miss when finally a good play was made, I agreed to join him. Afterwards Ryan asked me if I would like to do something together again which I agreed to but never heard from him other than the one time he agreed to come over to play games at my place. Esther also had been there and she seemed more determined to get him to notice her than to actually playing the game to win.

Another time Kurt Y, a guy I had met at Program Uniting Singles who had cerebral palsy which made him very dependent upon his crutches came over with Samuel X, a friend of his who suffered from seizures which prevented him from being able to drive. Samuel X is the guy I had found more attractive than Matt G, my coworker, whom

I thought I would definitely consider for more than friends if he had expressed an interest but he never had. Esther had been over then too which made them quite uncomfortable as at one time she had tried to pressure one of them into becoming her boyfriend.

Other than these times the only times I felt I was successful having people over was when it was my birthday in which I usually had at least a handful of people over. The first year I remember Samuel M, my Bible study leader, had even come over though he was pretty allergic to cats, Betsy Q whom I remember making a scene when Isaac, my cat jumped up on the table where we were playing as he had farted in front of her, Nicole Q my friend from college who brought me a homemade cake, and Trudy Q also had come. Trudy had brought me another homemade cake and a gift which was The Game of Things which I had played with her and some of her friends a few months earlier and had fallen in love with. The Game of Things has several decks of cards which list scenarios of things a person should or shouldn't do (ex. Things you shouldn't say in a crowd, things you shouldn't say to your in-laws, things you shouldn't do at a job, etc.). Then each player wrote an answer to the scenario and then a player would guess who wrote what and if they guessed correctly they got to continue guessing but if wrong the next person got to try guessing. Trudy had also brought lasagna which she learned was my favorite food. For several weeks afterwards I enjoyed my birthday as I finished off my cakes and the leftover lasagna.

On my birthday, my final year in Rosemary City I remember having my sister Abby, Ma, Uncle Larry, and some friends whom I first made at RCEFC but whom had switched to Rosemary City Gospel which included Kimberly I, the pastor's wife—Libby V, and the pastor's parents—Aiden and Amy V. That year I remember we played The Game of Things which Abby and Kimberly I were hands down the best as unlike me who used writing utensils to get the right answers of who wrote what instead were just able to successfully guess the correct answer. Speaking of The Game of Things, I remember another friend, Wioletta, (pronounced Violetta) whom I had met through a young adult group at Solid Foundation Based Church in Pansy City, had joined me playing the game along with her boyfriend, Earl, and another friend of theirs. Wioletta I remember would draw pictures of the choices to choose from. One of the scenarios was "What things should you not do at your job" and from the pictures that she drew which I kept I know one of the answers was doodling, another was goofing around, another was yell at your boss and my answer was to speak poorly of the boss's children. Wioletta was another good friend I had made and remember hanging out with rather frequently until she moved to Colorado for a job.

For about two and a half years I had gone to Samuel and Lisa M's Bible study until they discontinued it. The studies proved to be thought provoking and valuable in getting to know them and about a dozen more people in Rosemary City. During these studies, I learned how Samuel worked at Christian Fiscal Organization for a period but currently was working at International Trucking while Lisa worked in the radiology department at Western Cities Medical. Often, she was on call so she would not always be there for the Bible study. The studies they held in their dining room and while we gathered snacks to eat they would let us all get to see their young son, Elijah, whom had been born about eight months before I joined their study, and then before we would officially start the study, Samuel and Lisa would take Elijah and put him to bed singing him a children's Bible song.

It was at Samuel and Lisa M's Bible study that I met Betsy Q, a dark haired and eyed skinny woman several inches taller than me who was pretty outspoken about her opinions. While I know she shared once with me how she didn't want me to feel intimidated by Samuel when he disagreed with me as she saw I was quieter, I remember being more intimidated by her the one time when she strongly suggested I shouldn't let my fear of losing my job influence my sharing my faith. Maybe it was because he would laugh at himself while Betsy was always so serious. Also, I remember how she invited me a few times to join her in watching Packer games once she learned how much I loved watching football. The one time it was at her house which was a larger, older place and as she had been unemployed at that time I remember the house as being dark and cool as she was working on conserving money. Another time was when she was house sitting and she invited me over to use their indoor pool while watching the game. It was this time when I shared with her about how I wanted to help my family know why I believed what I did and why I knew that suffering was not so much because of a lack of perfect prayers – which Satan would twist – but that it was to help our faith grow. Betsy then helped me look for Bible verses and stories to share my beliefs and to explain why God allows suffering. These bible verses I have included at the end of the book in case you are interested in what we found.

For that first year that I lived in Rosemary City, I kept going to Rosemary City Evangelical Free Church in the mornings and Rosemary City Alliance Church in the evenings until Pastor Rob moved to Pennsylvania. Then Rosemary City Alliance discontinued the two evening services, and the young adult events changed hands a few time until the group was only meeting once a month on Tuesdays. It just became too hard to remember which Tuesday night it was being held each month since I had stopped attending Rosemary City Alliance due to its being too big to really connect regularly with anyone I knew, so I quit going. Also I had thought I'd try to save gas money once I had a car again, by making the trip to both churches in the morning instead of going to both morning and evening services at two different churches, but the crowds were just too big at Rosemary City Alliance during the morning services. I felt like I never really got to connect with anybody on a weekly basis there, so I decided that I would just go to Rosemary City Evangelical Free Church instead.

ROSEMARY CITY GOSPEL

A couple years after I started going to Rosemary City Evangelical Free Church, I started to hear how they were going to plant a new church that was going to meet downtown Rosemary City in the Organization Providing Towards Health. As I had moved again to an apartment closer to that neighborhood, I was excited. Also I thought this would probably give me an even better chance of helping and actually getting to know the people in a church. After all the new church would be a lot smaller to begin with and I thought it would surely need people to help get it going which I offered to help do. By the time I learned about the church plant though, the church planters, Pastor Victor and Libby V, already had most of their family members and some additional friends lined up to provide them the needed team to make the planting go smoothly.

So while I wasn't put in charge of any area during the church plant, I would always help anyway with set up as I would arrive early. After arriving early I would start by helping set up about a dozen rows of chairs. Then I would help put out several Bibles per row and a church bulletin on every other chair. Once that was done I would help set up tables for snacks, by helping make coffee and setting out napkins, plates, plastic silverware and beverage cups, etc. After the service, I would then help restack the chairs and repack the Bibles, the unused snack items, etc. By helping most weeks with that, I was able to get to know Pastor Victor and Libby V, better. Also, I got to know Libby V's parents Reggie and Angel I as well as Pastor Victor's parents Aiden and

Amy V better. As I helped with set up, I also got to know some of the other planting staff better like Ike and Kimberly I whom I had gotten to know a little bit through Rosemary City Evangelical Free Church's AWANA events. Kimberly reminded me a bit of Abby, with her ready smile, her willingness to listen, and her advice which came across as suggestions and never as things I needed to do. When both Kimberly and Abby came for the party I threw for my birthday in January 2012, I discovered they both also had a knack for being able to guess accurately who had written answers in playing The Game of Things. (I first played this game with Trudy Q from Rosemary City Alliance and loved it, and then as Trudy knew that she got it for my birthday in 2011.)

The new church, Rosemary City Gospel, also started having a few community groups, which let us dig deeper into the sermons during the week that we heard on Sunday. I chose to go to a couple of these and that is how I got to know Chad S and Stacy X, a dating couple who were constantly ribbing each other. Stacy was a tall skinny lady with lovely honey brown hair which reached to the middle of her back. She always seemed to laughing as she had no problem ribbing everyone she met so the group was always lively. She particularly loved to tease me about talking so much that others couldn't join the conversation. As Stacy started inviting me to hang out with her more especially when Chad would travel which often would be weekly, I started to get to know her well enough to feel comfortable giving her as hard of a time as she gave me. Often she would fix up a meal or take me out for a meal. Afterwards sometimes we would play games. She was the one who finally taught me how to play Backgammon. Other times she would suggest that we hit garage sales. That was when I learned how horrible she was at directions as once we were only a few blocks from her home and she had no idea. Needless to say, while I would let her pick the garage sale from Craigslist, I would then give her directions to help her get there. After all I loved exploring and would as soon as I learned enough streets start taking streets I never took before in an effort to see if it could be used as a preferred route sometime. That might be why I do not remember taking a detour after the storm I mentioned in the last chapter as I easily was able to find alternative streets on my own to get to where I wanted to go. Stacy and I during those times also learned how we had a few more things in common as she struggled with a bad back and had family in the Rose City area too.

When Stacy and Chad finally set a date for their wedding, I was invited and I helped her with her rather elaborate decorations along with several others of her friends and family. Some of the decorations included gluing down "grass" on small logs tied and glued into a triplet of various heights and then gluing on a bird. She also had bought a bunch of picture frames which she had spray painted a silver metallic color and had put in pictures of her and Chad at various points in their lives up till that date. The night before her reception she about drove everyone crazy who were helping her set up as she was downright determined on making everything perfectly centered and just how she had mentally pictured how everything was to look. Everything had to be centered just right, nothing even slightly lopsided or uncentered. Then the day of her wedding, everyone ended up waiting close to another hour for her to finally be ready to march down the aisle of chairs which were set out on her parents front lawn in Rose City as that was where her wedding was taking place. She had Pastor Victor officiate her wedding and many other couples from Rosemary City Gospel also were there. Many of her guests were muttering and joking about the delay but Chad just waited patiently up front by Pastor Victor until Stacy arrived.

The group where I met Chad and Stacy had been held at Pastor Victor V's parents, Aiden and Amy V's, place so I got to know them better as well as Natisha E who was a skinny, petite lady with dark brown hair and eyes. Natisha several months later shared about how she had ended up meeting Alan I online. Within a year of my knowing Natisha, she moved to Alan's town of Hydrangea City. Alan had been a country boy, whom Natisha would excitedly share about getting to ride horses and four-wheelers out at the farm his parents owned that he helped run. Then a few months later I received an invitation to their country-style wedding. I invited Uncle Larry to join me at Alan and Natisha I's wedding, which he did the driving to get me to. Their wedding was being held out in a field which they had several people help direct us out to where they had us park way out in the field over by where they were planning to hold the ceremony. There were about a dozen rows of chairs set up which along the outside were lined with big round bales which they had decorated with flowers. The reception afterwards was then held in a nearby tent. As I saw how the wedding was being held in the field, it prompted me to ask Uncle Larry if there would be a chance that someday I could have my wedding at his farm. He said sure, but he offered only the yard, which was right on a street corner. I didn't think I would actually like that though because there would not be much privacy from passersby and the backdrop would be a building or a road instead of the wide-open space and bushes on the rest of his farm. The only way I would have considered it would be if he planted bushes around the perimeter of the yard so that it would be more appealing for a wedding, though even putting up round bales to fence up the area would have worked too if the bales were decorated beautifully. Anyway, Natisha told me that she now is waiting for me to announce my wedding so she can come.

Other community groups I went to were held at Pastor Victor and Libby V's place and then another one at Rob and Noelle Y's place. It was while I was going to the community group being held at Rob and Noelle's place that I found out how Abby's cancer had come back and was now in her liver. When I heard that, I finally decided that no matter how much I did not want to move again, I would feel better if I was living closer to Abby. My decision was based on how I felt I would be able to bond better with Susannah and work on getting a better relationship with Nathan if I wasn't living two hours and a tank of gas away from them. Up till then I hadn't as I would let myself remain frustrated about Nathan's foul vocabulary, how his playing pool at bars led him to drinking and bar fights, and his continuous job hopping or unemployment which resulted when he grew tired of a job before he got another job lined up. I did not understand how Abby could put up with Nathan's almost continuous video game playing which caused her to cook meals after working a typical full time job, plus doing laundry, and cleaning. I felt she should have at least requested his help doing most if not all of these things but she loved to cook and she wanted things put away or done according to her standards which is why she never required more from Nathan. So as I was at Rob and Noelle's community group the one week, I had shared with them about how Abby's cancer had returned and shared how I felt I needed to move back to Rose City. So, Aiden V offered to help me get a truck to move all my things and to get a work crew together to load the truck as long as I got everything packed, found someone to drive the truck to Rose City and some people to help unload it for me.

BACK TO ROSE CITY

It was while I was truly starting to feel like I had made a true friend in Stacy and was getting established in Rosemary City that Abby called me just days before the last weekend of October 2012, after she had Ma take her to the emergency room because her stomach hurt horribly. In the emergency room the doctor found tumors growing in her liver. As Abby had only been off chemo for only about two or three months, I became scared again that unless God worked a miracle, which if it was his will he could have, then Abby's time on earth was definitely getting short and I would be losing my best friend.

Living two hours away from Abby did not feel like a good option anymore. Every time I came to visit her while the doctors were treating her the prior several months, she would apologize for not having been good company during my visit. Since my lease was up where I was renting, I decided to move to Rose City. That way I could continue to help Abby do laundry, entertain Susannah, and wash dishes while she was undergoing treatments and then to hang out with her and her family when she wasn't, so that she would feel like we were getting some quality time together and not always feeling like she wasn't good company whenever I came around.

Anyway, once I decided that I wanted to move over by Abby, I updated my team leaders about how Abby's cancer had spread. Again, they continued to tell me that they would help me however they could. I told Amber N and Ian H, the team leaders in charge of the department I worked, that I wanted to look into the possibility of changing jobs to the North Central Second-Hand Retail Store in Rose City. Less than a year earlier I knew they had helped a prior North Central Second-Hand Retail Store team member make the move to Rose City as she wanted to move there with a friend but only survived living in Rose City for less than a year as she said it was too little, seeing as how it was less than a third of the size of Rosemary City and had none of the numerous additional cities all around it that made the city of Rosemary City feel more like ten times the size of Rose City. Amber N and Ian H then offered to get me the information to see if Noah R, the store team leader in Rose City, would be willing to let me make the switch by hiring me over at the Rose City location. So they gave me the number of the North Central Second-Hand Retail Store in Rose City and told me to give Noah a call. As I talked with Noah, he asked me when I would be in town next so I told him the following weekend which was the last weekend in October, at which point he encouraged me to swing by the store that Saturday as he was going to be in working. That Saturday was the day when my friend Stacy from Rosemary City Gospel church had offered to give me a ride to Rose City when she heard Abby's cancer had returned because she already was planning to visit her family in Rose City that weekend.

That Saturday as I was visiting Abby in Rose City, after I had just finished reading my morning Bible devotion and Susannah, my niece had just awakened, I got a call from Ma. She was distraught because of a phone call she had just gotten from Uncle Larry saying Grandma Nancy was doing poorly. By this time, Ma had found an apartment of her own to live in Rose City, around the end of 2011. So to stretch her money, Ma had been in line to receive some food from Monthly Church Food Distribution, a ministry of the church that back in 2006 had formerly been known as Rose City Alliance provided, which, for a fifteen-dollar donation, would provide a big box of food (worth a lot more than the fifteen-dollar donation). Ma asked if I would please come and stand in line for her so she could go out to the farm and be there with Grandma Nancy, and she asked me to later bring Drew Y, an Amish horse farrier, out to the farm to trim Cinnamon's hooves. I then asked Abby if it would be okay, as I would have to take her car.

Abby said yes, so I took Susannah with me as I waited in line. After getting the food, I then dropped off the food and Susannah at Abby's and went to pick up Drew. After Drew trimmed Cinnamon's hooves, I took him to his next client's farm and dropped him off before going back to Abby's to clean up so I could be ready to meet with Noah. I also followed up with Ma to find out more about how Grandma Nancy was doing. Ma told me how Grandma Nancy kept seeing me and Abby there with her and would get frustrated when she would have religious conversations with me and I would not answer. Grandma Nancy also expressed concern that Abby and I would not come to her funeral.

Once I got cleaned up I drove to Rose City's North Central Second-Hand Retail Store and had them page Noah up to the front so he could meet with me. When I first met with Noah, I was a bit intimidated by his height, as he was about a foot taller than me. He quickly put me at ease, however, as he was very easy going and as he had me share about why I wanted to switch to Rose City (because of Abby and now Grandma Nancy's failing health). He made sure I knew and was okay with the fact that he could not guarantee me a certain number of hours any more than any of his other seasonal hires. In our conversation, I also learned that he and his wife were homeschooling their seven kids. Noah also reminded me a little of Dr. Reuben F, as both were tall and had black hair, who had been the person who got my family to accept my going off to college. He then gave me a quick tour of the backroom and told me that whenever I wanted to start working at the Rose City North Central Second-Hand Retail Store he would have Dan S, the team leader of the department I would be working, give me some hours.

Based on how well that weekend went plus how Grandma Nancy's and Abby's health were failing, I asked Amber N and Ian H, Petunia City team leaders, if it would be okay for me to switch to Rose City starting November 5th as they did not have a schedule out for that week yet even though it was less than two weeks out. They told me that would be fine, so I told Noah that I would like to start working at his store on Monday, November 5th. He told me just to come in at 9:00 a.m. on the fifth and they would get me started.

The last weekend in October I had planned to participate in

Buttercup City Evangelical Free Church's missionary conference and present my position at CODCL there. Due to my sister's health, however, I told them that I would not be able to. CODCL was ramping up for their 2012 fall conference where over nine hundred students were expected to attend. Between still being involved in this part of CODCL and in dealing with Abby's health, I just did not have time to come up with anything for a table at the church's missionary conference. In addition, I was planning to move to Rose City, which would mean I would no longer be working for CODCL. When I had talked with Michael, my boss at CODCL about Abby's cancer returning and my desire to move to Rose City to be near her, he was totally understanding. I had made sure he knew I fully intended to continue helping up to the CODCL conference though.

I did go to the missionary conference at Buttercup City Evangelical Free Church, though, just to be able to spend time with my friends but first I wanted to get out to the farm to have an actual "religious conversation" in person with Grandma Nancy. So I went to visit her and sat through a movie with her that Ma had playing on a portable DVD player, all the while praying that I would have a chance to share my beliefs with her again about being born again and believing Jesus is our Savior. When the DVD temporarily stopped, I felt I had time to have my conversation with her then. That was when God prompted me to remind her that I knew she knew the following Bible verses:

John 14:6. *Jesus answered, 'I am the way and the truth and the life. No one comes to the father except through me.*

1 John 4:4. *You, dear children, are from God and have overcome them, because the one who is in you is greater than the one who is in the world.*

Luke 23:39-43. *One of the criminals who hung there hurled insults at him: "Aren't you the Messiah? Save yourself and us!" But the other criminal rebuked him. "Don't you fear God," he said, "since you are under the same sentence? We are punished justly, for we are getting what our deeds deserve. But this man has done nothing wrong." Then he said, "Jesus, remember me when you come into your kingdom." Jesus answered him, "Truly I tell you, today you will be with me in paradise."*

Then I shared with Grandma Nancy how – like the criminals but compared to Jesus who did no wrong – we definitely are not perfect, so our sufferings are just and are more deserved. But all we need to do is admit that to Jesus and ask Jesus to remember us and forgive us for our sins. Grandma Nancy smiled and nodded with each Bible verse and explanation I gave her. This was unlike previous times when I had not been thoughtful enough to reassure her that she knew the verses as well as I did, but instead had tried to help her see them as I did and not simply agree to disagree on our views of them.

After sharing the verses in Luke's gospel with Grandma Nancy, I realized I had come to see them as the perfect example of what Christians refer to as the steps to salvation: The ability to see and repent of one's sins, and putting one's trust in Jesus for salvation, which results in becoming a child of God. These steps happened at the end of the criminal's life on the cross next to Jesus, but they can happen for anyone at any stage in one's life. From this story in Luke, we can see how, compared to Jesus, none of us have lived good lives. This means that since Jesus suffered death on the cross, then our suffering – while sometimes deserved, is minimal compared to his undeserved suffering. My sharing this story with Grandma Nancy was not to indicate to her that I thought she was close to death as much as I thought how neatly this passage displays how easily one can trust in God, be forgiven, and be accepted into God's family. I also shared this passage with Abby before she passed on. It is my hope that they and all who read this book will see themselves as more like the second criminal than the first by seeing how we suffer due to our wrongs but Jesus suffered unjustly and then to ask Jesus to remember them as he enters his kingdom.

After I shared the Bible verses with Grandma Nancy, I then headed to Buttercup City Evangelical Free Church. While there, I connected with Luke and Betsy S, my first youth group leaders. Betsy told me how their former neighbors, Yale and Noreen S, were also there at the conference and that they attended a church in Rose City which maybe would be a good church for me when I moved back to Rose City since I was looking for a different church. I agreed to meet Yale and Noreen S so Betsy S introduced us. The two of them shared how their pastor really believed in outreach to the community. I hoped I could find a church that could reach out to Nathan and Abby, especially as Abby continued her battle with cancer. Yale and Noreen also shared how there was another woman, Rina Y, who worked at North Central Second-Hand Retail Store who attended their church, Church Based on Christ the Solid Rock. That Sunday I decided to check out Church Based on Christ the Solid Rock. Pastor Ryan P was preaching on Luke 6:46-49: *"Why do you call me, 'Lord, Lord,' and do not do what I say? As for everyone who comes to me and hears my words and puts them into practice, I will show you what they are like. They are like a man building a house, who dug down deep and laid the foundation on rock. When a flood came, the torrent struck that house but could not shake it, because it was well built. But the one who hears my words and does not put them into practice is like a man who built a house on the ground without a foundation. The moment the torrent struck that house, it collapsed and its destruction was complete."* Pastor Ryan preached using this passage about how suffering and trials in life test what type of foundation our life is built on – sand or Christ the solid rock. I wished Grandma Nancy could have heard this sermon. For several years, she believed that suffering came from Satan snatching up her prayers and putting evil twists to all of her words which had multiple meanings. After the service, Yale and Noreen saw me and introduced me to Rina.

My friend, Aiden V, from Rosemary City Gospel Church had lined up a U-Haul to bring my things from Rosemary City to Rose City and had found people to load it for me. I quickly looked at a couple apartments and chose to move into one that was already vacant and did not require a roommate to make the rent affordable. It was an upstairs apartment, however, and the only way to get there was to climb about thirteen steps. I had hoped to find a lower-level apartment, as Ma continually reminded me of how Uncle Larry was not supposed to climb stairs. But since I only had a week to look, this was the best option that I had found. Then I called Betsy S from Buttercup City Evangelical Free Church, Nissa I from the church formerly called Rose City Alliance, and Noreen S from Church Based on Christ the Solid Rock to see if any of them would be able to help me find people to unload the U-Haul into my new apartment. Betsy said that another couple who regularly attended their church was also moving that weekend so she was pretty sure that any available people would be moving that couple instead. I only reached Nissa's answering machine so I left a message. (I did not see that Nissa had emailed me offering help until Ma told me several weeks after I had gotten everything moved. (Ma had started to attend the church formerly called Rose City Alliance Church after I had convinced her to join me there for a few weekends when I was in Rose City prior to my eventual move back to Rose City. Ma had been upset when she learned I decided to attend Church Based on Christ the Solid Rock instead of the church formerly called Rose City Alliance Church.) Noreen told me that her husband, Yale attended a men's group at Church Based on Christ the Solid Rock and she was sure he could find a group of men to help me unload the U-Haul, and he did. A group of six to twelve men helped me move all my things into my new apartment including my friend Nora V from the church formerly called Rose City Alliance's husband, Robbie.

The Friday before my move as Matthew M, my friend from Petunia City North Central Second-Hand Retail Store, was helping me pack up my things over in Rosemary City, Ma called me to let me know Grandma Nancy had passed away. Grandma Nancy I was told did not want any funeral or memorial service other than a few brief words shared among family members.

Once I got moved and settled into my apartment in Rose City, I nervously called Noreen S, as I wanted to make sure I had a group from church to be plugged into to help keep me spiritually strong more than just on Sundays, since I was now living so close to my family and closer to Abby during her illness. Unless I desperately need something or have a specific reason to call people on the phone (like for a person's birthday or anniversary), I still struggle with calling people simply out of the blue, especially if I am not sure where my relationship stands with them. And this is why my call to Noreen was so out of the ordinary for me. However, part of why I think my discomfort level was lowered with calling Noreen was because Betsy from Buttercup City Evangelical Free Church was such good friends with her and because Noreen's husband, Yale, had during our first meeting discovered how he knew Uncle Larry whom he had bowled with a number of times over the years. From that call, Noreen connected me to the women's Bible study she attended on Wednesday nights. The first night I attended the Bible study, Robin T, the leader, asked everyone to introduce themselves and tell what they do for a living. From the introductions, I met Noreen R who had just written a book and gotten it published and I met Trinity F who had edited Noreen's book. After the study, I shared with Trinity how I had written my story down and asked if she would like to read it. I hoped that she would and that it would help me to get it published. Trinity did read it and edited it, and upon returning my story to me, she told me how the publisher she works with wanted me to send the book to him when I finished looking through the editing she had done.

Meanwhile, North Central Second-Hand Retail Store gave me between thirty and thirty-nine hours each week for the first month or so after I moved to Rose City, but then could only schedule me for twenty to twenty-nine hours after that. Whenever they had a lot of people call in sick or unable to work for whatever reason, Noah would tell his team leaders to give me a call, as he was sure I would pick up the hours. Except for maybe a few times when I was to be Abby's ride to the hospital for chemotherapy, I usually picked up the shifts. After working at the Rose City North Central Second-Hand Retail Store, I started to notice how the store did not follow the price points on everything which Petunia City team leaders had insisted we follow so I started to question my team leaders Dan S then Noah R about if we really weren't going by the price lists that North Central Second-Hand Retail Store's headquarters provide each of their stores on those items. Dan S said that, "No, Rose City North Central Second-Hand Retail Store didn't go by those price points as it has a smaller market than the stores in the Rosemary City area have."

Noah R, though, thought we should at least try the new prices. As he had just separated a favorite team leader from North Central Second-Hand Retail Store, I did not share with my fellow team members how Noah felt we should at least try the new price points as he was not very popular among many of my fellow team members at that time. As I had Noah's approval though and later a couple other team leaders I continued to insist we try to mark up the items. Then about the time my strongest opposing team member ended up getting separated from North Central Second-Hand Retail Store, I decided I had enough stress from Abby's illness so I shouldn't create more stress by continuing to push for the price points the North Central Second-Hand Retail Store headquarters requested. Then as my strongest opposing team member who worked full time got separated, her full time position became available and Noah told the team members in a meeting that anyone interested in the full-time position should let him know, so I did. That was in March of 2013 when I again became full-time so that I could get benefits including health insurance. I was glad I finally had insurance because shortly after this I found a swollen lymph node under my left arm. I contacted Rose City Clinic to meet with a doctor to have the lymph node checked out. The doctor then ordered several tests including an ultrasound and a MRI of the lymph node but after all the tests were done, I was told that all looked normal, though they want me to annually have an MRI to continue to make sure I remained cancer free.

God has continued to provide lessons for me in my walk with him. Many of my coworkers at the Rose City North Central Second-Hand Retail Store tend to complain a lot. Some complain about managers and they seem to be always complaining about other coworkers. During one of my devotional readings in *Our Daily Bread*, God had me read in Titus 3:1-2: *Remind the people to be subject to rulers and authorities, to be obedient, to be ready to do whatever is good, to slander no one, to be peaceable and considerate, and always to be gentle toward everyone.* From this passage I have been encouraged to ask people to not be negative, to try to avoid gossip (myself included), and to respect my team leaders even when I disagree with them. After all, the team leaders have more experience than I do in the areas which I may disagree with them on. Then as I continue to struggle with coworkers who share too much information about their personal lives, use language they should not use, or are disrespectful, God had me read Titus 3:3: *At one time we too were foolish, disobedient, deceived and enslaved by all kinds of passions and pleasures. We lived in malice and envy, being hated and hating one another.* This passage I use to remind me of the times when I read books I shouldn't, did things I shouldn't, started to care less about what language I used, and let my temper get the best of me. That has helped me to give my coworkers a bit of slack when I disagree with their behaviors.

However, some of my coworkers have expressed disdain for Jesus, including one who admits that is why she wears the star of David. Then a few days later, she mentioned to another coworker how she struggles with believing in something she cannot sense with one of her five senses. I asked her if she believed in the wind and she said yes because she can feel it. Since I struggle with feeling comfortable conversing with this coworker, I just dropped the conversation at that point. But since then, I have wanted to ask her various questions which ultimately point to Jesus and which I have remembered from various sources through the years. One question would be that if she were to walk in the woods and find a watch on the ground, would she think that it somehow made itself or would she recognize there had to be a maker who made it. Then I would point that everything is created—in nature and otherwise—thus there is a maker of it all. Another question I might ask her is if she believes in George Washington. Since he lived and died so long ago, there is basically the same amount of proof of his existence as there is of the existence of God and Jesus so how could she deny the existence of God. Finally, I would want to ask her about believing in all the messages which are present in a room due to TV and radio waves. The messages are all still being presented in the room whether one has a radio or TV tuned in to any or all of them. In the same way, God is present and it is only by tuning into his creation (and especially his Word) around us that we really can be aware of his presence. In recent days, I have since realized how my having a part time job with North Central Second-Hand Retail Store instead of the full-time laboratory job at the Medical Facility of Combined Practices was a blessing as it turned out North Central Second-Hand Retail Store was able to let me transfer to Rose City while if I had still been working at the laboratory I probably would have had to apply for a job in that field in the Rose City area and hope to get a job offer.

Additionally, in 2013 after returning to Rose City, I signed up to take an Education to Provide Fiscal Harmony class which a friend recommended as it would give me sound financial advice to help me get out of debt and know how best to invest the settlement I got from my car accident. From that, I learned to throw every last dollar that I could find at my debt while being faithful to give back to God, pay all current bills, buy necessities and give myself a little bit of spending money. The buying of necessities and spending money I find to be the hardest but thanks to food pantries like at Catholic Second-Hand Retail Store's and Monthly Church Food Distribution I managed to survive by getting creative so that I rarely felt the need to buy additional groceries. As for extra spending money, I rarely had any trouble with that as I just would tell myself to avoid going into stores. I usually was pretty successful at avoiding stores unless I had to buy the cats food or litter but when I would go, I would try to remind myself how I didn't have additional spending money to buy anything else. Working at North Central Second-Hand Retail Store though meant occasionally I would actually end up buying something as it just was too irresistible. Especially when it comes to DVDs, though, I lately tend to splurge. Finally December 2016 I paid off my last medical bill and college loan. Afterwards, for a month and a half I splurged quite a bit as I felt like celebrating a number of things: being debt free, finding a job as clinic security which merged my interests in law enforcement and the medical field, as well as how Christmas and my birthday were coming up. Those are the two events in the year I tend to let myself splurge a bit more than normal especially since Abby died. When Abby was alive, I splurged more as I would get her things which I thought she would like, for example when she was into stamping, stamps, or into making jewelry, beads, etc.

STRETCHING OUT

After moving to Rose City, the one day I attended a meeting at Church Based on Christ the Solid Rock where they had people break into groups. The leaders of the meeting had us break up into groups of five and then decide who in each group would play the role of a mother, a father, and their three kids, with the father being the wage earner. The groups had to decide if they were going to buy or rent a place to live, determine the method of transportation, determine if the mom was going to stay home to watch the youngest kid, and decide what was to happen with the other kids if mom stayed home and dad was working. That activity reactivated my dream of making a difference in people's lives by having a place for them to hang out, play games, watch movies, etc. It made me realize I needed to stretch myself and renew my efforts to become a part of the community. So, I contacted the youth pastor of this church, Michael N, and asked him how I could help him. He told me there was a need to watch some fifth and sixth grade students who had about an hour between when their group got finished with their youth group meeting and when their older siblings' groups got finished with their youth group meeting.

The first night was difficult for me and the four pre-teen kids I ended up watching. I was only briefly introduced to them and as I never had worked with fifth or sixth graders before, I was not sure what I was supposed to do so I probably came across as hovering and the kids I was watching liked to find someplace to hang out together without me being present. I tried to think of things to do together but with my awkwardness I was never able to overcome it to actually connect with the kids. Later one of the other youth group leaders took to hanging out with us for a while and would start a game of dodgeball which the kids really enjoyed and the group of kids would often grow larger as more kids wanted to stay to play dodgeball. Then when a few weeks later Michael announced they were having a talent night at the church, I signed up to read one of Abby's poems. By the time Abby married Nathan she had written over two hundred poems. Ma had helped Abby get the poems published in a book called *America: Our Struggles Lead Us to Victory* under the pen name of Marie Maria. The poem I chose to read that night was titled "If She Could Face Her Problems" which is about how this lady often feels like an outsider always looking in and portray pretty accurately how too often I feel when I'm around other people.

After reading the poem, I read a prayer I wrote on April 17, 2013. The prayer was based on my feelings watching the four kids that first night after youth group and was also based on the sermon the previous Sunday. The prayer went like this:

> "Dear Lord, despite all of us having had these types of feeling at some point in our lives and to some extent, thank you for reassuring us in Psalms 139:2 that *you perceive my thoughts from afar.* And thank you for your reassurance in Psalms 139:16 that says, *Your eyes saw my unformed body. All the days ordained for me were written in your book before one of them came to be.* I want to thank you for how in Ephesians 1:11 you tell us, *In [you] we were also chosen, having been predestined according to the plan of [you] who works out everything in conformity with the purpose of [your] will.* Help us to always remember how you tell us in 1 John 4:4b *that the one who is in you is greater than the one who is in the world,* when doubts and fears come our way. God please help us, as we stretch ourselves to minister through Jesus to others here on earth as we seek to do your will

for our lives, just as you ministered to those who entered your path. In Jesus' name we pray! Amen!"

I still feel out of place, but I know that if I am serious about the "mission house" idea that I feel God has laid on my heart, then I need to continue to work on getting comfortable around other people better. In the meantime, I also have again occasionally been trying to establish myself in my community by trying to start hosting game nights followed by a movie with friends and their friends.

At what ended up being one of my final game nights in the spring of 2014, my friend from church and North Central Second-Hand Retail Store, Rina Y and I played the game of Life and she got to have the career of police officer without having to go to college. That prompted me to start looking into if being a police officer might be a job for me as the ladies I went to Bible study with at Church Based on Christ the Solid Rock had a number of times expressed how with my college degrees, I could surely find a more career type of job than the retail job I held. As the team leaders at the North Central Second-Hand Retail Store had always treated me so well and were so flexible plus how over the years doing the work at the North Central Second-Hand Retail Store my back had been improving I hadn't really been sure I wanted to switch jobs, especially as using my Dairy Science degree could mean less social life or even worse milking cows again or as the Laboratory Science degree had ended rather disastrously in Rosemary City making me feel like I put people's lives in danger which made laboratory work quite unappealing. Also pretty much anything else in the medical field seemed pretty unappealing thanks to my laboratory experience in Rosemary City. Besides I felt I already rarely stuck to a job with the two years in Rosemary City working for the North Central Second-Hand Retail Store and CODCL being the longest I had worked at any job. Thankfully now between the two North Central Second-Hand Retail Store locations I ended up working a total of over 6 years at one job!

Thanks to playing the Game of Life though with Rina, I got my first stirring of interest in doing something outside of retail at the North Central Second-Hand Retail Store and church. To determine if a career in law enforcement was an option I first went to the six-week Citizens Police Academy class the Rose City Police Department held once a week on Tuesdays. Then about week four I decided I would apply to volunteer with the department as an auxiliary police officer.

As I considered a career in law enforcement, I prayed that God would help me to see if it was his will or just something I was spurred toward because I knew several people working or volunteering with the police department. These people included my coworker, Nigel T, fellow church members at the Church Based on Christ the Solid Rock Clinton and Raya C who are auxiliary members almost as long as I have been alive, the current police chief whom I first knew as an usher at the Church Based on Christ the Solid Rock whom always made me feel welcome at the Church Based on Christ the Solid Rock as he has a ready smile as he helps people find a seat. Additionally, I knew there was another officer at Church Based on Christ the Solid Rock as at a women's event at church his mom had told us that she was his mom as she shared how people thought she looked too young to be his mom. Also, I didn't want it to be because my favorite movie at that time was Courageous a movie which depicted several deputies hanging out fairly regularly with each other which was especially appealing as other than work, I didn't have much if anything in common with most of my coworkers, other than Rina, so I didn't really hang out with any of them as most of them seem more comfortable partying and pushing the law both of which I wasn't comfortable with. As I prayed about whether law enforcement was a career I wanted or God's will, God had me realize how being an officer would give me a chance to impact my community and help me grow to become a better parent for when I finally start to foster children. Also, after I rode with Officer Marty Q, I realized that law enforcement wasn't so much about being strict on laws but could be used to eliminate fear which I came to realize was the root of what drove Grandma Nancy in her overprotectiveness.

Also before I had applied to the police auxiliary, I had talked to Noreen S, my Church Based on Christ the Solid Rock friend, about what I thought would be the benefits of joining the police auxiliary. Some of them were: I could get to know and help my community more as I had heard that we could help at the local fair, sport events, parades, etc.; that we always were to be paired up with another auxiliary member-thus forced socialization. As I tended to take a while to get comfortable with those that I do not know, I felt that always working with at least another member of the auxiliary would stretch my comfort zone which was something I felt I still definitely needed.

So it was on June 28th, 2014 that the Rose City Police Departments' auxiliary set up to interview me to see if they thought I would be a good candidate. My friends, Clinton and Raya C, from the Church Based on Christ the Solid Rock were part of the interview panel as were Nicky C and Autumn L whom I had never met before but was quickly at ease around. As the interview ended Raya made a comment about if I would want to wear the auxiliary ball cap which came with the position. I had commented that I haven't had a problem with wearing ball caps especially when milking cows as it kept one's hair clean. That's when I learned that Nicky also had been raised on a farm as he agreed with me. After the interview, they had me sit out in the lobby for a few minutes as they determined whether they would bring me on to the auxiliary. They had and since then I have come to know many of the officers and other members of the auxiliary as I volunteer for as many of the events as I can, often using vacation days and days off from the North Central Second-Hand Retail Store to do so.

I have found a few events which I don't enjoy all that much like helping with the winter parade where my feet freeze and demolition derby as I can't understand why people would purposely do something which could put them in a position where they could get seriously injured as I had been in my accident. On the other hand, I have found some events which leave me feeling quite energized like helping kids learn safety, giving them the opportunity to play with the lights on a police vehicle, helping them cross the street safely on Halloween and working at the fair where I'm reminded of the few years Ma and Uncle Larry had taken us on what was the closest we came to taking vacations while growing up on the farm. I also enjoy parking cars for the mayor's dairy breakfast at the fairgrounds and making certain that barricades are respected at parades, 5K walks, movies in the park, etc.

While volunteering with the police auxiliary, Officer Marty Q, the liaison officer for the police auxiliary when I joined has been active in fundraising for the Program Providing Cognitively Disabled Hope and Confidence as he spearheaded basketball games and later night golf opportunities. For the basketball game Officer Marty would recruit officers to play against the Program Providing Cognitively Disabled Hope and Confidence basketball players as he tries to help the Program Providing Cognitively Disabled Hope and Confidence raise funds needed to allow the athletes to continue to play for free, be provided free travel to events around the state and provide the athletes a free meal when they go to an event in another town. For the golf game, Officer Marty would recruit officers and community residents to play the game while the Program Providing Cognitively Disabled Hope and Confidence athletes helped man the holes and help keep the golfers from losing their balls by rounding the balls up before they stopped glowing. As my sister Sandy qualifies for the Program Providing Cognitively Disabled Hope and Confidence, I began to help Officer Marty more with these events and signed up to volunteer with the Program Providing Cognitively Disabled Hope and Confidence as I hoped to get Sandy involved in the Program Providing Cognitively Disabled Hope and Confidence as she still rarely does anything socially unless Ma or Dora or both do it with her so doesn't have too many friends of her own. Also, Officer Marty recruites officers, both regular and auxiliary, and he has said even citizens could join him biking from Rose City over to Jasmine City for the Program Providing Cognitively Disabled Hope and Confidence state games in what is called the Torch Run where police officers and deputies from all over the state come. They also bring along at least a trailer, in case a person can't bike the whole way which when I join in biking I always have to take advantage of as I overheat about half way over. While I have gotten Sandy to participate in a few of the Program Providing Cognitively Disabled Hope and Confidence events of bowling, bocce ball, and swimming, I have yet to get her to go to the state games which are quite spectacular seeing all the support from around a hundred or more police officers and deputies all over the state for these hundreds to thousands of athletes.

As a result of volunteering with the police auxiliary and my back getting where some weeks I almost can forget I have an injured back, I started to look into what it would take to get into law enforcement. The North Central Second-Hand Retail Store also developed a website to help their team members to dream bigger and look into ways to grow educationally. Due to those things, I had sent in a message on that website about my frustration with trying to overcome my debt to pursue an education toward become an officer in law enforcement. As Tim H, one of the people who had put together the website had worked for thirty years as a police officer, they put me in touch with him. Due to my conversations with him and his suggestion of looking at additional fields in law enforcement including as a correctional officer, I had. So, I started to apply to a number of positions, especially in Rose City, Birch County and since Pine and Ash Counties are on the northern border of Rose City I started to look into jobs in those counties, too. Once I interviewed for a position in Snapdragon City, a city over half hour north in Pine County, I realized how I felt that if I got hired I'd probably end up moving over there to save on gas money since the job was with Snapdragon City and not just with Pine County. When I realized that, I decided I might as well apply to positions in the Jasmine City area as that was where my niece lived. I hadn't gotten the job in Snapdragon City or any I interviewed for in the Jasmine City area but when I applied for a part time position at the Rose City Clinic as a Security Officer, I did get hired for it.

In fact as I interviewed for the position, it was one of my most laid back interviews which I felt really comfortable at, which in past interviews that were as laid back had always ended up getting the position. During the interview, I had learned how Chad R, the security officer manager who was interviewing me, and I had several things in common which got me really excited for the opportunity to work there. These similarities were that both of us had been involved in a car accident, we both shared the same beliefs of being a born again Christian and he had worked as an Ash County deputy while I was a former Ash County resident considering working as a deputy. When I shared with a number of my friends these things about Chad, without including his name, my friend Noreen S from the Church Based on Christ the Solid Rock had asked me if the person I was talking about was Chad. I replied, "It was, I take it you know him?" Noreen had then shared how her one daughter was a very good friend of one of his daughters so their kids grew up hanging out all the time together.

Then as I started in October 2016 training for the Security Officer position, Ma mentioned how Silas X, a guy she and Uncle Larry used to deliver the local free newspaper with, worked in the Rose City Clinic Security office. He ended up being the one doing the majority of the training and was so outgoing and friendly, usually greeting everyone he saw by name that I began to feel inspired hoping, that I also will get to the point that I would also. Additionally, I got to realizing how when I had delivered a locally subscribed paper for a few months back in 2013, I used to see Silas delivering the local free newspaper. I remembered how he was so friendly and would always wave when he would see me.

From the first day on the security officer job, I would ask some of the other security officers if there would be any chance I could go from part time to full time. Silas would always say he was sure I would be able to as the Rose City Clinic was in the middle of buying the Catholic Hospital. When Isaac J, another security officer who was hired the same time I was, mentioned that he might be headed to Poppy City, Silas emphasized how if a person decided that they wanted to move on, he hoped we would before he stuck a lot of time into training us as he realized how much time it took for new security officers to learn all they needed to learn to be comfortable doing the job. Isaac ended up remaining in Rose City and he was my partner on the weekends I was hired to work. He was pretty enthusiastic and made it so that our shifts were never boring even when there weren't anybody else in any of the buildings we would check.

After working part time for three months a couple full time positions were posted, one a 5PM-3AM position in the hospital and the other a 10PM-8AM position through the Free Hotel for Cancer Patients, so I applied to them. Both jobs were on one week Wednesday-Tuesday and off one week Wednesday-Tuesday. I ended up getting the full-time position working at the Free Hotel for Cancer Patients which provides free lodging for cancer patients that live over 40 miles away from Rose City as long as a doctor sends a recommendation and there is no criminal history in their background. I wasn't sure I liked the hours as much as the hospital's hours as I tended to usually wake shortly after dawn cracked when the room would start to brighten and in the spring when I'd hear the robins and other birds start to sing. Working with the cancer patients who stay at Free Hotel for Cancer Patients has been rewarding when I actually get to visit with the patients which isn't often as they usually are in their rooms the entire time I'm there, but staying up overnight has been an extremely uphill ability to develop. While the job seems more like a hotel desk clerk or housekeeping position than security, I have been grateful for the opportunity to get back into a more medical field as I move more towards a career in law enforcement. It also has given me more appreciation for the police officers of Rose City as they rotate into working overnights from 6PM-6AM to days 6AM-6PM every eight weeks.

Also, since I haven't had TV much less cable since my first year in Rosemary City in 2010, while working at the Free Hotel for Cancer Patients I have gotten to watch some cable TV. From that I have run across several renovations shows, which appeals to my creative side and looks like something I may like to do someday. After all, I love to learn new things and love to give almost anything at least a try, plus my creative side looks like it could possibly prove to be an advantage. On the other hand, though, I really struggle with spending money which would not be the greatest asset when renovating. I also have gotten to start watching more movies and as I've been encouraged to start a blog I have gotten to further develop my writing as I share some of my thoughts which some of the movies stimulate. Afterall, my favorite movies are ones which cause me to really stop and think about what God wants to teach me from what I just watched.

CHANGES AFTER GRANDMA NANCY DIED

Once Grandma Nancy passed life became a bit interesting. Us grandkids heard how we were supposed to get an inheritance from her once her old farmhouse was sold. I remember how I got to thinking from my portion of her inheritance I might finally be able to buy myself a home which I had been dreaming of since I got my settlement after my accident in 2011. Abby though felt quite sad as she sensed she would not be alive to enjoy her portion of the settlement which proved to be true. After the old farmhouse sold though, we learned that the legal document did not include us grandkids. So as Ma was living on disability at the time, we learned how she wasn't able to split with us her inheritance or she would lose her disability. The only way she wouldn't lose her disability would be by putting it in a trust which she would have to have someone dole out the money only as she needed it or if she wanted, she could use it to buy a house or car. So she chose to put the money in the trust, bought herself an Avalanche which she had been wanting and put my oldest sister Dora in charge of giving her money as she needed it. As Ma had a horrible habit of bouncing checks my friend, Nissa I from Rose City Alliance who has for quite a few years taught Education to Provide Fiscal Harmony, told me not to continue to bail Ma out by my paying for her bounced checks. For that reason, several months earlier I had told Ma I no longer would provide her with the $20/bounced check that she needed more frequently than I liked. My refusal to bail

304

her out, distressed Ma and obviously caused her to turn to others to keep helping her. No doubt my refusal was the reason she did not put me in charge of providing her funds from her inheritance out of the trust fund. As for Uncle Larry, he also did not share his inheritance as he felt it was Ma's responsibility, instead he started to use it for vacation packages and cruises and then sometime around 2016 led him to move with a few friends down to a state further south-east where they started a campground.

Then over a year after Grandma Nancy died, on April 21, 2014, I received an innocent-enough sounding question. Uncle Larry had sent me this text: "If I would ever sell the farm, what are your ideas?" I had just finished working at the North Central Second-Hand Retail Store for the day and was heading to my friend Rina Y's to grab a bite to eat before the two of us would head to the Bible study we went to every Monday which was held at the Church Based on Christ the Solid Rock. My mind raced with all the possibilities of what the question could mean. Was he wondering if I wanted to buy it or just wondering if I would back him on the decision to sell it?

So, I began to text him back but decided to try calling him, hoping he was still close to his phone since I had just gotten the text while walking out of the North Central Second-Hand Retail Store to my car. Sure enough, he picked up the phone. I then asked him what he meant by his text and he asked me if I would be okay with his selling the farm. I told him how I would be and how over the years I had been telling Ma, Grandma Nancy, and Dora that I felt it would be best for Dora and Sandy if they were encouraged to check out opportunities off the farm. So I told Uncle Larry I was excited about what it could mean for Dora and Sandy if he were to sell the farm.

Meanwhile, I decided not to ask Uncle Larry if he was wondering if I wanted to buy the farm as I was trying hard to finish paying off my school loan and to become a part of the Rose City community which a thirty-minute commute just wouldn't be ideal. While I wanted a place that was mine, I wanted it in Rose City and I was settled now in my decision to follow baby steps learned in my class of Education to Provide Fiscal Harmony that recommended a person completely pay off all their debts before buying a home. And even though I loved the cows when I was growing up, I knew they would cut into any possibility of my having a social life if I were to take over caring for them.

After hearing Uncle Larry was considering selling the farm I went to work looking into options for transitioning Dora and Sandy to living and working elsewhere since I knew it would require a lot of work as Sandy had a disability and Dora had probably never looked farther off the farm other than when she considered going to classes to learn genealogy around 2005. As I wasn't sure where to begin—in Birch County where Ma and I was living or Ash County where Dora and Sandy were currently living, I nervously debated and finally decided to swing by the police station to ask for advice. I ended up talking to Sergeant Arnold K, who with some help from the ladies in the front office got me some leads in Ash County to look into. When I talked with the Ash County representatives they directed me to Birch County as they thought it sounded like Dora and Sandy wouldn't be Ash County residents much longer while Birch County insisted it should be Ash County's responsibility to help them. Ultimately Birch County was the one that actually helped Dora and Sandy as before we knew it the three-week deadline before Uncle Larry sold the farm arrived so they were living in Birch County instead of Ash County.

As I started to look into helping my sisters following Uncle Larry's news, I had hosted another game night the following Thursday, April 24, Uncle Larry came and played games with Rina and me at my apartment. I waited until Rina left before I asked Uncle Larry for more information about what his plans were for selling the farm. That was when I learned Uncle Larry had already found a neighbor who had approached him about buying the farm a few years earlier, and so now that Uncle Larry was ready to be finished farming, he asked the neighbor if they were still interested. As they still were, Uncle Larry accepted their offer. By the time he talked to me that Thursday, Uncle Larry had already received the down payment and was just waiting to close the sale, which he said was going to happen in three weeks on May 15. He confirmed with me that I was still planning on coming to the farm on Sunday, April 27, which is when he wanted to share the news with all the family. He also told me he already had made plans to move to Jasmine City.

The next day, Friday, I had off, so I swung by Rose City's Organization Providing Needs to Seniors and Handicapped to see what resources they had to offer in Birch County for my sisters. It was then that I learned that Dora and Sandy's guardian needed to be the one actually doing the paperwork and legwork to help them, and since I was not their guardian, I couldn't do this for them. The Organization Providing Needs to Seniors and Handicapped also told me that it would probably take close to seven months' minimum to get Sandy qualified for disability. People at some of the other programs in Birch and Ash Counties for people with disabilities that I talked with told me they would require Sandy to be on disability in order to provide her with a coach who could help her with housing and a job. Needless to say, I started to get overwhelmed and stressed with what looked like seven months' of work that was going to have to be crammed into about three weeks' time.

The next day at work I was so worked up and stressed out while working at North Central Second-Hand Retail Store that when the opening team leader, Dan S, saw me while I was on one of my breaks, he could tell something was up. As he was leaving, he took time to find out what was causing me to feel that way. I ended up sharing with him how that morning Ma had failed to pick up my niece, Susannah, from my place at the time I had asked her to (noon), nor had she even made it there by the time she had promised me she would be there (12:30), but in reality it was 12:55 before she had gotten to my place. Thankfully, Rina had spent the morning with me so when I left at 12:40 she was there to watch Susannah until Ma eventually showed up. I also told Dan I had told Susannah that we could have a picnic together that day, which she got really excited about, until I realized that even though it was sunny outside, there was a nasty wind that whipped through just often enough to make having a picnic not possible that day. I also realized that I had not made sure Susannah had something other than slippers to wear if we went anywhere. So I ended up canceling the picnic which made Susannah cry, pout, refuse to take a time out, turn off my movie

I was watching with Rina, and refuse to listen to anything I told her to do that day until I pretended to call her dad to tell him how poorly she was behaving. Finally, I also shared with Dan how Uncle Larry had sold the farm and was closing on it on May 15, giving my family only three weeks to clean out the farmhouse and find housing, jobs, and get Sandy on disability. Then I told him how the Organization Providing Needs to Seniors and Handicapped said it would probably be close to seven months before Sandy would get disability to get housing and then be qualified to get assistance getting a job. When I learned that, I then felt that would mean I would have to house Dora and Sandy at my place as Ma would only be able to keep them a maximum of two weeks at her place. Dan said to me, "You have worked too hard to get to where you are and you need to make sure your family knows that will NOT be an option. Otherwise, of course they will bring your sisters to your place. Then from track history with your family you probably will have your sisters at your place for at least those seven months."

In the following weeks, other friends and coworkers echoed Dan's sentiments about not letting my sisters stay with me as it could lead to them overstaying their welcome. They reminded me that my apartment is too small for more than just one person to live there comfortably. Eventually my sisters trying to come live with me did become an issue once my sisters stayed the maximum length allowed at Ma's. The Monday following the three week move out time and two weeks at Ma's, I had gotten a voicemail from Ma which went like this: "Hey Renata, I'm bringing your sisters out tonight. I hope to see you around 8:30 or 9:00. Please welcome them. This is a family project helping the girls adjust. I appreciate it. God loves you, the girls love you, and I love you. During the day they will be at my place but they really need someplace to stay overnight. It doesn't make sense to pay an extra $240 (a week) unless you have the extra $240 for me to spend to do so. You know the thing we all need to do is to help family out and I have reached the limit that I can help them out. God loves you and so do I."

After that call, it took all my friends' support and prayers for me to stand my ground and stick to my decision not to let them stay at my place. My friends continually reminded me how there were better options in town for places for Dora and Sandy to stay at, as well as it wouldn't be in my best interest either for them to stay at my place. It helped a little that after I got that call when I asked, Noah gave me the rest of the day off. With that free time I remember calling the Temporary Home for those Without, the Shelter for New Mothers, the Second-hand store's Catholic Homeless Sanctuary, the Restarter Homeless Program and Christian Shelter for Abused Women looking to see if any of them would be able to take in my sisters. From these calls the only place that I was able to get ahold of which said they had room available so they would be able to help me at that time was the Christian Shelter for Abused Women. They told me that they had a room available which they offered to provide my sisters as long as my sisters helped with some chores and attended church and Bible studies which they required of all adults who came to stay there. I was offered a chance to get a tour along with my family, so I arranged to meet Ma, Dora and Sandy so that they could go with me on the tour. So when I went to meet my family I parked in a two hour parking space, thinking that would be plenty of time. Then Ma offered to drive all of us over together to the Christian Shelter for Abused Women in her vehicle which I foolishly accepted in order to save gas, to show that I was trying to unite the family while maintaining personal boundaries. At the tour of the Christian Shelter for Abused Women we saw a fully furnished room with two twin beds, two dressers and two closets which could house my sisters for three weeks to six months while they worked on getting on their feet. The shelter also provided a kitchen, bathrooms and living room which my sisters would share with other female residents. After the tour, as we were driving back I learned that Dora insisted that she still was only willing to consider my place. When I told them that was NOT an option they accused me of turning my back on my sisters in their time of need. I felt cornered seeing as how I had rode with them over to the Christian Shelter for Abused Women and so I had to ride with them until they drove me back to my car. Unfortunately, once they learned my place still was not an option, instead of dropping me off at my car Ma drove to an apartment complex which occasionally rent out apartments by day. There Ma inquired about being able to put Dora and

Sandy up for $35/night. The person she needed to talk to was gone for the day though, so it looked like Ma, Dora and Sandy were planning to continue to ask me to put them up for the night. Since it was now more than two hours since I joined Ma, I told her I needed to go for a walk and walked back to my car.

Once I got back to my car, I called Noreen S from the Church Based on Christ the Solid Rock and explained to her how my day had gone. She told me that she was proud of me for remaining strong. When I expressed my concern that Ma still planned to bring Dora and Sandy to my place that night, Noreen shared a story about how at one point in her life she had had a similar difficult situation which resulted in her calling the police to have them talk to the person who would not respect her when she said no. That made me feel a bit better and as on the prior Friday I had joined a friend who was having a garage sale with a friend, I went over to the location of the garage sale to pick up my things that had not sold. As I had brought quite a few things to my apartment while I helped clean the old farmhouse, like additional books, family pictures a large chest freezer and favorite toys of Abby and mine, I had decided to get rid of quite a few things as my apartment started to feel a bit cramped, too much like how it felt living at the farm my final years there and like I was a hoarder which hadn't been helped any by a comment made in November 2013 by Ruthanne T, the wife of my Monday Bible study leader at the Church Based on Christ the Solid Rock, about how many things I had when she helped me move some of my things to the one bedroom apartment that I had been living at.

After talking to Noreen, I then went to where the garage sale had been held to gather my things. I apologized to the homeowners for my not coming earlier when I said I would and shared some about my day. Once I had everything in my car since I was so upset, I took absolutely everything in my car over to where I worked at the North Central Second-Hand Retail Store and donated all of it as I had already prepared myself to not have any of the items. Since then, I wished I had kept more of the books and yarn, but obviously it is too late and at least my apartment was no longer as cramped feeling.

Once I had gotten rid of those things, I gave my friends Nora V and Clinton C, a call and talked with them about how miserable I was feeling, like I was a bad sister and daughter for refusing to let my sisters move in with me. They both reassured me that I was doing the right thing.

During this disagreement about my sisters getting to stay with me, I thought back to when Robin M had let me move in with her and wondered if she felt the way I was feeling. I was grateful for what she had done and I wondered if Robin was more gracious towards me then I was being toward my sisters. Later I realized there had been a big difference between my sisters and me when we went about looking for a place to stay. I had already taken the initiative to get a job, had learned to drive, and had started making friends through church. My sisters, on the other hand, resisted leaving the comfort of the farm until forced to and gave up on learning to drive or to get at least a part-time job to be able to gain some financial independence. I also had a dream when I was looking to live off the farm to go off someday to college to become a veterinarian.

When Uncle Larry first announced to my family back in April 2014 that he had sold the farm, Dora and Ma had been quite upset. Dora said she figured she would have to get a job working at home, because Sandy would not be able to work at the North Central Second-Hand Retail Store because she wasn't comfortable around strangers. I shared with Dora how Sandy used to be comfortable around strangers when she went to school, until she had been encouraged to be content to never leave the farm or never interact with anybody other than family even the farm's business people which occasionally came out to the farm. Then Dora and Ma brought up the fact that teachers had taught Sandy to cheat while they accused Dora of helping Sandy cheat. Later that week I learned from Ma that Dora thought I was happy with how things were turning out for them. While I had been excited about the new opportunities which Dora and Sandy would be able to have, I had never been happy about how it all fell into place, especially once I realized there were only three weeks left before the farm sold. I said I would have preferred that it had been Dora and Sandy's decision to leave the farm when they wanted to, instead of how that decision ended up being dumped on them, pushing them quickly to transition into finding someplace else to live.

After I had successfully been able to keep my boundaries of not letting my sisters live with me, Rosemary from Restarter Homeless Program (RHP) put in some effort to also help my sisters find alternative options of where to live and was able to convince the Catholic Second-Hand Retail Store's Catholic Homeless Sanctuary to take in my sisters for a couple weeks. After those couple weeks, Rosemary found an apartment manager who would allow my sisters to live in one of his apartments while they went through RHP's program at putting together a six-month plan on what they needed to do towards getting a job, onto disability, and housing of their own. So, Dora and Sandy lived at that apartment for six months and as after six months both of my sisters finally ended up getting accepted for disability, Ma was able to talk the apartment manager where she lived to let them live in her apartment complex since there were so many open apartments. Up to around then her apartment complex only allowed for those over 55 to live there.

While Dora and Sandy still have some ways to go towards becoming independent, friends of ours are excited about the progress we are seeing. Dora has found she enjoys playing cards with the seniors at Ma's apartment complex, and she and Sandy have been attending church with Ma. Also, they both have gone down to watch a parade by themselves, as well as walks and took a bus to a Program Providing Cognitively Disabled Hope and Confidence event by themselves. Sandy has also started accepting hugs from some people who do not know how our family never gave out hugs other than Ma. Also, Ma has started accepting help from neighbors and friends of mine with cleaning as well as their giving other assistance to Dora and Sandy. Also, my friend Nora V, who has been leading a prayer-like group that Ma has been attending, recently led Ma in prayer with her friend Clinton C to where Ma admitted she was a sinner and accepted Jesus' gift of salvation through his sacrifice of dying on the cross for our sins. As Nora said, Ma is now her sister and my sister through Christ!

Additionally, during this trying time of helping my sisters adjust, my friend Nora V informed me how she and several friends of hers were launching a Groups Helping Individuals Overcome Hurts, Habits and Hangups group and invited me to attend. I had. From attending, I continued to become comfortable sharing about the hurts and hang-ups which I struggle with. As I share, I gain new insight into why I continue to struggle with them, and have learned ways to start letting them go and thus heal from them.

When my sisters finally got permanent housing, I asked Sergeant Arnold K if I could ride along with him as I wanted to update him with my sister's situation. While talking to him that evening I heard how he and at least three other officers attend the Church of Believers. As I had been feeling like I did not have many peer opportunities at the Church Based on Christ the Solid Rock, I thought I'd check out the Church of Believers. At the Church of Believers, I found they had several Bible studies for mixed groups which allowed children to also come. As I became certified for foster care and occasionally would have Susannah when I went to church, I loved how they had children ministry groups during the Sunday service also until 4th grade. This made me not feel like I had to choose between ministry and watching Susannah as Susannah loved the children ministry groups. So, I started to attend the Church of Believers after the Church Based on Christ the Solid Rock let out until the pastor at the Church Based on Christ the Solid Rock left to minister to another church. As by that time I had gotten to know a fair number of the congregation at the Church of Believers, after attending a couple Bible studies and volunteering with their toddlers, I started to attend the Church of Believers as my main church.

THE BIBLE ON SUFFERING

Back several years ago I had shared with Betsy Q, a friend from Rosemary City Alliance Church whom I met at Samuel and Lisa M's bible study, and some of my other friends how the sufferings and trials which came into my family's lives had been viewed by at least Grandma Nancy as being caused by Satan getting to her prayers and distorting them. For example, Grandma Nancy felt that if she prayed to Jesus all the people who claimed to be Jesus would take her prayer and answer it as they willed, which then would be the reason trials and sufferings had happened to those of us in her family. Additionally, she stopped feeling like she could pray The Lord's Prayer as Jesus taught it in Matthew 6:9-13: *"Our Father in heaven, hallowed be your name, your kingdom come, your will be done, on earth as it is in heaven. Give us today our daily bread. And forgive us our debts, as we also have forgiven our debtors. And lead us not into temptation, but deliver us from the evil one."*

Instead after having prayed the prayer as it is written above and then hearing an owl hoot, Grandma Nancy then felt the need to spell out who to make sure Satan didn't turn it into something related to an owl and potential evil linked with owls. Also as a dairy farmer, it's important that cows remain pregnant as much as possible to earn maximum income. In farming terms, a pregnant animal is a bred animal, so Grandma Nancy then started spelling out bread to make sure Satan wouldn't try to make things pregnant which shouldn't be pregnant. Once she started feeling to spell out those words, numerous other words followed to the point that eventually she felt she had to spell ordinary conversation and most of her prayers to keep Satan from misconstruing her prayers and conversations.

After becoming a Christian, I recognized that Satan was relying on her being and remaining fearful. But when a person is fearful, they cannot fully trust God is caring for them. So to show Grandma Nancy and other family members how God uses trials and suffering to develop and display a person's character and their devotion to him, Betsy and some of my other friends helped me look up some verses dealing with suffering. Following are the verses which I highlighted in Bibles and gave to each family member Christmas 2011.

> Genesis 50:19-20. *"But Joseph said to them, "Don't be afraid. Am I in the place of God? You intended to harm me, but God intended it for good to accomplish what is now being done, the saving of many lives."*

> Esther 4:14 (Esther's people are about to be destroyed.) *"For if you remain silent at this time, relief and deliverance for the Jews will arise from another place, but you and your father's family will perish. And who knows but that you have come to your royal position for such a time as this?"*

> Job 1:20-22 (Job, a "blameless and upright man," gets multiple reports of death and the loss of his children and his livestock.) *"At this, Job got up and tore his robe and shaved his head. Then he fell to the ground in worship and said: "Naked I came from my mother's womb, and naked I will depart. The Lord gave and the Lord has taken away; may the name of the Lord be praised." In all this, Job did not sin by charging God with wrongdoing."*

John 16:33. *"I have told you these things, so that in me you may have peace. In this world you will have trouble. But take heart! I have overcome the world."*

Acts 14:22b. *We must go through many hardships to enter the kingdom of God," they said.*

Romans 5:3-4. *Not only so, but we also glory in our sufferings, because we know that suffering produces perseverance; perseverance, character; and character, hope.*

Romans 8:18. *I consider that our present sufferings are not worth comparing with the glory that will be revealed in us.*

Romans 8:28. *And we know that in all things God works for the good of those who love him, who have been called according to his purpose.*

Romans 8:35-39. *Who shall separate us from the love of Christ? Shall trouble or hardship or persecution or famine or nakedness or danger or sword? As it is written: "For your sake we face death all day long; we are considered as sheep to be slaughtered. "No, in all these things we are more than conquerors through him who loved us. For I am convinced that neither death nor life, neither angels nor demons, neither the present nor the future, nor any power, neither height nor depth, nor anything else in all creation, will be able to separate us from the love of God that is in Christ Jesus our Lord.*

2 Corinthians 1:3-4. *Praise be to the God and Father of our Lord Jesus Christ, the Father of compassion and the God of all comfort, who comforts us in all our troubles, so*

that we can comfort those in any trouble with the comfort we ourselves receive from God.

   1 Thessalonians 3:4. *so that no one would be unsettled by these trials. For you know quite well that we are destined for them.*

   1 Thessalonians 3:7-9. *Therefore, brothers and sisters, in all our distress and persecution we were encouraged about you because of your faith. For now we really live, since you are standing firm in the Lord. How can we thank God enough for you in return for all the joy we have in the presence of our God because of you?*

Of course, the ultimate example of suffering is how Jesus – being innocent – was willing to suffer inhumane brutality in order to take our sins upon himself so that he could be the Lamb of God which takes away our sins. Joni Eareckson Tada writes about suffering in her book *"The God I Love, A Lifetime of Walking with Jesus."* On page 286 she says, "[True wisdom is] found not in being able to figure out why God allows tragedies to happen. True wisdom is found in trusting God when you can't figure things out."

These are just a few texts that explain why God allows suffering and that have helped me over the years as trials have come my way. I hope they can help you, too, during any and all trials God may allow into your life to develop and display your character and your devotion to him.

THE BIBLE ON BELIEFS

The following are some additional Bible verses having to do with believing, which Betsy Q and other friends helped me gather:

All of the Gospels are Jesus sharing about what is needed to be a true follower of his, but select verses I chose to include here are:

> Luke 18:10-14. *Therefore, brothers and sisters, in all our distress and persecution we were encouraged about you because of your faith. For now we really live, since you are standing firm in the Lord. How can we thank God enough for you in return for all the joy we have in the presence of our God because of you?*

> Luke 23:42-43 *Then he said, "Jesus, remember me when you come into your kingdom." Jesus answered him, "Truly I tell you, today you will be with me in paradise."*

> John 1:1-4 *Then he said, "Jesus, remember me when you come into your kingdom" Jesus answered him, "Truly I tell you, today you will be with me in paradise."*

> John 1:14 *The Word became flesh and made his dwelling among us. We have seen his glory, the glory of the one and only Son, who came from the Father, full of grace and truth.*

John 1:16-17. Out of his fullness we have all received grace in place of grace already given. For the law was given through Moses; grace and truth came through Jesus Christ.

John 3:16-18 For God so loved the world that he gave his one and only Son, that whoever believes in him shall not perish but have eternal life. For God did not send his Son into the world to condemn the world, but to save the world through him. Whoever believes in him is not condemned, but whoever does not believe stands condemned already because they have not believed in the name of God's one and only Son.

Acts 4:12 Salvation is found in no one else, for there is no other name under heaven given to mankind by which we must be saved."

Acts 13:38-39 "Therefore, my friends, I want you to know that through Jesus the forgiveness of sins is proclaimed to you. Through him everyone who believes is set free from every sin, a justification you were not able to obtain under the law of Moses.

Romans 1:16-17 For I am not ashamed of the gospel, because it is the power of God that brings salvation to everyone who believes: first to the Jew, then to the Gentile. For in the gospel the righteousness of God is revealed—a righteousness that is by faith from first to last, just as it is written: "The righteous will live by faith."

Romans 3:10-12 As it is written: "There is no one righteous, not even one; there is no one who understands; there is no one who seeks God. All have turned away, they have together become worthless; there is no one who does good, not even one."

Romans 3:20-24 *Therefore no one will be declared righteous in God's sight by the works of the law; rather, through the law we become conscious of our sin. But now apart from the law the righteousness of God has been made known, to which the Law and the Prophets testify. This righteousness is given through faith in Jesus Christ to all who believe. There is no difference between Jew and Gentile, for all have sinned and fall short of the glory of God, and all are justified freely by his grace through the redemption that came by Christ Jesus.*

Romans 3:27-28 *Where, then, is boasting? It is excluded. Because of what law? The law that requires works? No, because of the law that requires faith. For we maintain that a person is justified by faith apart from the works of the law.*

Romans 3:31 *Do we, then, nullify the law by this faith? Not at all! Rather, we uphold the law.*

Romans 6:23 *For the wages of sin is death, but the gift of God is eternal life in Christ Jesus our Lord.*

Romans 10:9 *If you declare with your mouth, "Jesus is Lord," and believe in your heart that God raised him from the dead, you will be saved.*

Romans 10:13-15. *for, "Everyone who calls on the name of the Lord will be saved. "How, then, can they call on the one they have not believed in? And how can they believe in the one of whom they have not heard? And how can they hear without someone preaching to them? And how can anyone preach unless they are sent? As it is written: "How beautiful are the feet of those who bring good news!"*

Ephesians 2:5 *made us alive with Christ even when we were dead in transgressions—it is by grace you have been saved.*

Ephesians 2:8-9 *For it is by grace you have been saved, through faith—and this is not from yourselves, it is the gift of God— not by works, so that no one can boast.*

Galatians 2:16 *know that a person is not justified by the works of the law, but by faith in Jesus Christ. So we, too, have put our faith in Christ Jesus that we may be justified by faith in Christ and not by the works of the law, because by the works of the law no one will be justified.*

Hebrews 10:25. *not giving up meeting together, as some are in the habit of doing, but encouraging one another—and all the more as you see the Day approaching.*

James 2:19. *You believe that there is one God. Good! Even the demons believe that—and shudder.*

1 Peter 3:18. *For Christ also suffered once for sins, the righteous for the unrighteous, to bring you to God. He was put to death in the body but made alive in the Spirit.*

EPILOGUE

God used Abby's battle with cancer to show me how short life can be. He has reminded me how, with life-altering experiences like cancer, one can try to improve their interactions with their loved ones by forgiving past grievances and debts and by encouraging other loved ones to love each other better. He also reminded me of how he is the master healer and even if the prognosis for someone with cancer is no more than a few more months of life, God can still give them a year or more to live. On the other hand, life can end as unexpectedly as in an accident, which he obviously has spared my family from several times. Abby's battle with cancer also prompted me to give my family Bibles in order to share with them why I believe what I believe and to share some of the many stories and verses in the Bible that explain why God allows trials which I am sharing with you in the chapters titled The Bible On Beliefs and The Bible on Suffering.

As for my family, my oldest two sisters and Uncle Larry will finally no longer be stuck living on the farm as Uncle Larry found a buyer for the farm. I am a bit excited thinking of what their futures may now hold as I remember back to 2005. Back in 2005 I had offered to help Dora go to college at Rose City to study genealogy. I had mentioned Rose City to Dora as it was the closest college which would make it possible for Dora to could continue to live at the farm while going for a degree in genealogy. At that point Dora had then told me how she would have to go to the College at Jasmine City in order to take classes for genealogy not Rose City as Jasmine City is the campus which offered the genealogy degree not Rose City.

She seems to have a gift for genealogy as she is able just from reading newspapers, to talk with Ma, Uncle Larry, and Grandma Nancy (when she was alive) about people in the state where Ma grew up which Dora probably never had ever met – to figure out who is related to whom and where they have lived, and other things having to do with their genealogies. When I offered to help her go to college, she first told me she was not smart enough and then told me how the family needed her on the farm instead. Of course, my family never refuted this. As for Sandy (my sister with the mental disability), she had been okay with being on the farm 365 days a year the ten years prior to the sale of the farm. For both Dora and Sandy, I had always felt saddened whenever I thought about how isolated they were on the farm. I felt they were missing out on developing relationships with people who could help them stretch themselves beyond what they were able to do or be, to become all God wants them to be, and who could help them by giving them a listening ear and bring them back to God and his truths, much like I have had people help me do these things over the years since I left the farm in 2001. While I would like to convince them of these things and had tried, I have come to realize I cannot make them change their minds. Instead, I need to ask God to help me have serenity to know what I cannot change and courage to know what I can change and wisdom to know the difference. As I've taken Groups Helping Individuals Overcome Hurts, Habits and Hangups classes this has been further honed into me. Also, I continue to hope they get a personal relationship with Jesus Christ our Savior and to try to help them so that they will see that the One who wants to live in them is stronger than the one who is in the world. Maybe and hopefully at some point it will prompt them to minister to people who struggle with similar problems. That is ultimately what I see as the reason God has allowed me to undergo all the trials I have, so that I can minister to people with similar trials like those who may be struggling socially, or with depression, family tension, job loss, recovery from an accident, cancer in their family, etc. So my prayer is that through my story and through everything, God may be exalted and that you will be inspired not to give up but will look to see how you can be used by God to allow your trials to benefit others. Thank you for reading my story and may God richly bless you and the ministry which he currently has you in and in everything God has in store for you in the future!

About the Author

Renata grew up on a dairy farm in a small town where she was home schooled and home churched. She has gotten a degree in Dairy Science and Clinical Laboratory Science as she considered becoming a veterinarian and had seen the need for both during her time on the farm. She enjoys volunteering with numerous organizations as she tries to bless others as God blessed her and spending time with her cats.

Printed in the United States
By Bookmasters